Women's Rights

Women's Rights

Reflections in Popular Culture

Ann M. Savage, Editor

Issues through Pop Culture

An Imprint of ABC-CLIO, LLC

Santa Barbara, California • Denver, Colorado

Library of Congress Cataloging-in-Publication Data

Names: Savage, Ann M., editor.
Title: Women's rights : reflections in popular culture / Ann M. Savage, Editor.
Description: Santa Barbara : Greenwood, [2017] | Series: Issues through pop culture | Includes index.
Identifiers: LCCN 2017003777 (print) | LCCN 2017006019 (ebook) | ISBN 9781440839429 (hard copy : alk. paper) | ISBN 9781440839436 (ebook)
Subjects: LCSH: Women's rights. | Feminism. | Women in popular culture.
Classification: LCC HQ1236 .W65286 2017 (print) | LCC HQ1236 (ebook) | DDC 305.42—dc23
LC record available at https://lccn.loc.gov/2017003777

ISBN: 978-1-4408-3942-9
EISBN: 978-1-4408-3943-6

21 20 19 18 17   1 2 3 4 5

This book is also available as an eBook.

Greenwood
An Imprint of ABC-CLIO, LLC

ABC-CLIO, LLC
130 Cremona Drive, P.O. Box 1911
Santa Barbara, California 93116-1911
www.abc-clio.com

This book is printed on acid-free paper ∞

Manufactured in the United States of America

With an immense amount of love and gratitude, for my mother Sophie, and in memory of my father Leonard.

Contents

Acknowledgments

I am thankful to all of the feminists who have fought hard to make the world a more welcoming place for women.

I am grateful for the meaningful feedback from Kevin Hillstrom, the ABC-CLIO Acquisitions Editor, and John Mugge for his detailed editing and thoughtful feedback. I am also grateful for John's volunteer work at Planned Parenthood and the Humane Society of Indianapolis! I am appreciative for Butler University graduate Maggie Monson's careful and detailed fact checking and editing.

I am thankful for the support of so many valuable friends who help keep me sane. There are too many to mention, but I especially want to thank Kristin Swenson for being such a supportive department chair and loving friend. I am enormously indebted to Allison Harthcock for her support, love, and friendship.

I am thankful to my family. To all of my big sisters—Cathy, Debbie, Cindy, and Bonnie—thank you. Thanks also to my brothers-in-law, nephews, and niece. I am also grateful for my beagle mutt, Edie, for keeping me warm and making me smile every day.

I am most grateful for my incredibly supportive and loving parents, Sophie and Leonard Savage. I love them immensely and always will.

Introduction

The status of women as less than men is memorialized in the United States' Declaration of Independence, which asserted, "All **men** are created equal." The use of the word "men" was deliberate and referred specifically to white, land-owning males. The Declaration purposely excluded women, people of color, religious minorities, and the poor. Despite this, women, including women of color and sexual minorities, have lobbied, fought, and died for their full humanity to be recognized by the government and their fellow citizens. Beginning in 1948, women began to organize more formally on behalf of women's rights. What is now considered the first convention for women's rights organized by women was held in the small town of Seneca Falls, New York. At this gathering, 68 women and 32 men signed the Declaration of Sentiments, modeled on the Declaration of Independence, which professed, "All men **and women** are created equal." Taken for granted in the 21st century, this new Declaration was greeted with hostility and was quite controversial. Over 70 years later, women were finally granted the right to vote with the passing of the 19th Amendment to the Constitution in 1920. Despite these gains, women were still denied full legal status or civil rights for decades to come.

As late as the 1960s, women were still denied many basic rights and faced many obstacles to full equality. Women could not keep their job while pregnant, file a claim for workplace sexual harassment, refuse to have sex with their husband, serve on a jury, get a credit card on their own, or even run in the Boston Marathon. Not until more than 50 years after the 19th Amendment would there be another surge of activism on behalf of women's rights. Journalist Betty Friedan's book *The Feminine Mystique* (1963), which described the disaffected life of many suburban women, calling it the "problem that has no name," is widely credited for igniting what came to be known as the Women's Liberation Movement. Women demanded legal status equal to that of men. Now known as the second wave of feminism, the movement was one of the most successful in fundamentally changing society in ways never imagined. By the 1970s, more and more women were moving into the workforce, and gender roles were being challenged.

Through all of this historical change, popular culture (which includes television, music, literature, film, news reports, and, more recently, the Internet) played a significant roll in changing the public's opinions of women and gender roles in general. Popular culture serves as a mirror of what is happening in a culture at any particular time while simultaneously disseminating ideas and perspectives that influence public attitudes about social issues. This anthology seeks to introduce readers to the women and events in popular culture that made the most significant contributions to the advancement of women's rights.

ONE

Television

The introduction of television in the 1950s transformed American life. Audiences no longer imagined pictures in their mind when listening to radio dramas, comedies, and mysteries; rather, television delivered the images right into audiences' homes. Although women's lives were still relegated to the domestic, television was a window into the world and a glimpse of how other people lived.

As time passed and women's rights became a more prominent issue in American society, however, television increasingly emerged as a cultural touchstone for understanding the frustrations, fears, demands, and dreams of women from all socioeconomic backgrounds. Using both humor and drama, diverse television programs such as *I Love Lucy* (1951–1957), *Maude* (1972–1978), *Murphy Brown* (1988–1998), *Roseanne* (1988–1997), and *Ellen* (1994–1998) explored and commented on momentous changes in women's lives during the second half of the 20th century, just as shows like *Parks and Recreation* (2009–2015), *How to Get Away with Murder* (2014), *Inside Amy Schumer* (2013–), and *Orange is the New Black* (2013–) have done for audiences of the 21st century.

Television has played an important role in transforming American culture and the reimagining of gender roles. Despite the splintering of television audiences as technology and creators deliver multiple options and channels for audiences' viewing pleasure, the small screen remains a force in U.S. culture as a vehicle for potential political and cultural change.

THE GOLDBERGS (1949–1956)

The Goldbergs was an American situation comedy about a Jewish immigrant family living in a tenement in the Bronx, and was popular in the 1950s, during television's infancy. Creator, writer, and star of *The Goldbergs*, Gertrude Berg (neé Edelstein; 1899–1966) was the force behind a multimedia entertainment empire forged in her likeness: by the time of the 1950s television show, her Jewish immigrant matriarch character, Molly Goldberg, had captured hearts for decades in a variety of formats and genres. *The Goldbergs* was originally a radio show, and Berg's durable characters went on to populate not only television but also a Hollywood film, a Broadway show, and commercial products ranging from cookbooks to coloring books and puzzles.

Berg's subject was American immigrant life from the Depression to the post-war era, and her fan base was legion. At the height of its popularity, the program was viewed by 40 million people a week.

The Molly Goldberg character was developed from skits about fictional Jewish immigrant Maltke Talnitzky, created by a teenaged Berg to occupy guests on rainy days at her father's Catskills resort. Berg's natural skill with dialogue, keen sense of dramatic structure, and sensitivity to cultural issues served her well when she adapted the skits for radio and television. Talnitzky eventually evolved into Molly Goldberg, a loving matriarch whose quaint customs and humorous malapropisms were matched with a fierce intelligence and an open-minded worldview.

Each episode of *The Goldbergs* opens with Molly Goldberg leaning out her tenement window and shouting "Yoo-hoo!" to her neighbors, before directly addressing the audience with a pitch for the program's sponsor. After speaking with her television audience family, Molly retreats into the apartment to join her television family: her doting husband Jake, who gives her the run of the household; her brother Uncle David, whose old-world charm creates a perfect comic foil for Molly's explorations of American culture; and Sammy and Rosie, two accent-less children who are fully assimilated into the burgeoning youth culture of the American 20th century. The program also featured a seeming cast of thousands playing neighbors, shopkeepers, bellboys, and the like; Berg's ear for language and eye for television imagery led her to hire widely from her New York life, making the show's secondary characters into a realistic representation of mid-20th-century American life.

The story of *The Goldbergs* followed the story of the United States: its industrial and cultural shifts mirrored those in the world both inside and outside radio and television. When CBS reported the German invasion of Poland on September 1, 1939, the news broadcast was followed immediately by an announcement that thanked "Oxydol, sponsor of *The Goldbergs*." When the actor playing Sammy was drafted, the character was drafted too, and a special episode was recorded at Grand Central Station. The program responded to the brutal devastation of *Kristallnacht* by airing an episode in which a brick is thrown through the Goldbergs' window during a Passover Seder. And the show was pulled from the air for a year when Berg refused to fire Philip Loeb, the actor who played Jake, when he was identified as a Communist in *Red Channels: The Report of Communist Influence in Radio and Television*.

Berg made inestimable contributions to 20th-century entertainment media. In addition to being the face and voice of *The Goldbergs* for decades, she wrote an episode each morning before making her family breakfast, eventually penning more than 10,000 *Goldbergs* scripts. As a pioneer in the world of both radio and television, Berg understood that entertainment media is a balancing act between performers, producers, and sponsors. Her autobiography vividly describes her performing all these roles: while acting and cueing her fellow actors, Berg would also be improvising on the fly in order to conform to the sponsor's mood and to the ticking clock of the live broadcast. *The Goldbergs'* witty banter, focus on family dynamics, and foregrounding of sponsored products established televisual conventions and industry practices that are still in use more than 60 years after Molly gave her first "Yoo-hoo!"

Leah Shafer

FURTHER READING

Berg, Gertrude. 1961. *Molly and Me: The Memoirs of Gertrude Berg.* New York: McGraw Hill.

Smith, Glenn D., Jr. 2007. *"Something on My Own": Gertrude Berg and American Broadcasting, 1929–1956.* Syracuse: Syracuse University Press.

THE HAZEL SCOTT SHOW (1950–1959)

The Hazel Scott Show was a variety show that premiered in the United States in July 1950 on the DuMont Network, to critical acclaim. The 15-minute program was broadcast three times weekly and hosted by renowned jazz artist Hazel Scott (1920–1981), an accomplished pianist and performer in movies and radio. As a black woman, her starring position was notable during a time when the roles of both women and blacks in broadcasting were minimal. Her appearance as an intelligent and sophisticated woman was also a challenge to prevailing stereotypes of blacks. The program showcased Scott's musical skills, setting her in a luxurious penthouse, wearing elegant clothing. The show was canceled on September 29, 1950, largely due to Scott's blacklisting because of false accusations of ties to the Communist Party. None of the episodes are known to exist today and are presumed destroyed.

As suggested by the show's title, Hazel Scott had a recognizable name in the entertainment industry. A piano prodigy, she was known for "swinging the classics," or giving jazzed tones and beats to classical works. This unorthodox practice was popular, but also a subject of debate. In Scott's case, the criticism was twofold. She was accused of "corrupting" a high art form and failing to perform "authentic" black culture, as well as of co-opting white culture to fit into white society. She was also critiqued for her physical performance, particularly her intensity while playing, which was considered more appropriate for male entertainers.

Scott had the reputation of being very outspoken about her social views. Her onscreen characters in film matched her stage persona—dignified and cultured—and she refused to play stereotypical black submissive roles. A proponent of civil rights, she was one of the earliest artists to refuse to perform for segregated audiences, and her promotion of racial integration made her a progressive symbol. Overall, her status as host on her own show contrasted with stereotypical representations of black women, such as the black domestic.

In June 1950, Scott's name appeared in *Red Channels*, a right-wing publication that listed names in the entertainment industry and their supposed affiliations with Communist and Communist front organizations. Nearly all of those listed were politically progressive, but many, like Hazel Scott, did not identify as Communist (Stabile, 2011). This was during the height of the Hollywood blacklist, when artists were barred from employment due to suspected affiliation with the Communist Party. The rationale for blacklisting was an underlying fear that media for public consumption, like cinema, radio, and television, could contain underlying subversive and anti-American messages. Although Hazel Scott voluntarily defended herself before the House Un-American Activities Committee (HUAC) and denounced *Red Channels*, the show's sponsors pulled their support, resulting in its cancellation. The accusations not only instigated the end of her show but her career on the American screen as well. Film historian Donald Bogle has suggested that had *The Hazel Scott Show* survived, popular black images might have changed altogether to reflect emerging progressive attitudes (Bogle, 2001: 18–19).

Monica Murtaugh

FURTHER READING

Bogle, Donald. 2001. *Prime Time Blues: African Americans on Network Television*. New York: Farrar, Straus and Giroux.

Mack, Dwayne. 2006. "Hazel Scott: A Career Curtailed." *Journal of African American History*, 91(2): 153–70.

McGee, Kristin A. 2009. *Some Liked It Hot: Jazz Women in Film and Television, 1928–1959*. Middletown, CT: Wesleyan University Press.

Stabile, Carol. 2011. "Women and the Broadcast Blacklist." *Communication Currents*, 6(5): 266–85. https://www.natcom.org/CommCurrentsArticle.aspx?id=1705.

THE BEULAH SHOW (1950–1953)

The Beulah Show was a half-hour comedy series aired by the American Broadcasting Company (ABC). The show centers on Beulah, a black domestic servant for the Hendersons, an archetypal white suburban family. The standard plot formula in this episodic series often entails a family problem or conflict that is eventually resolved—although not without first getting magnified—by Beulah's cleverness and genuine desire to set things right. Beulah was played by three prominent female black actors during that time period: Ethel Waters (1896–1977), Hattie McDaniel (1895–1952), and Louise Beavers (1902–1962). Although the show garnered some accolades, it also received much backlash for its stereotypical portrayal of black characters. The National Association for the Advancement of Colored People (NAACP) requested local stations and sponsors to boycott it. Only four episodes have been made publicly available, and many more are presumed lost.

Like many other early television shows, *The Beulah Show* originated as a radio series in 1945. Beulah was voiced and created by Marlin Hurt, and briefly by Bob Corley (both white and male actors), before Hattie McDaniel, the distinguished first black actor to win an Academy Award, took over the role. Hurt and Corley performed the role as part of their specialty in dialect humor. Having white actors portray black characters was a staple in pre–World War II American comedy, with roots in the minstrel shows, or minstrelsy, of the 19th century. Minstrelsy is a form of comedic variety entertainment performed by black actors or, more typically, by white actors in blackface, establishing recognizable caricatures of black people that carried over into modern media. Such denigrating black stereotypes served as models for comedic representations of blacks, pitting them as distinct "other" and objects for white entertainment. Although the radio show was critiqued for its use of stereotypes, a 1950 review of the television series found similar faults with the show's "stereotyped" concepts (Gould, 1950: 46).

The televised version of *The Beulah Show*, although notable for featuring a black woman as the leading star in her own weekly network series, is still accused of perpetuating black stereotypes. Historians have pointed out that Beulah's character as a domestic servant is a typical stock representation of blacks, and particularly black women, in media. One common stereotype of black domestic roles, including Beulah's, is a lack of family or life outside of her work, which reduces domestic characters to mere extensions of the family they are serving rather than independent persons (Berger, 2010: 21–22). Essentially, Beulah represents an anachronistic fantasy image of black womanhood as the always-helpful caretaker of the white household. Nevertheless, it has been observed that the female actors who took on the role of Beulah succeeded in bringing their own lives and personalities to the character, making Beulah more than just a flat caricature, as well as in showcasing blacks in black roles (Bodroghkozy, 2012: 21–29).

Monica Murtaugh

FURTHER READING

Berger, Maurice. 2010. *For All the World to See: Visual Culture and the Struggle for Civil Rights.* New Haven: Yale University Press.

Bodroghkozy, Aniko. 2012. *Equal Time: Television and the Civil Rights Movement.* Champaign, IL: University of Illinois Press.

Bogle, Donald. 2007. *Brown Sugar: Over One Hundred Years of America's Black Female Superstars.* New York: Continuum.

Gould, Jack. 1950. "Billy Rose Gives First Show on TV." *The New York Times,* October 4.

I LOVE LUCY (1951–1960)

I Love Lucy starred real-life couple Lucille Ball (1911–1989) and Desi Arnaz (1917–1986). The situation comedy centers on the lives of club singer and bandleader Ricky Ricardo (Arnaz) and frustrated housewife Lucy Ricardo (Ball), who live in a New York City apartment building. Throughout the series, Lucy often finds herself involved in screwball antics due to her insatiable appetite for adventure. The couple's neighbors, landlords, and best friends, Fred (William Frawley, 1887–1966) and Ethel (Vivian Vance, 1909–1979), are another mainstay of the show, and they are regularly involved in the weekly storylines. Ethel frequently finds herself involved in Lucy's high jinks, with Ricky and Fred often bailing the duo out of trouble.

Originally a serious film actor, Ball gained attention for her comic talent in her role as a wife in the radio comedy *My Favorite Husband* (1948). Broadcast network CBS approached her about developing a show for television, but Ball would only do it if her husband Arnaz could play her television husband. When CBS resisted, claiming that audiences would not accept a Cuban foreigner with an accent, Ball and Arnaz took a vaudeville show on the road to persuade the network to think otherwise. Eventually, CBS gave in. In addition to starring a multiethnic couple, the show was groundbreaking in several other ways. Ball and Arnaz were not only the stars, but they were actively engaged in the production of the show and insisted on the use of film, which provided greater visual quality, as opposed to the less expensive live broadcast standard of kinescope. To make this happen, Ball and Arnaz agreed to pay cuts, but they also retained creative control and full ownership rights to the show, which led to the launch of their own company, Desilu Productions. Capturing the series on film also allowed for syndication, unlike most other shows from the time period of which no recordings were made. The show also veered from traditional production methods at the time

One of Madame Tousauds's most popular wax images is television icon Lucille Ball as her character Lucy Ricardo in the critically acclaimed *I Love Lucy*. Ball was an entertainment trailblazer on screen, as well as behind the scenes. In addition to multiple self-produced sitcoms, Ball was the first woman to run a major television studio, Desilu Productions. (Jveccl/Dreamstime.com)

by including Ball's preference for a live studio audience instead of a canned laugh track. Additionally, the show was one of the first on American television to include Spanish dialogue.

During the course of the show, Lucille Ball became pregnant with her second child. Her pregnancy was written into the script, but the network banned the use of the word "pregnant" and instead insisted on the use of the word "expecting." This was only the second time in television history that a woman was shown pregnant on a television show, the first being *Mary Kay and Johnny* (1947–1950). Similarly, and also typical of the time, scenes in the bedroom restricted the couple to separate twin beds instead of a double bed.

The chemistry among the show's stars, and especially Ball's impressive physical slapstick comedic talent, led to a successful six seasons and numerous Emmy Award nominations and wins. Desilu Productions went on to produce other groundbreaking television hits, including *The Untouchables* (1959–1963), *Star Trek* (1966–1969), and *That Girl* (1966–1971). After the couple's divorce in 1960, Arnaz sold his share of the company to Ball, who then became the first woman to head a major studio. Ball would continue to work in television, starring in a variety of self-produced sitcoms, until 1986. *I Love Lucy* is considered one of the most successful and groundbreaking television sitcoms of all time, and Lucille Ball remains a celebrated and revered comedic talent.

Ann M. Savage

See also: *That Girl*.

FURTHER READING

Ball, Lucille, Betty Hannah, and Lucie Arnaz Hoffman. 1996. *Love, Lucy*. New York: Putnam.

Banks, Miranda J. 2013. "I Love Lucy: The Writer-Producer." In *How to Watch Television*, 244–52. Edited by Ethan Thompson and Jason Mittell. New York: New York University Press.

Edwards, Elisabeth. 2011. *"I Love Lucy": A Celebration of All Things Lucy: Inside the World of Television's First Great Sitcom*. Philadelphia: Running Press Book Publishers.

Landay, Lori. 2016. "I Love Lucy: Television and Gender in Postwar Domestic Ideology." In *The Sitcom Reader: America Re-Viewed, Still Skewed*, 2nd ed., 87–97. Edited by Mary M. Dalton and Laura R. Linder. Albany, NY: State University of New York Press.

THAT GIRL (1966–1971)

Starring Marlo Thomas (1937–) as aspiring actor Ann Marie, *That Girl* was one of the first sitcoms to center on a single woman living alone. The storylines focus on Ann's pursuit of an acting career, picking up temp jobs to support herself, her relationship with her longtime boyfriend Donald Hollinger (Ted Bessell, 1939–1996), and her mischievous efforts to challenge the sexist status quo. The show's opening scenes typically set up scenarios in need of a bold young woman, and when the question is posed, "What woman would or could possibly accomplish such a thing?" the response was always *That Girl.*

When the show debuted in 1966, women on television were almost exclusively seen as supporting characters. If a woman was a lead in a show, too often her relationship with a man—whether as a wife, secretary, or girlfriend—was the primary element around which the program orbited. Moreover, if a female character was single, the husband was typically presented as deceased in order for audiences to accept such an unmarried status. A young woman living alone was viewed as unseemly and improper.

As an aspiring actor, Thomas kept receiving scripts in which female characters always served as an appendage to a man and never as the lead. Disappointed with such options, Thomas actively sought scripts that featured a woman as the center of the show and did not focus on the woman's need to establish some sort of relationship with a man. In fact, during the development process for *That Girl*, broadcast network ABC pushed for an aunt to live with Ann Marie, but Thomas kept pushing back. Eventually, ABC agreed to the character living alone on the condition that boyfriend (and eventual fiancé) Donald Hollinger had to leave her apartment at the end of every episode. There could never be the appearance of the couple sleeping together. Additionally, the character Ann Marie could never dismiss the idea of marriage or declare that she never intended to get married. ABC insisted that the script include the words "just yet" whenever Ann Marie declared her reluctance to get married, as in "I don't want to get married *just yet.*"

The response to the show was overwhelmingly positive, with Thomas often receiving letters from viewers who identified a "that girl" in their own families. The series aired during the height of the Women's Liberation Movement and the development of what is now known as the second wave of feminism. Thomas also regularly received letters from women seeking to escape abusive relationships, and she was disheartened to learn that there were no safe houses or pro bono law services available to women at risk. Through her experience of working (and producing) the show, as well as the letters she received from women throughout the course of the show, Thomas began to identify as a feminist. As the series neared its end, the network pressured Thomas to end the show's storyline with a wedding, but she refused. Instead, the final episode has Ann Marie taking boyfriend Donald to a women's liberation meeting.

Ann M. Savage

FURTHER READING

Conaway, Cindy, and Peggy Tally. 2014. "Friendship and the Single Girl: What We Learned about Feminism and Friendship from Sitcom Women in the 1960s and

1970s." In *How Television Shapes Our Worldview: Media Representations of Social Trends and Change*, 107–28. Edited by Deborah A. Macey, Kathleen M. Ryan, and Noah J. Springer. Lanham, MD: Lexington Books.

Lehman, Katherine J. 2011. *Those Girls: Single Women in Sixties and Seventies Popular Culture*. Lawrence, KS: University Press of Kansas.

Pilato, Herbie J. 2014. *Glamour, Gidgets, and the Girl Next Door: Television's Iconic Women from the 50s, 60s, and 70s*. Lanham, MD: Taylor Trade Publishing.

Thomas, Marlo. 2010. *Growing Up Laughing: My Story and the Story of Funny*. New York: Hyperion.

JULIA (1968–1971)

In 1968, the NBC television network debuted the situation comedy *Julia*, the first sitcom to feature a black family. Created by white, liberal writer-producer Hal Kanter (1918–2011), *Julia* starred Diahann Carroll (1935–) as a middle-class widowed mother to Corey, her six-year-old son. Following the death of her husband in the Vietnam War, Julia takes a job as a nurse at the health clinic of an aerospace company and moves into an integrated apartment building in Los Angeles. The show's premise revolved around Julia's efforts as a working single mother and the experiences she and Corey faced with the white world in which they lived, both good and bad. Though Julia and Corey had white friends on the show, their experiences with bigotry were thinly veiled attempts to blend entertainment with teachable moments about contemporary race issues.

The sitcom attempted to portray lighthearted situations concerning race issues; however, viewers wrote to Kanter protesting that *Julia*'s representation of a middle-class single black mother living in a posh apartment on a nurse's income did not accurately portray the "real" black experience. Many white viewers contested the accuracy of *Julia*, claiming that the lead character demeaned white motherhood because she was portrayed as more beautiful and smarter than Marie Waggedorn, Julia's white neighbor. In contrast, black women argued that *Julia* was unrealistic in other respects. They asserted that Carroll's character did not illustrate the race struggle that many blacks of the 1960s were fighting to overcome. Many also contended that presenting Julia as a widow undermined the role of black men in the family and society in general, and that it perpetuated the stereotype of black households being fatherless and run by overbearing matriarchs. Although Kanter aimed to introduce the first show about African Americans, critics claimed that he overlooked some harsh actualities of black family life, especially those that involved gender and class factors.

Cries for a more realistic representation of a black family rang loudly in fan mail, the popular press, and in public critiques of Diahann Carroll. By season three, Kanter attempted to respond to viewer criticisms by taking the show in a more pragmatic direction and introducing Steve Bruce, Julia's steady boyfriend, played by Fred Williamson (1935–). Kanter wanted to incorporate a black father figure by having Steve and Julia wed in the fourth season, and intended to dramatize the conflict of Julia wanting to maintain her career while married; however, the show's ratings continued to drop, and NBC cancelled *Julia* at the end of its third season.

Kate L. Flach

FURTHER READING

Acham, Christine. 2004. *Revolution Televised: Prime Time and the Struggle for Black Power.* Minneapolis: University of Minnesota Press.

Bodroghkozy, Aniko. 2012. *Equal Time: Television and the Civil Rights Movement.* Chicago: University of Illinois Press.

Shabazz, Demetria Rougeaux. 2005. "Negotiated Boundaries: Production Practices and the Making of Representation in *Julia*." In *The Sitcom Reader: America Viewed and Skewed*, 151–164. Edited by Mary M. Dalton and Laura R. Linder. Albany, NY: State University of New York Press.

THE MARY TYLER MOORE SHOW (1970–1977)

The Mary Tyler Moore Show is considered one of the greatest sitcoms of all time, and it played an important role in increasing public acceptance of women in the workplace and as independent individuals. The show centers on actress Mary Tyler Moore's (1936–2017) character, Mary Richards, who, after a broken engagement, moves to Minneapolis to take a new job at WJM, the lowest-rated local television station. As an example of the morality of the time period, in the original script Mary moves to Minneapolis as a divorcée, but CBS network executives were so worried that mainstream America would not be accepting of a divorcée that they insisted the storyline be changed. Although Mary applies for a secretarial position, she is hired as an associate producer. Mary's stint at WJM starts off rocky as she clashes with her cantankerous boss, news director Lou Grant (Ed Asner, 1929–).

The second main setting of the show is Mary's apartment, where she develops friendships with her landlord, Phyllis Lindstrom (Cloris Leachman, 1926–) and another tenant, Rhoda Morgenstern (Valerie Harper, 1939–). The show focuses on Mary as she navigates her career and personal life in a time when women's roles in society are moving away from the more conservative and traditional role of a homemaker.

The Mary Tyler Moore Show addressed many issues in relation to women's changing role in the culture at the time. As one of only a few sitcoms with a focus on a single woman living alone and pursuing a career, the show is still considered groundbreaking in challenging traditional views of women in contemporary society. The show addressed topics such as birth control and premarital sex, equal pay for women, homosexuality, divorce, addiction, and sex work. The show was also trailblazing in its portrayal of the affirming relationships Mary develops with other women. The character arc of Rhoda Morgenstern decidedly follows the arc of the

1970s Women's Liberation Movement. The show was also pioneering in terms of who was behind the scenes. By 1973, at a rate still rarely seen today, 25 out of the 75 writers on the show were women.

Lasting for seven seasons, *The Mary Tyler Moore Show* was highly acclaimed and won numerous awards, including 10 Emmys, several Golden Globes, and a Peabody Award. Feminist actor, writer, and producer Tina Fey and media mogul Oprah Winfrey have both cited *The Mary Tyler Moore Show* as being influential in their lives and careers. The final episode of the series, in which new management at the fictional television station fires the majority of the staff, prompting emotional farewells, is still cited as one of the best finales in television history.

Ann M. Savage

See also: *30 Rock*.

FURTHER READING

Bodroghkozy, A. 2004. "Where Have You Gone Mary Richards? Feminism's Rise and Fall in Primetime Television. *Iris*, 49: 12.

Crozier, Susan. 2008. "Making It After All: A Reparative Reading of the Mary Tyler Moore Show." *International Journal of Cultural Studies*, 11(1): 51–67.

Dow, Bonnie J. 1996. *Prime-Time Feminism: Television, Media Culture, and the Women's Movement since 1970*. Philadelphia: University of Pennsylvania Press.

Films for the Humanities & Sciences (Firm), Films Media Group, and Public Broadcasting Service (U.S.). 2011. *Independent Woman*. New York: Films Media Group.

Landay, Lori. 1998. *Madcaps, Screwballs, and Con Women: The Female Trickster in American Culture*. Philadelphia: University of Pennsylvania Press.

Moore, Mary Tyler. 1995. *After All*. New York: Putnam.

MAUDE (1972–1978)

Maude centers on the life of audacious and brash self-identified liberal feminist Maude Findlay (Bea Arthur, 1922–2009) and her life in upstate New York with her fourth husband, Walter Findlay (Bill Macy, 1922–) and daughter, Carol Traynor (Adrienne Barbeau, 1945–).

An unapologetic advocate of gender and racial equality, Maude is a dedicated progressive who often has the last word in arguments with her husband, with the phrase "God'll getcha for that, Walter." As is typical for other shows crafted by *Maude* writer and producer Norman Lear in the 1970s, the sitcom deals with topical social issues and includes storylines about alcoholism, domestic violence, rape, equal opportunity employment, birth control, mental health, and suicide. With lyrics comparing Maude to Lady Godiva, Joan of Arc, and Betsy Ross, the theme song is arguably a feminist anthem, with the phrase "That uncompromisin', enterprisin', anything but tranquilizing, Right-on Maude." At the same time, however, the show also rightly portrays the progressive Maude as being blind to her own status and racism. She is a white upper-class liberal who sometimes comes off as patronizing and as the righteous "savior" of people of color or the working class. Jokes are often made at her expense in her inability to see her own contribution to social hierarchies and inequality.

A decidedly feminist character, Maude finds herself pregnant at 47 years old in season one, and she decides to have an abortion. Although abortion was legal in New York at the time, the episode aired just two months before the *Roe v. Wade* Supreme Court decision that made abortion legal in all 50 states. Decades later, *Maude* is still one of only a handful of American television series to ever have a character confront her unintended pregnancy by opting for an abortion. Most unwanted pregnancies on television tend to end in miscarriages. Titled "Maude's Dilemma," the watershed episode was pre-empted by 30 stations.

Maude was one of several successful spinoffs of the popular and top-rated, groundbreaking Norman Lear sitcom *All in the Family*. *All in the Family* centers on the home life of a white, blue-collar, cantankerous bigot named Archie Bunker (Carroll O'Connor, 1924–2001) and his dedicated wife, Edith (Jean Stapleton, 1923–2013); their liberal daughter and son-in-law; and the comings and goings of neighbors, friends, and extended family members. Maude is Edith's cousin, who only appears twice on *All in the Family*. However, Maude's progressive politics coupled with her bold and forward style erupt in sparks when engaging in conversation with conservative Archie. These entertaining clashes, coupled with actor Bea Arthur's unquestionable talent, led Norman Lear to offer her a sitcom of her own.

Ann M. Savage

See also: Women's Liberation Movement.

FURTHER READING

Dow, Bonnie J. 1996. *Prime-Time Feminism: Television, Media Culture, and the Women's Movement since 1970.* Philadelphia: University of Pennsylvania Press.

Lentz, Kirsten Marthe. 2000. "Quality versus Relevance: Feminism, Race, and the Politics of the Sign in 1970s Television." *Camera Obscura*, 15(1): 44–93. https://muse.jhu.edu.

McGee, Dyllan, Rachel Dretzin Goodman, and Public Broadcasting Service (U.S.). 2014. *Makers Episode 1: Women in Comedy.* San Francisco: Kanopy Streaming.

Tally, Margaret J. 2004. "Television Women from Lucy to Friends: Fifty Years of Sitcoms and Feminism." *The Journal of American Culture*, 27(2): 253–55.

ONE DAY AT A TIME (1975–1984)

One of the first television shows to prominently feature a divorced working mother with children, *One Day at a Time* centered on the lives of Ann Romano

(Bonnie Franklin, 1944–2013) and her two teenage daughters, Julie (Mackenzie Phillips, 1959–) and Barbara Cooper (Valerie Bertinelli, 1960–). The apartment building superintendent, Dwayne Schneider (Pat Harrington, 1929–2015), also played a lead role in the sitcom, mostly providing comic relief. Created by Whitney Blake and developed by renowned writer-producer Norman Lear, the show dealt with a variety of topical social issues as single mother Ann struggled to support her family and raise her two teenage girls. Storylines included such controversial topics as teen sex, teen suicide, birth control, and alcohol and drug use.

Mirroring the 1970s Women's Liberation Movement, the show explored changing gender roles and addressed contemporary political issues of the time. Having married at 17, new divorcée and feminist Ann relocates with her teenage daughters to Logansport, Indiana, in hopes of a fresh start. She takes back her maiden name and for the first time in her life sets out in search of a full-time job. She struggles to make ends meet, faces sexism in her job search and everyday life, and tackles a variety of challenges that come with raising two girls during their tumultuous teen years. Ann finds herself balancing her own embracing of the changing roles of women with her daughters' rebellion, particularly older child, Julie, who pushes cultural norms further and faster than Ann is comfortable with. Julie challenges Ann with her interest in premarital sex, dating older men, and drug use. Over the course of the show's nine-season run, the characters deal with many life changes: marriages, job changes, death, and births. By the end of the series, both girls marry and have children of their own while mother Ann moves to London with her new husband Sam (Howard Hesseman, 1940–).

The show was positively received by viewers, and its creators were inundated with letters from women who declared a clear identification with the storylines and characters. As made clear through the lyrics in the theme song, "Hold on tight, we will muddle through, one day at a time," many women identified with the struggles Ann went through. Although the show was progressive, the three assertive female characters ultimately move into traditional normative roles of wife and mother by the end of the series. The show was also plagued by Mackenzie Phillips's drug and alcohol addictions, a situation that forced writers to write the character Julie in and out of the show on several occasions.

Ann M. Savage

See also: Women's Liberation Movement.

FURTHER READING

Dow, Bonnie J. 1996. *Prime-Time Feminism: Television, Media Culture, and the Women's Movement since 1970.* Philadelphia: University of Pennsylvania Press.

Fortini, Amanda. 2013. "Bonnie Franklin." *The New York Times Magazine,* December 29, P30.

Spangler, Lynn C. 2003. *Television Women from Lucy to Friends: Fifty Years of Sitcoms and Feminism.* Westport, CT: Praeger.

ROSEANNE (1988–1997)

Roseanne is one of the few shows in television history to focus on a working-class family with overweight parents, living in a modest home, who consistently struggled throughout most of the series to make ends meet. Set in a small fictional town in Illinois, the show centers on wisecracking mother Roseanne Conner (Roseanne Barr, 1952–); her husband, Dan Conner (John Goodman, 1952–); and their three children, Becky (Lecy Goranson, 1974–, and Sarah Chalke, 1976–); Darlene (Sara Gilbert, 1975–); and D. J. (Michael Fishman, 1981–). Roseanne's sister, Jackie Harris (Laurie Metcalf, 1955–), is another prominent character. The show was based on the stand-up comedy of Barr, who found herself often battling with *Roseanne*'s producers to ensure that the show maintained a feminist working-class ethic. Storylines grappled head-on with domestic violence, birth control, sexual abuse, worker's rights, and inconsistent employment. The show was also one of the first to include recurring gay characters as well as have an on-screen lesbian kiss.

Comic, actress, and producer Roseanne Barr at a book signing. Roseanne is best known for her role in the sitcom of the same name, which centered on the working-class Conner family. (Turkbug/Dreamstime.com)

One of the unique things about *Roseanne* was the amount of screen time spent on working-class concerns and especially family economics. Throughout the series, both parents cycle through a variety of different and transient jobs as they struggle to make ends meet. In all of her jobs, Roseanne consistently challenges her bosses regarding unfair working conditions and unreasonable expectations. While working at a plastics factory, for example, Roseanne challenges her boss to remove production quotas. When he breaks his promise to do so, she walks off the job, eventually followed by her sister, Jackie, as well as several other coworkers. When working at a diner in a shopping mall, Roseanne consistently pushes back on her boss's confining rules.

As a feminist, Barr also insisted that storylines on *Roseanne* address gender inequality in the home as well as more broadly. One story arc focuses on the complexity of domestic abuse through Jackie's relationship with a boyfriend. In another episode, Roseanne's teenage daughter, Becky, approaches her in need of birth control. After some debate and lots of humor, Roseanne supports Becky in her choices with her own body. At one point, the series even addresses the issue of child sexual abuse. As a child, Roseanne was molested by her father, and when he passes away, audiences see Rosanne grapple with complex emotions as an adult. *Roseanne* successfully addressed complex and difficult social issues, all the while emphasizing comedy over drama.

In Roseanne Barr's pursuit of delivering a show with a feminist working-class sensibility, though, she was often at odds with the show's producers. In the press, Barr was portrayed as an overbearing and difficult woman to work with, and the public largely bought this image of her. She paid a public and personal price to keep the show true to her vision. Although the show was critically acclaimed and consistently at the top of the ratings, it was never nominated for an Emmy Award for Outstanding Comedy Series. However, the actors, including Roseanne Barr, did win a total of four Emmys. Additionally, the show was recognized by the Golden Globe Awards and Screen Actors Guild Awards, and it won a Peabody Award in 1992.

Ann M. Savage

FURTHER READING

Films for the Humanities & Sciences (Firm), Films Media Group, and Public Broadcasting Service (U.S.). 2011. *Independent Woman*. New York: Films Media Group.

Gilbert, Joanne R. 1997. "Performing Marginality: Comedy, Identity, and Cultural Critique." *Text and Performance Quarterly*, 17(4): 317–30.

Karlyn, Kathleen Rowe. 1995. *The Unruly Woman: Gender and the Genres of Laughter*. Austin, TX: University of Texas Press.

MURPHY BROWN (1988–1998)

The sitcom *Murphy Brown* starred actor Candice Bergen (1946–) as the title character, an investigative journalist who works as a news anchor for *FYI*, a fictional CBS television news magazine show. Created by Diane English (1948–) as a decidedly feminist sitcom, the show centers on recovering alcoholic Murphy Brown as a career-driven, hard-hitting reporter who attains great success in a male-dominated profession. After a stint in rehab at the Betty Ford Clinic, Murphy Brown returns to the network. Her coworkers include anxiety-ridden producer Miles Silverberg (Grant Shaud, 1961–); perky reporter Corky Sherwood (Faith Ford, 1964–), whose job seems to be mostly based on her good looks rather than her talent; old-fashioned hard-news anchor Jim Dial (Charles Kimbrough, 1936–); and her longtime investigative collaborator Frank Fontana (Joe Regalbuto, 1949–). A consistent and memorable part of the series is the revolving door of oddball applicants for the position of Brown's secretary. English orchestrated this scenario as a way to include a diverse array of celebrity guest stars, including Bette Midler, Rosie O'Donnell, and Sally Field. As a sitcom centered on a news magazine show, many of the show's storylines focused on current events and used Murphy Brown's sarcasm as a form of political satire.

The series is representative of 1990s feminism: a working baby-boomer woman, who is comfortable with her success, not helpless or naïve, enjoys sex, and who has multiple sexual partners through the course of the series. The series garnered the greatest national attention at the end of the fourth season in 1992, when Murphy finds herself pregnant and chooses to become a single parent. At a public event in May of that year, Vice President Dan Quayle criticized the character Murphy Brown, during a speech on family values, for choosing to be a single parent. "Bearing babies irresponsibly is, simply, wrong," Quayle told his audience. "It doesn't help matters when prime-time TV has Murphy Brown—a character who supposedly epitomizes today's intelligent, highly paid, professional woman—mocking the importance of fathers by bearing a child alone and calling it just another 'lifestyle choice.'"

Quayle's critique was widely reported and triggered a national debate on single parenthood and family values. Stunned that the vice president was making an example of a fictional television character, creator Diane English addressed the matter at the start of the next season. In an episode focusing on Murphy Brown's preparation of a segment on the diversity of the American family, the fictional news magazine incorporated actual television footage of Quayle's comments.

The critically acclaimed show earned 62 Emmy nominations during its run, winning a total of 18. Candice Bergen became the only actor in television history to win five Emmys for playing the same character. The show won numerous other awards as well as a Peabody in 1991.

Ann M. Savage

FURTHER READING

Douglas, Susan J. 2010. *Enlightened Sexism: The Seductive Message That Feminism's Work Is Done.* New York: Times Books.

Dow, Bonnie J. 1996. *Prime-Time Feminism: Television, Media Culture, and the Women's Movement since 1970.* Philadelphia: University of Pennsylvania Press.

Films for the Humanities & Sciences (Firm), Films Media Group, and Public Broadcasting Service (U.S.). 2011. *Independent Woman.* New York: Films Media Group.

Walkowitz, Rebecca L. 1997. "Reproducing Reality: Murphy Brown and Illegitimate Politics." In *Feminist Television Criticism: A Reader,* 325–36. Edited by Charlotte Brunsdon, Julie D'Acci, and Lynn Spigel. Oxford: Clarendon Press.

THE WOMEN OF BREWSTER PLACE (1989)

The Women of Brewster Place, based on Gloria Naylor's 1982 eponymous novel, was a 1989 American television miniseries that explored the lives of African American women living in a housing project on Brewster Place. The series was so well received that it led to a weekly TV show, *Brewster Place*, which was short-lived due to low ratings.

Brewster Place explored the diverse experiences African American women can face even within the same community. Mattie (Oprah Winfrey, 1954–) moves to the neighborhood in old age when she loses her house after her son skips bail; Ciel (Lynn Whitfield, 1953–) suffers post-traumatic stress when her toddler daughter fatally electrocutes herself; Cora (Phyllis Yvonne Stickney; no birth year available) struggles as a single mother to raise six children by different fathers; Sophie (Olivia Cole, 1942–) gossips maliciously about the neighborhood's lesbian couple, Lorraine (Lonette McKee, 1954–) and Theresa (Paula Kelly, 1943–); and Melanie "Kiswana" Browne (Robin Givens, 1964–) moves to Brewster Place to reconnect to her African roots.

The primary threats to the Brewster women are men, who are generally depicted as either absent or violent. Every child is fatherless. The men who do not leave are often vicious, such as C.C. Baker, who brutally rapes Lorraine. (In Naylor's novel, C.C. and his friends gang-rape Lorraine, but such violence may have been deemed too graphic for television.) An exception is Brewster's handyman, Ben, who is both present and kind, but he is killed by Lorraine when she discovers him in an alleyway after her rape. Lorraine may be so traumatized from her assault that she believes Ben is her rapist, or she may not know whom she attacks. Ben's murder may also be a metaphor for the need for women to dismantle the patriarchy (which Ben, at that moment, embodies). The episode presents a more sanguine alternative: instead of killing individual, innocent men (as Lorraine does), women unite to smash systemic patriarchal oppression (as Mattie does when she leads the neighborhood women in tearing down the wall against which Lorraine was raped). The series presents communal sisterhood as the answer to the violence men visit upon women. As Mattie reflects in a voiceover, "We did a lot of laughing here and some crying. Most important, though, we learned that when women came together, there was power inside us we never felt before."

Eden Elizabeth Wales Freedman

FURTHER READING

Bobo, Jacqueline, and Ellen Seiter. 1991. "Black Feminism and Media Criticism: *The Women of Brewster Place.*" *Screen*, 32: 286–302.
Christian, Barbara. 1990. "Naylor's Geography: Community, Class, and Patriarchy in *The Women of Brewster Place* and *Linden Hills.*" *Reading Black, Reading Feminist*, 348–73. Edited by Henry Louis Gates Jr. New York: Meridian/Penguin.
Glickman, Marlaine. 1989. "Black Like Who?" *Film Comment*, 25(3): 75–76.
Naylor, Gloria. 1982. *The Women of Brewster Place*. New York: Penguin.

ALL AMERICAN GIRL (1994–1995)

Predated only by *Mr. T and Tina*'s short run of five episodes in 1976, *All American Girl* was the second sitcom centered on an Asian family and starring an all-Asian cast. The show was promoted as based on the comedy of feminist Margaret Cho (1968–), whose work included stories about her family, particularly her mother; their life running a bookstore; and the cultural gap and struggles between immigrant parents from Korea raising American-born children. Set in San Francisco, the show finds Americanized and rebellious daughter Margaret (played by Margaret Cho) often at odds with her traditional mother Katherine Kim (Jodi Long, 1954–). Father Benny Kim (Clyde Kusatsu, 1948–) often acts as mediator between Margaret and her mother, and eccentric grandmother Yung-hee Kim (Amy Hill, 1953–) provides comic relief. Younger brother Eric Kim (J. B. Quon, 1980–) and obedient and reserved older brother Dr. Stuart Kim (B. D. Wong, 1960–) provide contrast to Margaret's antics. Much of the series focuses on Katherine's displeasure with Margaret's rebellion against tradition as well as her choices in suitors. Katherine's preference is for Margaret to take the more traditional route by settling down with a professional and polite Korean American man.

At just 26, Cho found herself at the center of a national network sitcom and felt responsible for the success of the show. But she did not have the level of creative control she would have preferred. As a result, Cho was often at odds with network executives who consistently rejected storylines based on her comedy. Cho also widely detailed in the media an incident in which network executives told her that her face was too big for the camera and requested that she lose weight in order to achieve what they deemed an acceptable look for primetime. Eager to keep the show, Cho went on a drastic and unhealthy diet and nearly died after losing 30 pounds in just two weeks. Cho also found herself being criticized for being both "too Asian" and "not Asian enough." Cho also wrangled with executives about the perpetuation of Asian stereotypes. The show and Cho faced criticism from the broader Asian community about what many saw as cli-chéd representations of Asians—particularly the roles of Katherine and Stuart. Korean Americans in particular were critical of the show's poorly spoken Korean dialogue. None of the writers had Korean backgrounds, and Cho was the only Korean American cast member.

The show was canceled after just one season, but Cho went on to have a successful career in stand-up as well as acting. She has completed numerous successful stand-up comedy tours around the country and has written two books. Cho is politically active and has been a strong advocate for gay and women's rights. She has also spoken openly about her difficult experience working in the entertainment industry. In both her memoir, *I'm the One That I Want*, and her stand-up routines, Cho has chastised the entertainment industry for its racism and sexism and its partiality for thinness and whiteness.

Ann M. Savage

All American Girl star Margaret Cho on a red carpet in 2009. Cho, an outspoken feminist, is candid about the pressures television executives put on her about not only her appearance, but also the direction and content of the show. (Aaron Settipane/Dreamstime.com)

FURTHER READING

Cho, Margaret. 2001. *I'm the One That I Want*. New York: Ballantine Books.

Cho, Margaret. 2005. *I Have Chosen to Stay and Fight*. New York: Riverhead Books.

Karlyn, Kathleen Rowe. 2011. *Unruly Girls, Unrepentant Mothers: Redefining Feminism on Screen*. Austin, TX: University of Texas Press.

Lee, Rachel C. 2004. " 'Where's My Parade?': Margaret Cho and the Asian American Body in Space." *TDR*, 48(2): 108–32.

Mizejewski, Linda. 2014. *Pretty/Funny: Women Comedians and Body Politics.* Austin, TX: University of Texas Press.

ELLEN (1994–1998)

After years of speculation and months of anticipation, in April 1997 Ellen DeGeneres's (1958–) character Ellen Morgan came out as lesbian in a two-part episode of the sitcom *Ellen*, titled "The Puppy Episode." When DeGeneres's character came out of the closet with a love interest played by actor Laura Dern (1967–), it was widely described as a groundbreaking moment in television history. The highest-rated episode of the series, with 42 million viewers, "The Puppy Episode" went on to win a Primetime Emmy Award for Outstanding Writing for a Comedy Series, as well as a Peabody Award. Just one year later, however, the show was canceled because of declining ratings, due in part to the failure of audiences to accept storylines centered on a lead lesbian character.

DeGeneres started her career as a stand-up comic. Eventually she caught the eye of a producer of top-rated late-night talk show *The Tonight Show Starring Johnny Carson*. After she concluded her stand-up routine on the show, legendary host Carson called her over to the couch next to him (usually reserved for guests rather than comics paid for stand-up routines). DeGeneres was the first woman to receive the much-sought-after invitation. Her success on *The Tonight Show* led to several comedy specials and, in 1994, the development of a sitcom for ABC. At first titled *These Friends of Mine* (the name of the series was changed to *Ellen* beginning in the second season), the Ellen Morgan character was seemingly heterosexual and dating men. Eventually, as DeGeneres considered coming out in real life, she also began to consider having the character Ellen come out on the television sitcom. Although the network promotions for "The Puppy Episode" never explicitly indicated that the character would be coming out, DeGeneres made many pre-broadcast hints about this possibility. In the highly anticipated episode, Ellen meets a lesbian played by Laura Dern and begins to have feelings for her. Eventually, Ellen comes out to Dern's character in a more public way than she anticipated, by declaring her sexual identity through an airport microphone. Although the ratings were high and there was a positive response, ABC chose to start the episode with an "adult content" warning, and several advertisers pulled out of the episode. Soon after, the ratings of the show declined, with some attributing this to the show being too much about Ellen being a lesbian as well as ABC's discomfort with the content. The show was eventually canceled at the end of the fifth season in 1998.

The dual coming out—Ellen as character and Ellen in real life—was greeted with a great deal of media attention, including appearances on top-rated talk shows, in news magazines, and elsewhere in the press. DeGeneres appeared on the cover of the April 1997 edition of *Time* Magazine with the headline "Yep, I'm Gay." After revealing her lesbianism, it took years for DeGeneres to get another job. In 2001, she attempted a second sitcom titled *The Ellen Show*, which lasted only one season. In 2003, she launched her daytime talk show *The Ellen DeGeneres Show*, which has been on the air for more than 13 years and has won numerous awards and accolades.

Ann M. Savage

FURTHER READING

Dow, Bonnie. 2001. "Ellen, Television, and the Politics of Gay and Lesbian Visibility." *Critical Studies in Media Communication*, 18(2): 123–40.

Herman, Didi. 2005. "'I'm Gay': Declarations, Desire, and Coming Out on Prime-Time Television." *Sexualities*, 8(1): 7–29.

McCarthy, Anna. 2001. "Ellen: Making Queer Television History." *GLQ*, 7(4): 593–620.

Peterson, Valerie V. 2005. "Ellen: Coming Out and Disappearing." In *The Sitcom Reader: America Viewed and Skewed*, 165–76. Edited by Mary M. Dalton and Laura R. Linder. Albany, NY: State University of New York Press.

THE L WORD (2004–2009)

The L Word was "the first prime-time commercial television drama to focus on the lives of lesbian and bisexual women" (McFadden, 2010: 1). Airing on the premium cable network Showtime, *The L Word* followed the lives of six core female characters in West Hollywood, California, as they coped with the everyday life challenges of love, break-ups, pregnancy, marriage, bigotry, and death. The main cast members included Shane McCutcheon (Katherine Moening, 1977–), a heart-throb/womanizer hairstylist; a biracial couple consisting of an art curator turned university dean named Bette Porter (Jennifer Beals, 1963–) and Tina Kennard (Laurel Holloman, 1971–), a movie executive; Bette's famous older half-sister, Kit Porter (Pam Grier, 1949–); and writer/radio host Alice Pieszecki (Leisha Hailey, 1971–). The first season centers on Jenny Schechter (Mia Kirshner, 1975–), a young writer who moves to California with her boyfriend and ends up falling in love with a woman. Upon *The L Word*'s success, creator Ilene Chaiken (1957–) subsequently produced three seasons of the reality show *The Real L World*, which aired on Showtime from 2010 to 2012.

In an interview, Chaiken, who also served as executive producer of the series, explained that she always intended for *The L Word* to run on Showtime as she did not want to be constrained by the regulations of broadcast television. Depictions of queerness on television had been introduced in the 1970s; however, most representations centered on the experience and visibility of gay male characters (consider, for example, *Will & Grace*). *The L Word* gave visibility to the gay female experience, and the show was greeted with much praise. It is often credited with playing a pivotal role in the mainstreaming of gay rights. However, the show also received recurring criticisms for its lack of diversity in the cast and an unrealistic representation of lesbians' lives. Critics pointed out that the characters all lived in upper-scale areas of West Hollywood but were rarely depicted working. Likewise, the show privileged femme cisgender (a person whose self-identity corresponds to her biological sex) representations in all its main cast members and ultimately failed to show the full gender spectrum, including the symbolic absence of masculine "butch" lesbians.

Despite these perceived shortcomings, *The L Word*'s influence in popular culture is impossible to ignore. At the annual 2016 Gay & Lesbian Alliance Against Defamation awards, actor Ruby Rose related the major role that *The L Word* played in her life: "When I was young, 12, I came out. I couldn't see anybody on the screen that was anything like me. I couldn't find anyone gay. It was before *The L Word*." She credited the show with saving her life and said, "It made me feel like I existed." Her statement underscores the importance of mediated representations of identity for viewers across the world. *The L Word* continues to have a large following online. There are multiple fan sites dedicated to the show, and Showtime reports continued stable viewership.

Giuliana Sorce

FURTHER READING

Cefai, Sarah. 2014. "Feeling and the Production of Lesbian Space in The L Word." *Gender, Place & Culture*, 21(5): 650–65.

McFadden, Margaret. 2010. "'L'" is for Looking Again: Art and Representation on *The L Word*." *Feminist Media Studies*, 10(4): 421–39.

McFadden, Margaret T. 2014. *The L Word*. Detroit: Wayne State University Press.

On Top Magazine Staff. 2016. "Taylor Swift Presents Ruby Rose with GLAAD Media Award." *On Top Magazine*, April 3. http://www.ontopmag.com/article/22537/Taylor_Swift_Presents_Ruby_Rose_With_GLAAD_Media_Award.

30 ROCK (2006–2013)

Tina Fey (1970–) was a popular cast member and first female head writer of the long-running variety show *Saturday Night Live* (SNL). In the early 2000s, she teamed with renowned SNL producer, Lorne Michaels (1944–), to develop a sitcom that centered on television show producer Liz Lemon (played by Fey), who works on a show not unlike *SNL*. The show's other characters included eccentric actors Jenna Maroney (Jane Krakowski, 1968–) and Tracy Jordan (Tracy Morgan, 1968–), even odder show writers, and a self-absorbed network executive, Jack Donaghy, played by frequent SNL guest star Alec Baldwin (1958–). Fey's Lemon is a quirky but appealing nerd with a strong neurotic streak.

A self-identified feminist, Fey used her positions as producer and writer on *30 Rock* to parody the absurdity of female stereotypes, particularly through the Jenna Maroney character as well as her own character's obsession with age. Fey's show not only forefronted female storylines, it consistently raised feminist issues related to women in the workforce, gender norms, body ideals, and gender double standards. In one episode, for example, Liz Lemon lobbies for the use of "herstory" instead of history when arguing with Jack Donaghy. In another episode, when Liz asks Jack for his signature, instead of the usual colloquialism of asking for his "John Hancock" she instead asks for a "Lucretia Mott," referencing the influential 18th-century suffragette. When Jack refers to a woman as a businessman, Liz responds with "businesswoman." Challenging the cultural secrecy and shame surrounding menstruation and feminine hygiene products, Liz deliberately drops tampons on the floor and demands that people "deal with it."

Fey's Lemon feminism (sometimes referred to as Lemonism in popular culture press) was of course limited, representing a privileged form of feminism from the perspective of a white, middle-class, heterosexual woman who did not have to worry about or choose to campaign for other more marginalized groups such as transgender people, people of color, or the working

Saturday Night Live alum, comic, and writer Tina Fey with *30 Rock* co-star Alec Baldwin at the 59th Primetime Emmy Awards in 2007. Fey's character, Liz Lemon, is often at odds with Baldwin's conservative, profit-minded, television executive Jack Donaghy. The show won a total of sixteen Emmys. (Featureflash/Dreamstime.com)

poor. Although the show received criticism for perpetuating the tropes of women as baby-crazy and relationship-focused, there was no question that this was Tina Fey's work, even if it was not the most progressive form of feminism.

30 Rock won the Emmy for Outstanding Comedy Series for the first three years of the series, three Emmys for Outstanding Writing for a Comedy Series, and several acting Emmys. The series was honored with multiple Golden Globe Awards and Screen Actors Guild Awards as well as a Peabody.

Ann M. Savage

FURTHER READING

Davidauskis, April. 2015. "'How Beautiful Women Eat': Feminine Hunger in American Popular Culture." *Feminist Formations*, 27(1): 167–89.

Fey, Tina. 2012. *Bossypants*. New York: Back Bay Books/Little, Brown.

Mizejewski, Linda. 2012. "Feminism, Postfeminism, Liz Lemonism: Comedy and Gender Politics on 30 Rock. (Essay)." *Genders*, 55: NA.

Mizejewski, Linda. 2014. *Pretty/Funny: Women Comedians and Body Politics*. Austin, TX: University of Texas Press.

PARKS AND RECREATION (2009–2015)

In this critically acclaimed comedy series, *SNL* alum Amy Poehler (1971–) starred as Leslie Knope, a determined and idealistic mid-level bureaucrat in the Indiana Parks and Recreation Department in the fictitious town of Pawnee, Indiana. Set in the offices of the neglected and underestimated parks department, altruistic Leslie works tirelessly on behalf of the community to mold Pawnee into a crown jewel of Indiana. Her disinterested, antibureaucracy, libertarian boss, Ron Swanson (Nick Offerman, 1970–), and her under-qualified and apathetic staff tend to provide inconvenient and unintended challenges in her efforts to attain her goals. Sarcastic office assistant April Ludgate (Aubrey Plaza, 1984–) tries to avoid working as much as possible, and media mogul wannabe Tom Haverford (Aziz Ansari, 1983–) has little interest in his job as second in command to Leslie. Naïve, childlike Garry Gergich (Jim O'Heir, 1962–), endlessly teased by his coworkers, is earnest but unaccomplished. And longtime parks department employee Donna Meagle (Marietta Sirleaf, 1970–) is more interested in dating and her Mercedes than helping Leslie move projects along. Other characters include dim-witted shoe shiner Andy Dwyer (Chris Pratt, 1979–); Leslie's best friend, nurse Ann Perkins (Rashida Jones, 1976–); Leslie's love interest and eventual husband Ben Wyatt (Adam Scott, 1973–); and obnoxiously upbeat state employee Chris Traeger (Rob Lowe, 1964–). Despite their shortcomings, Leslie's coworkers often end up rallying in support of her lofty goals.

A single-camera mockumentary sitcom, *Parks and Recreation* had storylines that often included social commentary and references to current events. Leslie, who unapologetically loves public service, is pro-woman, pro–Equal Rights, and determined to do things equitably. As an admirer of women in politics, her office is decorated with photos of Madeleine Albright, Hillary Clinton, Sandra Day O'Connor, Michelle Obama, and Nancy Pelosi. The names of feminist icons such as Naomi Wolf, Laura Mulvey, Susan B. Anthony, and Gertrude Stein also were mentioned in episodes throughout the series.

Leslie is not afraid to challenge the status quo, especially when it comes to gender and women's rights. When she finds herself as a voting member of Pawnee's anachronistic beauty pageant, she tries to overthrow the process by lobbying for a win for the most educated and community-minded contestant versus the traditional focus on the superficial. When a girl isn't allowed to join the boys-only Pawnee Rangers, Leslie establishes the Pawnee Goddesses in an effort to challenge exclusionary barriers and gender roles. By the end of the episode, the Pawnee Rangers folds, and all genders are welcome to be a part of the Pawnee Goddesses. In another episode, Leslie and April take jobs as garbage collectors to prove that women can do any job men can do. In a challenge to Valentine's Day, Leslie introduces Galentine's Day as a holiday for women to celebrate other women. When she decides to marry, Leslie refuses to change her last name. She consistently challenges the patriarchy and successfully makes progressive change.

Although she was not the originating creator behind the sitcom, feminist Poehler did help shape the show. She often provided creative input and wrote four episodes of the series. The show garnered 10 Primetime Emmy Award nominations, several Golden Globe nominations (with one win for Amy Poehler), and a Peabody Award. Poehler has gone on to act in films as well as to launch Amy Poehler's Smart Girls website. Smart Girls' aim is to create an online community that celebrates imagination and intelligence over fitting in and encourages girls to get engaged in activism, volunteerism, and the arts.

Ann M. Savage

FURTHER READING

Engstrom, Erika. 2013. "'Knope We Can!' Primetime Feminist Strategies in NBC's Parks and Recreation." *Media Report To Women*, 41(4): 6–21.

Galo, Sarah. 2015. "How Parks and Recreation Served up Prime-Time Feminism amid the Laughs." *The Guardian*, February 24. https://www.theguardian.com /tv-and-radio/2015/feb/24/parks-and-recreation-prime-time-feminism-laughs.

Ryan, Maureen. 2015. "What 'Parks and Recreation' Taught My Son about Feminism (And So Much Else)." *The Huffington Post*, February 23. http://www .huffingtonpost.com/2015/02/23/parks-and-recreation-finale_n_6732338 .html.

Thompson, Ethan, and Jason Mittell. 2013. *How to Watch Television*. New York: New York University Press.

SCANDAL (2012–)

Scandal centers on Washington, D.C., political crisis manager Olivia Pope (Kerry Washington, 1977–), a former White House aide who runs her own public relations firm, Pope & Associates. Considered the best in the business, fierce and strident Olivia manages crises for the powerful while trying to manage her own personal and professional life and that of her staff through the series' run. In the first season, Olivia helps struggling candidate Fitzgerald Grant III (Tony Goldwyn, 1960–) win the presidency, and soon after they begin an affair that is on-again, off-again throughout the series.

Scandal is one of the few dramas in television history to star a highly accomplished and bold professional African American woman as the lead, and producer Shonda Rhimes (1970–) is the first African American woman to create and produce a Top Ten network show. Inspired by real-life Washington, D.C., Republican crisis manager Judy Smith, producer Shonda Rhimes deliberately set out to create a show representative of the diversity of America.

Although broadcast networks have traditionally steered clear of anything that might be perceived as undesirable or not of interest to a white, middle-class audience, Rhimes's success with television hit dramas *Grey's Anatomy* and *Private Practice* gave her the clout to persuade ABC television network executives to give the green light for *Scandal*. Not only does the show have a rarely seen professional and sexual black woman as the lead, but the vice president is a woman, the Republican chief of staff is gay, and Olivia has an interracial affair with Fitzgerald. Most notably, this less typical casting is portrayed as merely ordinary rather than as a central theme of any storyline.

Television writer and producer Shonda Rhimes with one of her five NAACP Image Awards. Rhimes pushed television boundaries by casting women of color as the leads in shows such as *Scandal* and *How to Get Away with Murder.* (Carrienelson1/Dreamstime.com)

Rhimes skillfully weaves in social justice storylines throughout the show. Self-identified feminist Olivia actively seeks to challenge traditional gender norms and break barriers. When Fitzgerald refers to a woman as a bitch, Olivia swiftly reprimands him and asks him to consider how his word choice would be different if he were referring to a man. She challenges a senator when he victim-blames a rape survivor. Mirroring real-life politics, another storyline focuses on a female senator filibustering against efforts to defund women's health care provider Planned Parenthood. In the same episode, and without any handwringing or expressions of regret, Olivia unapologetically has an abortion. Among many other progressive storylines, the show also addresses equal pay for women and challenges the double standard women face when it comes to appearance.

Although it is widely celebrated and stridently feminist, some have criticized various elements of the show. Some feminists see Olivia and Fitzgerald's relationship as perpetuating myths of passion. The obsessive nature of the relationship and aggressive sex scenes are portrayed as desirable rather than as potentially dangerous or as signals of an abusive relationship. With the portrayal of all its diverse characters as successful, some have criticized the show for perpetuating the myth that hard work is all you have to do to succeed, without addressing how minorities regularly face obstacles of racism, sexism, or homophobia. The most common criticism is that most of the show's diverse characters are Republican when in reality the Republican Party lacks diversity and often blocks progressive policies. Despite these criticisms, the series has won numerous awards from Black Entertainment Television and the NAACP, as well as Primetime Emmy Awards and a Peabody.

Ann M. Savage

See also: *How to Get Away with Murder.*

FURTHER READING

Dolan, Jill. 2013. *The Feminist Spectator in Action: Feminist Criticism for the Stage and Screen.* New York: Palgrave Macmillan.

Goldman, Adria Y. 2014. *Black Women and Popular Culture: The Conversation Continues.* Lanham, MD: Lexington Books.

Silva, Kumarini, and Kaitlynn Mendes. 2015. *Feminist Erasures: Challenging Backlash Culture.* Houndmills, Basingstoke, Hampshire: Palgrave Macmillan.

Spark, Clare. 2015. "SCANDAL's 'Inclusive' Feminism." *YDS: The Clare Spark Blog,* November 21. https://clarespark.com/2015/11/21/scandals-inclusive-feminism/.

ORANGE IS THE NEW BLACK (2013–)

The Netflix comedy-drama series *Orange Is the New Black* (OITNB) is loosely based on the memoir *Orange Is the New Black: My Year in a Women's Prison* (2010) by Piper Kerman (1969–). The series begins with the imprisonment of white, middle-class Piper Chapman (Taylor Schilling, 1984–) in a minimum-security prison for criminal drug activity she engaged in 10 years earlier. As the series develops, audiences follow the lives of a racially and sexually diverse group of women in the fictional prison of Litchfield in upstate New York. Prominent figures in the series include African American transgender woman Laverne Cox (1984–) as Sophia Burset, the prison's hairstylist, and African American Uzo Aduba (1981–), who plays the innocent yet erratic Suzanne "Crazy Eyes" Warren.

When the series begins, Piper appears as a wholesome woman thrown into the unruly world of prison. As the series unfolds and Piper morphs into a prison regular, the other inmates' backstories are revealed, and the characters become more fully developed and multidimensional. Poverty, poor choices in men, and lack of opportunity surface as the major themes leading to their lives in prison. Series storylines address individual struggles of the various inmates while simultaneously unpacking social justice matters such as racism, transphobia, solitary confinement, overcrowding, and prison privatization as well as issues that plague female inmates specifically, such as pregnancy and childbirth in prison.

The show has been critically acclaimed and has received numerous awards, including several Primetime Emmy Awards, a Gay and Lesbian Alliance Against Defamation (GLAAD) award for Outstanding Comedy Series, and multiple Screen Actors Guild Awards as well as a 2013 Peabody Award. The show has also received NAACP Image Awards nominations

Despite the show's accolades for its breadth of diversity, many rightly point out that one of the few times the media represents so many women of color is when they are imprisoned. Another oft-criticized and highly problematic storyline appears in the fourth season, when rape survivor Tiffany "Pennsatucky" Doggett (Taryn Manning, 1978–) not only forgives but begins to have romantic feelings for her rapist, a prison guard. Some also criticize the show for perpetuating stereotypes by focusing on a white woman inmate with a "fish out of water" storyline.

Ann M. Savage

FURTHER READING

Artt, Sarah, and Anne Schwan. 2016. "Screening Women's Imprisonment: Agency and Exploitation in Orange Is the New Black." *Television & New Media*, 17: 467–72.

Belcher, C. 2016. "There Is No Such Thing as a Post-racial Prison: Neoliberal Multiculturalism and the White Savior Complex on Orange Is the New Black." *Television & New Media*, 17: 491–503.

Enck, Suzanne M., and Megan E. Morrissey. 2015. "If Orange Is the New Black, I Must Be Color Blind: Comic Framings of Post-Racism in the Prison-Industrial Complex." *Critical Studies in Media Communication*, 32(5): 303–17.

Schwan, A. 2016. "Postfeminism Meets the Women in Prison Genre: Privilege and Spectatorship in Orange Is the New Black." *Television & New Media*, 17: 473–90.

INSIDE AMY SCHUMER (2013–)

Two years into the critically acclaimed show *Inside Amy Schumer*, comedian Amy Schumer (1981–) skyrocketed to fame in 2015 when she starred in her first feature film, *Trainwreck*; won *Glamour* magazine's Trailblazer Award, and hosted the *MTV Movie Awards*. Acerbic, smart, sex-positive feminist comic, Schumer started with stand-up before landing the show *Inside Amy Schumer* on cable channel Comedy Central. With Schumer as creator, star, writer, and executive producer, the topical skit comedy show features a blend of comedy sketches, Schumer's stand-up bits, interviews with everyday people, novelty stars, and other comics. The skits target a variety of feminist-themed topics, including rape culture, women's tendency to over-apologize, beauty standards, and government encroachment on reproductive rights. In a culture where women are expected to be "shy" about their own desire for sex, Schumer is unapologetic about her own healthy sexual appetite, often referencing masturbation, one-night stands, and STDs.

In a 2015 spoof on the 1957 classic film *Twelve Angry Men*, the series addresses lookism and sexism in Hollywood as a group of men debate and deliberate on whether Amy Schumer herself is attractive enough to even be on television. This skit, as well as others, references an issue that Hollywood, in addition to the general culture, has been plagued with for decades. In another sketch, Schumer comes upon an outdoor luncheon with actors Julia Louis-Dreyfus, Tina Fey, and Patricia Arquette debating the age when female actors find themselves viewed as too old and "unattractive" by Hollywood. In yet another sketch, Schumer addresses the epidemic of rape in the military when she joins her boyfriend in a first-person shooter, role-playing video game and her character faces a variety of obstacles as well as ridicule when attempting to report a rape.

Despite Schumer's willingness to tackle topical gender issues, however, she has been accused of having a blind spot when it comes to race. Schumer has been known to make jokes that perpetuate problematic stereotypes of people of color. Schumer quickly responded to such criticisms by insisting that although she will likely no doubt make jokes that offend people, she is not racist. Many found this response defensive, with some critics describing her as another white feminist who fails to accept her white privilege. In August 2015, a gunman with a history of violence against women entered a Louisiana theater screening of Schumer's film *Trainwreck*, killing two people and injuring nine others. The shooting motivated Schumer to advocate for stricter gun control laws.

The show has been recognized with Primetime Emmy wins as well as a Peabody Award. The future of the series remains unclear. Although Comedy Central has green-lighted a fifth season, Schumer indicated on social media that there were no plans for production to begin in the near future.

Ann M. Savage

FURTHER READING

Bilger, Audrey. 2015. "Inside and Out." *Ms.*, 20 (Summer).

Marx, Nick. 2016. "Expanding the Brand: Race, Gender, and the Post-Politics of Representation on Comedy Central." *Television & New Media*, 17(3): 272–87.

Vagianos, Alanna. 2016. "Amy Schumer Nails the Absurd Difficulties of Shopping While Female." *The Huffington Post*, May 13. http://www.huffingtonpost.com/entry/amy-schumer-nails-the-absurd-difficulties-of-shopping-while-female_us_5735d853e4b060aa781a07cc.

HOW TO GET AWAY WITH MURDER (2014–)

How to Get Away with Murder is a popular television show produced by the ABC, ShondaLand Productions, and NoWalk Entertainment. The part-thriller, part-legal drama follows Annalise Keating (Viola Davis, 1965–), a criminal defense attorney and professor who selects five of her students to work at her firm as interns. Annalise's team often defends well-known clients notorious for their alleged crimes. While investigating the murder of Lila Stangard, Annalise discovers that Stangard was her husband's mistress. Through flashbacks and current-day scenes, the audience learns that Sam Keating (Annalise's husband, played by Tom Verica, 1964–) is murdered, and the interns are involved in disposing of his body. How and why these events come to pass is a mystery sustained well into the second season.

The show has received many accolades. Notably, lead actress Viola Davis won an Emmy, People's Choice Award, and two Screen Actors Guild Awards for her role as Annalise Keating, a powerful, complex character described as an antiheroine. The series also won a GLAAD Media Award for Outstanding Drama Series and an American Film Institute Award in 2015 for Best Television Program of the Year.

How to Get Away with Murder has received praise for racial, gender, and sexual diversity in its plotlines and cast of characters. *Vanity Fair* called the show "the boldest, nerviest show on television at the moment" for its depiction of complex, flawed, and powerful characters and for being "unafraid of diversity, strong women, and gay sex"

Actress Viola Davis won the 2015 Screen Actors Guild Award for Outstanding Performance by a Female Actor in a Drama Series for her portrayal of law professor Annalise Keating in ABC's *How to Get Away with Murder*. Davis's acceptance speech included a jab at a *New York Times* writer who dismissed her beauty as less than ideal. (Jaguarps/Dreamstime.com)

(Lawson, 2014). The show features two actors of color in leading roles, and prominent gay characters. Creator Peter Nowalk explains that "writing some real gay sex into a network show is to right the wrong of all of the straight sex that you see on TV" (Dos Santos, 2014). Nowalk's comment speaks to the normalization of heterosexual intimacy in mainstream American television and film. The inclusion of same-sex intimacy has sparked criticism from some viewers, however. In a comment typical of other critical viewers, one Twitter user called these scenes "too much." Shonda Rhimes, the show's executive producer, responded: "There are no GAY scenes. There are scenes with people in them."

Although the show has been described as breaking new ground in its depiction of sexuality, the series is also known for its diverse cast. During her acceptance speech at the 2015 Emmy Awards, Viola Davis thanked the show's writers and Shonda Rhimes for "redefin[ing] what it means to be beautiful, to be sexy, to be a leading woman. To be black." Davis is the first black actress to win an Emmy for Lead Actress in a Drama, illustrating the scarcity of roles historically available for black women—a dearth in representation that the show is rectifying.

Emily L. Hiltz

See also: *Scandal.*

FURTHER READING

Dos Santos, Kristin. 2014. "Why There Will Be Plenty of Gay Sex on *How to Get Away with Murder*," September 25. http://www.eonline.com/news/582921/why-there-will-be-lots-of-gay-sex-on-how-to-get-away-with-murder.

Lawson, Richard. 2014. "Is How to Get Away with Murder the Most Progressive Show on Television?" October 16. http://www.vanityfair.com/hollywood/2014/10/how-to-get-away-with-murder-gay-sex.

Lowder, J. Bryan. 2014. "What's with All the Bottom-Shaming in *How to Get Away with Murder*?" October 28. http://www.slate.com/blogs/outward/2014/10/28/why_are_how_to_get_away_with_murder_s_gay_sex_scenes_full_of_bottom_shame.html.

O'Connell, Michael. 2014. "*How to Get Away with Murder* Breaks DVR Records," September 30. http://www.hollywoodreporter.com/live-feed/how-get-away-murder-breaks-736778.

JANE THE VIRGIN (2014–)

Jane the Virgin (2014–) is a U.S. television series airing on the CW network. The comedy-drama follows the story of Jane Gloriana Villanueva (played by Gina Rodriguez, 1984–), a 23-year-old Venezuelan virgin who becomes pregnant when she is accidentally artificially inseminated during a routine gynecological exam. This surprising turn of events sends Jane's well-planned life into disarray. While Jane's complicated story is at the center of *Jane the Virgin*, three generations of women in her family are at the heart of the show: Jane; her free-spirited mother,

Xiomara (Andrea Navedo, 1977–); and devout grandmother Alba (Ivonne Coll, 1947–). The series brings women of color to the foreground on primetime television by focusing on multidimensional, multigenerational Latina characters. *Jane the Virgin* directly engages with issues of gender, race, class, sexuality, nationality, and the law.

Jane the Virgin is adapted from the Venezuelan telenovela *Juana la Virgen* (2002). The telenovela television genre blends comedy and drama in serialized storylines—storylines that carry over from one episode to the next—prominently featuring women in plots that revolve around heterosexual love, marriage, and family. Although internationally popular, telenovelas are not widely seen by English-speaking audiences in North America.

Jane the Virgin borrows some telenovela conventions yet also subverts the genre's standards. For instance, the show focuses on female characters, but their stories are not limited to their relationships with men and the nuclear family. Although some critics feel that Jane's love triangle and decision to have the baby outweigh the subversive possibilities, the narrative of *Jane the Virgin* is still predominantly driven by women's experiences. Additionally, the series does not shy away from critiquing gender roles. Jane negotiates societal expectations surrounding her position as a young, unmarried-yet-expecting woman of color. She struggles with "having it all" and balancing her personal goals against a child she wants, but who was not in her plan.

Jane the Virgin also engages with contemporary issues about race, ethnicity, and U.S. law. When Alba is hospitalized after being pushed down the stairs, doctors inform Xiomara that they intend to report Alba to Immigration and Customs Enforcement because she is in the country illegally. Xiomara protests, "That can't be legal!" The scene pauses, and the show's narrator interjects with text reading, "Yes, this really happens. Look it up. #immigrationreform." Audiences are reminded that issues like citizenship and immigration reform are matters impacting real people.

Jane the Virgin has achieved considerable critical success. It has been honored by the American Film Institute and the Peabody Awards, as well as acknowledged by the Golden Globe Awards, Critics' Choice Awards, and Primetime Emmy Awards. These accolades are especially notable because *Jane the Virgin* is the first show focusing on Latinas to receive critical and popular acclaim in the United States.

Katie Sullivan Barak

FURTHER READING

Lang, Nicole. 2015. "Abortion and 'Jane the Virgin': Ultimately, Giving Birth Is the One Choice That Matters on This Show," Salon, November 2. http://www.salon.com/2015/11/02/abortion_and_jane_the_virgin_ultimately_giving_birth_is_the_one_choice_that_matters_on_this_show.

Martinez, Diana. 2015. "*Jane the Virgin* Proves Diversity Is More Than Skin Deep," October 19. http://www.theatlantic.com/entertainment/archive/2015/10/jane-the-virgin-telenovelas/409696.

TRANSPARENT (2014–)

Transparent is an Amazon Studios television series created and directed by Jill Soloway (1965–), who was inspired by her father's real-life transition from male to female. The series follows the Pfefferman family as they learn that the patriarch they knew as Mort, played by Jeffrey Tambor (1944–), identifies as transgender and begins her journey to become Maura. In the first season, the show's narrative moves between the present and 20–25 years into the past, weaving radical gender politics and Maura's changes and growing pains seamlessly with the mundane ins and outs of a tight-knit Jewish family in Los Angeles. Marrying "the marginalized idea of gender transition to the familiar American concept of reinvention," Maura's coming out and subsequent journey into hormone replacement therapy and trans support groups serves as a catalyst for the other Pfeffermans to do some much-needed growing and exploring of their own (Levy, 2015).

The show's influence is largely marked by its departure from previous media depictions of transgender characters as sick villains, tragic victims, or laughable punch lines. The trans characters on the show are rich, complex human beings, with the attendant diversity of backgrounds and perspectives. Furthermore, Soloway explores many real-life political and personal issues confronting transgender people (trans-exclusionary radical feminist spaces, decisions about medical/surgical interventions, etc.) without preaching to her audience or detracting from the larger narrative. She has used the show's media spotlight to call attention to the lack of support given to the transgender community, calling it "a trans civil rights problem" (Berman, 2015).

The series has met with both critical and popular acclaim, with Soloway and Tambor receiving multiple award nominations and wins. Despite this praise, critics have skeptically noted the underrepresentation of actual transgender people onscreen and in the show's writers' room. The second season sought to remedy this shortcoming by increasing the number of transgender actors on the show (Alexandra Billings, Trace Lysette, and Hari Nef all have recurring roles in season two) and adding a transwoman to the writing team (Our Lady J, whom Soloway trained in a workshop explicitly geared toward developing writers with a transfeminine perspective). Additionally, "[e]very decision on the show is vetted by [trans activists and artists] Rhys Ernst and Zackary Drucker," who ensure that the representation of trans characters is authentic and avoids the easy pitfalls of familiar stereotypes (Levy, 2015).

Casely E. Coan

FURTHER READING

Berman, Eliza. 2015. "Jill Soloway's Emmy Speech: 'We Have a Trans Civil Rights Problem.'" *Time* Magazine, September 20. http://time.com/4041908/emmys-2015-jill-soloway-trans-civil-rights-problem.

Levy, Ariel. 2015. "Dolls and Feelings." *The New Yorker*, December 14. http://www.newyorker.com/magazine/2015/12/14/dolls-and-feelings.

Maciak, Phil. 2014. "That's Not the Way It Feels: *Transparent*'s Ensemble." *The Los Angeles Review of Books*, September 26. https://lareviewofbooks.org/essay/transparent-season-1.

Rochlin, Margy. 2015. "In 'Transparent,' a Heroine Evolves Further Still." *The New York Times*, November 27. http://www.nytimes.com/2015/11/29/arts/television/in-transparent-a-heroine-evolves-further-still.html?_r=0.

TWO

Popular Music

Popular music is often described as the "soundtrack of our lives." But more than merely a soundtrack, it also has the power to be an instrument of social change. In the realm of women's rights, for example, American women of all races, backgrounds, and sexual identities—from early blues singers like Gertrude "Ma" Rainey and Bessie Smith to modern-day artists like Ani DiFranco and Laura Jane Grace—have used their gifts as songwriters, musicians, singers, and performers to challenge traditional gender roles; testify about their life experiences; decry the injustices of racism, classism, and sexism; and proclaim their equality with men.

GERTRUDE "MA" RAINEY (1886–1939)

Known as the "Mother of Blues," Gertrude "Ma" Rainey was one of the first popular stage artists to play a major role in establishing the American blues sound. Considered one of the most important artists of blues history, Rainey brought a blended country and urban blues sound to mostly African American audiences across the south as a part of vaudeville and tent shows. Rainey was an audacious and imposing figure who appeared on stage with wild hair, a big toothy smile with gold-capped teeth, a showy necklace of gold coins, an ornate sequined dress—and sometimes with an ostrich plume in her hand. Sometimes referred to as the "ugliest woman in show business," Rainey eventually signed with Paramount Records and recorded more than 100 songs in which she wailed and moaned about cheating spouses, domestic abuse, and hard living.

Born Gertrude Pridgett in post-Reconstruction Georgia, Rainey was raised in poverty by her parents, who scraped out a meager living as singers in Columbus, Georgia, a frequent stop for minstrel shows. Influenced by her parents, Rainey developed a penchant for singing, and she had her public debut as part of the local talent show *Bunch of Blackberries*. Soon Rainey joined the traveling tent minstrel shows, where she met and married show manager William "Pa" Rainey and became a part of his *Rabbit Foot Minstrels*, a music collective that spread the blues throughout the South, and began to develop a following and admiration. When Rainey joined another traveling performing troupe, the Moses Stokes Company, she befriended a young Bessie Smith and took her under her wing. Smith, who admired Rainey a great deal, later became a blues legend in her own right. With Rainey's unique blending of blues genres, relatable song lyrics, and deep-throated moan-like singing style, she eventually landed a recording contract with Paramount Records in 1923. Developing a following beyond the South, Rainey recorded more than 100 songs for the label, including "Bad Luck Blues," "Moonshine Blues," and "See, See Rider" with blues legend Louis Armstrong.

Rainey also developed a reputation for subverting normative gender roles and for her open lesbianism. She was known to wear men's suits, and sang about women loving women and not needing men. In 1928's "Prove on Me Blues," Rainey sang, "Went out last night with a crowd of my friends, they must've been women, 'cause I don't like no men." On the cover of the record, Rainey is dressed in a man's suit flanked by two feminine women, with a police officer looking on. In 1925, Bessie Smith had to bail Rainey out of jail after the latter was arrested for hosting an "indecent" party where she engaged in sex with other women. Through her music, Rainey challenged gender norms and traditional expectations of women.

Paramount Records dropped Rainey in 1928, saying that her style of music had gone out of fashion. In her retirement, Rainey bought and managed two theaters, one in her hometown of Columbus, Georgia, and another in Rome, Georgia. Rainey was inducted into the Rock & Roll Hall of Fame in 1990 and the Blues Foundation's Hall of Fame in 1983. In 1994, the U.S. Postal Service issued a stamp in her honor.

Ann M. Savage

See also: Bessie Smith.

FURTHER READING

Davis, Angela Y. 1999. *Blues Legacies and Black Feminism: Gertrude "Ma" Rainey, Bessie Smith and Billie Holiday*. 1st Vintage books ed. New York: Vintage.

Lieb, Sandra R. 1981. *Mother of the Blues: A Study of Ma Rainey*. Amherst: University of Massachusetts Press. http://www.gbv.de/dms/hbz/toc/ht004707266 .PDF.

Rutter, Emily. 2014. "The Blues Tribute Poem and the Legacies of Gertrude "Ma" Rainey and Bessie Smith." *MELUS: Multi-Ethnic Literature of the U.S.*, 39(4): 69–91.

Wilson, August. 1985. *Ma Rainey's Black Bottom: A Play in Two Acts*. New York: Plume.

BESSIE SMITH (1894–1937)

Known as the "Empress of Blues," Bessie Smith started her professional career in 1912 when she joined the Rabbit Foot Minstrels traveling tent show, which was managed by William "Pa" Rainey and featured Gertrude "Ma" Rainey. Known as one of the greatest jazz-blues singers ever, her first recording, "Down-Hearted Blues," was released in 1923 on Columbia Records and went straight to number one. Smith soon became the most successful black performing artist of her time, releasing more than 200 recordings that addressed issues such as domestic abuse, failed relationships, and poverty. In 2014, premium cable channel HBO debuted the biopic *Bessie* starring rapper and actress Queen Latifah (Dana Owens, 1970–).

Born into poverty in Chattanooga, Tennessee, in 1894, Smith was just a child when both of her parents passed away. Raised by her aunt, Smith and her brother, who played guitar, began performing on the streets for tips. By 1912, Smith began as a dancer with the Moses Stokes Company and eventually joined Rabbit Foot Minstrels, where she met mentor Gertrude "Ma" Rainey. She settled in Phila-delphia by the early 1920s, and after signing with Columbia Records, Smith set out on tour with her own elaborate custom-built railroad car. Smith's career soared in the 1920s, and she became one of the highest earning black per-formers in the world. In 1929, she starred in the 16-minute film *St. Louis Blues*, the only film she is known to have appeared in. Like Rainey, Smith had several lesbian affairs despite being married and was known to partake in house parties where sex was engaged in casually.

As the Great Depression took hold in the United States, Smith's popularity waned because audiences had less money to spend on leisure activities. A more sophisti-cated form of jazz performed by the likes of Ethel Waters emerged as well, and Smith's

Harlem Renaissance jazz singer Bessie Smith with her trademark feathers. Smith's soulful voice and profound themes of love and loss earned her the title "Empress of the Blues." (Carl Van Vechten Photographs Collection, Library of Congress)

earthier, homegrown musical style no longer held the attention of audiences. Smith's long battle with alcoholism also had deleterious effects on her health and career. Smith died unexpectedly in 1937 in an automobile accident near Clarksdale, Mississippi. Some reports suggest that Smith might have been saved, but the first hospital she was transported to refusing to care for her because she was African American. Citing Bessie Smith as a major influence, in 1970 rocker Janis Joplin had a headstone made for Smith's unmarked grave reading "The Greatest Blues Singer in the World Will Never Stop Singing."

Ann M. Savage

See also: Gertrude "Ma" Rainey; Queen Latifah

FURTHER READING

Albertson, Chris. 2003. *Bessie.* Revised and expanded edition. New Haven: Yale University Press.

Calliope Film Resources, Inc., and California Newsreel Firm. 1989. *Wild Women Don't Have the Blues.* San Francisco, CA: California Newsreel.

Davis, Angela Y. 1999. *Blues Legacies and Black Feminism: Gertrude "Ma" Rainey, Bessie Smith and Billie Holiday.* New York: Vintage.

Scott, Michelle R. 2008. *Blues Empress in Black Chattanooga: Bessie Smith and the Emerging Urban South.* Urbana, IL: University of Illinois Press.

SISTER ROSETTA THARPE (1915–1973)

Although she has been referred to as the "Godmother of rock and roll," Sister Rosetta Tharpe is an often-overlooked contributor to the invention of rock music. Tharpe introduced the electric guitar to gospel music with guitar solos that were nothing short of rhythm-and-blues-influenced rock. Tharpe became gospel's first huge crossover recording star by displaying a blended musical style that was accessible to a wider audience. Little Richard, Elvis Presley, and Jerry Lee Lewis all cited Tharpe as an important influence on their own careers.

Born to cotton pickers in Cotton Plant, Arkansas, Tharpe was a musical prodigy who began performing at the age of four, with her mother, as part of a traveling evangelical troupe. In the 1920s, Tharpe and her mother moved to Chicago as part of the so-called Great Migration of African Americans out of the South and into the North. After settling in Chicago, they continued to perform religious concerts. After a short marriage to Thomas Thorpe, Tharpe moved with her mother to New York City in 1938. She signed with Decca Records and recorded four songs: "Rock Me," "My Man and I," "That's All," and "Lonesome Road." These were Decca's first gospel recordings, and they all became hits. Tharpe became the first successful gospel singer and is widely credited with popularizing gospel with secular audiences. In December 1938, Tharpe performed with John Hammond's Spirituals to Swing Concert at Carnegie Hall. Her performance caused a stir in the religious community. Singing gospel with blues and jazz musicians was unheard of, and a woman playing guitar was considered controversial. Nonetheless, she soon became a regular at the Cotton Club in Harlem, where she performed with jazz legend Cab Calloway.

Replacing the acoustic guitar with her electric, Tharpe's first recording to introduce gospel to mainstream music audiences was her 1939 hit "This Train." In the 1940s, she recorded secular hits "Shout Sister Shout," "That's All," and "I Want a Tall Skinny Papa." Because of her crossover success, she was invited to record for troops overseas during World War II, only one of two African American gospel artists asked to do so. In the mid-1940s, Tharpe paired with blues pianist Sammy Price and recorded "Strange Things Happening Every Day" and "Two Little Fishes and Five

Guitar virtuoso Sister Rosetta Tharpe came to fame through gospel music, but her guitar playing was a precursor to rock and roll, and influenced the likes of Chuck Berry, Elvis Presley and Little Richard. (AP Photo)

Loaves of Bread." "Strange Things Happening Every Day" was the first gospel record to hit number two on the rhythm and blues charts (referred to at the time as "race records"). Other Tharpe hits include 1944's "Down by the Riverside" and 1945's "The Lonesome Road."

When criticism of her secular recordings intensified from elements of the Christian community, which continued to make up the bulk of her fan base, she asked gospel singer Marie Knight to join her on tour. Tharpe and Knight subsequently recorded a series of gospel songs with Decca Records throughout the 1940s, with two of them making the top 10 of the rhythm and blues charts. Although she dabbled once again with secular music, Tharpe finished out her career mostly playing gospel and touring Europe and the United States. Tharpe died of a stroke in 1973 in Philadelphia.

Ann M. Savage

FURTHER READING

Calliope Film Resources, Inc., and California Newsreel Firm. 1989. *Wild Women Don't Have the Blues*. San Francisco, CA: California Newsreel.

Darden, Bob. 2004. *People Get Ready!: A New History of Black Gospel Music.* New York: Continuum.

Jackson, Jerma A. 2004. *Singing in My Soul: Black Gospel Music in a Secular Age.* Chapel Hill, NC: University of North Carolina Press.

Kozak, Oktay Ege. 2012. "The Godmother of Rock & Roll: Sister Rosetta Tharpe." *Bitch Magazine: Feminist Response to Pop Culture,* 57.

Wald, Gayle. 2007. *Shout, Sister, Shout!: The Untold Story of Rock-And-Roll Trailblazer Sister Rosetta Tharpe.* Boston: Beacon Press.

BILLIE HOLIDAY (1915–1959)

Still recognized as one of the greatest jazz voices of all time, Billie Holiday rose to fame in the 1950s with her unique blend of blues emotion and jazz riffs. Nicknamed "Lady Day" by frequent accompanist Lester Young in 1936, Holiday had a unique vocal style inspired by jazz instrumentalists. One of Holiday's signature songs, "Strange Fruit," is a powerful, haunting, and soulful political song that details the horrors of lynching. Holiday is also known for her hits "Summertime," "God Bless the Child," and her trademark gardenias nestled in her hair. The victim of drug abuse and poor business management, Holiday died broke at the young age of 44.

Born Eleanora Fagan in 1915, Holiday grew up in Baltimore, singing along to Bessie Smith and Louis Armstrong records. With an absent father and a mother who worked away from home, Holiday was often left in the care of others. In the late 1920s, Holiday's mother moved to Harlem, and Holiday joined her soon afterward. Renting a room in a brothel and while Holiday was just 14 years old, they both turned to sex work to make ends meet. After serving a short stint in prison for prostitution, Holiday changed her name and began singing in Harlem nightclubs. Just a few years later, in 1933, at the age of just 18, Holiday recorded two songs with band leader Benny Goodman and had her first hit with "Riffin' the Scotch."

Holiday's career began to take off when two of her swing-inspired jazz songs, "What a Little Moonlight Can Do" and "Miss Brown to You," garnered national attention in 1935. The success of these tracks landed her a recording contract with Columbia Records in 1936, where she recorded George Gershwin's jazz aria "Summertime" from the African American–centered opera *Porgy and Bess.* Holiday's "Summertime," now a jazz standard, hit the top of the pop charts.

Holiday was much more than a vocalist, however. She was actively involved in developing arrangements for her songs. After working with African American bandleader Count Basie in 1937, Holiday joined Artie Shaw's band in 1938, making her the first black woman to work with an all-white orchestra. This also marked the first time a lead African American female singer toured the segregated South with a white bandleader. Holiday faced racism at every stage of the tour, with racial slurs being hurled at her even while performing on stage. While working at Columbia Records, Holiday was introduced to Jewish schoolteacher Abel Meeropol's 1937 anti-lynching poem "Strange Fruit." Holiday wanted to record the poem as a song, but Columbia refused, so Holiday recorded it with Commodore Records. "Strange

Fruit" became Holiday's biggest-selling recording, and it was inducted to the Grammy Hall of Fame.

Holiday struggled with alcoholism for much of her career, and in the 1940s she developed a heroin habit as well. In 1947, she was arrested for possessing narcotics and served prison time. She was released in 1948 for good behavior, only to be arrested again in 1949. Despite her substance abuse problems and a consensus that the peak of her career had passed, Holiday was able to move to Verve Records, where she recorded more than 100 new songs in the 1950s. Like many other early blues and jazz artists, Holiday saw little of the royalties from her work. Holiday's abuse of drugs and alcohol, as well as her stormy relationships with men, eventually took their toll. Diagnosed with heart disease and cirrhosis of the liver, Holiday was hospitalized shortly after giving her final live performance in New York City on May 25, 1959. Accused of smuggling heroin into the hospital, Holiday was put under arrest and handcuffed to her hospital bed by the Federal Bureau of Narcotics. Holiday is said to have died broke with just $750 taped to her leg and $.70 in the bank.

Ann M. Savage

FURTHER READING

Davis, Angela Y. 1999. *Blues Legacies and Black Feminism: Gertrude "Ma" Rainey, Bessie Smith and Billie Holiday.* New York: Vintage.

Greene, Meg. 2007. *Billie Holiday: A Biography.* Westport, CT: Greenwood Press.

Margolick, David, and Hilton Als. 2000. *Strange Fruit: Billie Holiday, Café Society, and an Early Cry for Civil Rights.* Philadelphia: Running Press.

Seig, Matthew, Robert G. O'Meally, Toby Byron, Richard Saylor, Ruby Dee, Buck Clayton, and Harry Edison. 2009. *Lady Day: The Many Faces of Billie Holiday.* Berlin, Germany: EuroArts Music International.

WILLIE MAE "BIG MAMA" THORNTON (1926–1984)

With a powerful voice and an immutable presence, Willie Mae "Big Mama" Thornton burst onto the American music scene in 1952 with "Hound Dog." This recording lasted seven weeks at number one on the Rhythm and Blues charts and eventually sold almost 2 million copies. A singer-songwriter who acquired the nickname "Big Mama" because of her commanding voice and her sizeable swagger, Thornton's musical contributions to the development of rock and roll are indisputable. In addition to the rock classic "Hound Dog," written by Jerry Leiber and Mike Stoller, which Elvis Presley would record just four years later with much greater success, Thornton was also the first to record her self-penned "Ball 'n' Chain." Citing Thornton as a major influence in her work, rock icon Janis Joplin recorded "Ball 'n' Chain" in 1968 with much wider acclaim and success. The Rock and Roll Hall of Fame has listed both "Hound Dog" and "Ball 'n' Chain" as two of the "500 Songs That Have Shaped Rock 'n' Roll." Yet because she lived during a time of significant racial bias, Thornton never received the accolades, monetary reward, or credit she deserved.

Born in Ariton, Alabama, in 1926 as one of seven children, Thornton was raised in the Baptist church by her minister father and choir member mother. Although she started out singing in the church, as did all of her siblings, Thornton had a keen interest in rhythm and blues artists of the time. A young teenager when her mother died, Thornton quit school and took a job at a saloon to help support the family. Thornton eventually left Alabama in 1940 and headed to Harlem, where she landed some gigs as the "New Bessie Smith." A self-taught drummer and harmonica player, Thornton had a commanding stage presence, was a frequent improviser, and often engaged in gospel-influenced call-and-response routines with her band. Similar to other women blues performers before her, Thornton also played with her gender expression. She often dressed as a man but never explicitly identified herself as lesbian. In 1948, Thornton moved to Houston, where she ended up signing with Peacock Records and recorded "Hound Dog," the song that made her a star. Like many blues performers before her, though, Thornton would receive little compensation for the song's success. She also never saw any royalties from Janis Joplin's recording of "Ball 'n' Chain," although Joplin's recording did draw renewed interest in Thornton.

Thornton continued to record and perform into the 1960s with various band incarnations that included well-known blues performers such as Buddy Guy and Muddy Waters. In 1969, Thornton signed with Mercury Records and released her most successful album, *Stronger Than Dirt*, which reached 198 on the Billboard Top 200 chart. In 1973, Thornton recorded her first gospel album. Her album *Saved* included gospel staples "Oh Happy Day," "Glory, Glory Hallelujah," and "Swing Low, Sweet Chariot." Thornton died in 1984 of heart and liver complications largely due to alcohol abuse.

Ann M. Savage

FURTHER READING

Jones, Dalton Anthony. 2015. "Death Sentences: From Genesis to Genre (Big Mama's Parole)." *Women & Performance: A Journal of Feminist Theory*, 25(1): 59–81.

Mahon, Maureen. 2011. "Listening for Willie Mae 'Big Mama' Thornton's Voice: The Sound of Race and Gender Transgressions in Rock and Roll." *Women and Music: A Journal of Gender and Culture*, 15(1): 1–17.

Spörke, Michael. 2014. *Big Mama Thornton: The Life and Music.* Jefferson, NC: McFarland & Company.

ODETTA (1930–2008)

Born in 1930 in Birmingham, Alabama, Odetta Holmes's (known more commonly as Odetta) raspy, deep, emotional voice was unmistakable whether singing

Singer, songwriter, and civil rights activist Odetta. Civil rights leader Martin Luther King, Jr. referred to her as "The Queen of American Folk Music." (AP Photo)

folk, jazz, blues, or soul. Dubbed the "Queen of American Folk Music" by civil rights leader Martin Luther King Jr. and identified as an inspiration by civil rights activist Rosa Parks, Odetta was dedicated to music that had a focus on social change, equality, and liberation.

Although born in Alabama, Odetta spent most of her childhood in Los Angeles, where her mother moved after her father's death. The move west was her first brush with blatant racism, as African Americans were asked to move to another railroad car to make more room for whites. This experience never left Odetta and was an impetus for her commitment to social justice. As Odetta was interested in music from a very young age, her mother encouraged her to get formal training when a young teacher recognized Odetta's potential and talent. Odetta's mother enrolled her in classical music lessons, encouraging a move toward opera. Odetta was engaged in formal training throughout her childhood and even had professional performing jobs as a teenager. Although she found value in her formal music training, Odetta was much more interested in the music happening on the streets and in juke joints and coffeehouses.

Already working professionally, Odetta released her first solo album, a mix of spirituals and blues called *Odetta Sings Ballads and Blues*, in 1956. American folk singer Bob Dylan later cited Odetta, and particularly this first solo release, as a major influence on his own career. Folk singer Joan Baez and blues rocker Janis

Joplin have also cited Odetta as a significant inspiration for their work. Although many of the songs that Odetta covered over the years weren't originals, she made them her own.

Odetta was known for singing for the voiceless: workers, women, African Americans, and the poor. At the 1963 March on Washington for Jobs and Freedom, she performed now well-known versions of "Oh Freedom," "On My Way," and "We Shall Overcome," with the latter becoming the anthem of the Civil Rights Movement. Similar to her involvement in that movement, Odetta spoke out against the Vietnam War and covered antiwar songs like Dylan's "Masters of War." Odetta also lent her voice to the United Nations Population Fund (UNFPA), singing a feminist anthem in support of women's reproductive rights worldwide called "Thirty-Four Million Friends." In "Hit or Miss," another feminist anthem, Odetta sang of women's need to be themselves instead of trying to fit into some narrow definition of what it meant to be a woman. Singing at numerous civil rights marches, she made Lead Belly's 1942 prison chain-gang work song "Take This Hammer" another signature song of hers. Odetta's music has been described as "the soundtrack of the Civil Rights Movement" ("Odetta Biography," 2014)

As Odetta aged and times changed, she slowly faded from public life and popularity. In 1999, though, she was awarded the National Medal of Arts by President Bill Clinton, and in 2004 she was a Kennedy Center honoree. In 2008, after becoming the first African American to be elected president of the United States, Barack Obama invited her to sing at his inauguration. Sadly, though, she died just before his inauguration, at the age of 77.

Ann M. Savage

FURTHER READING

Alcorn, Stephen, and Samantha Thornhill. 2010. *Odetta, the Queen of Folk.* New York: Scholastic Press.

Ford, Tanisha C. 2015. *Liberated Threads: Black Women, Style, and the Global Politics of Soul.* Chapel Hill, NC: University of North Carolina Press.

"Odetta Biography." 2014. Biography.com. http://www.biography.com/people/odetta-507480#later-career.

Odetta, Renee Poussaint, Camille O. Cosby, and National Visionary Leadership Project. 1997. *Odetta: National Visionary 2002.* Washington, DC: National Visionary Leadership Project.

ARETHA FRANKLIN (1942–)

Known as the "Queen of Soul," with 20 number-one hits on the rhythm and blues charts and 17 top-10 hits on the pop charts, Aretha Franklin is one of the most critically acclaimed and best selling music performers in history. Franklin's hits include iconic songs like "Respect," "Think," and "(You Make Me Feel Like a) Natural Woman." Franklin is a self-taught, gifted pianist with an emotive and impassioned vocal style. With a career spanning more than 60 years, she has inspired generations of musical artists and has been showered with awards and accolades including 18 Grammy wins, including a Grammy Lifetime Achievement Award. In 2005, she was awarded the Presidential Medal of Freedom.

Born in 1942 in Memphis, Tennessee, Franklin spent most of her early life in Detroit, Michigan. Like many other blues and soul singers before her, Franklin first began performing in public by singing gospel songs in church—in Franklin's case in her pastor father's Baptist church. She eventually also joined her father on traveling gospel caravan tours. At the age of 18, inspired by the likes of Sam Cooke and Jackie Wilson, Franklin won a recording contract with Columbia Records. She soon released her first secular records, which featured a mix of standards, doo-wop, and rhythm and blues. Experiencing only moderate success at Columbia, Franklin decided to move to Atlantic Records in 1967. Franklin's first release with the Atlantic label landed her multiple hits, including "I Never Loved a Man (The Way I Love You)," "Do Right Woman, Do Right Man," and "Baby I Love You." In April 1967, Atlantic released Franklin's version of the Otis Redding song "Respect," which shot up the charts and became her signature song. With its lyrics of self-dignity, the song became heralded as a feminist and civil rights anthem. In her 13 years with Atlantic, Franklin had a string of other hits as well, including "Chain of Fools," "Think," and "Spanish Harlem."

In 1980, Franklin moved to Arista Records, which was helmed by legendary music producer Clive Davis. Franklin recorded 10 albums with Arista, including releases where she tried a more contemporary and youthful sound with the release of *Who's Zoomin' Who?* in 1985, which had three hits, "Freeway of Love," "Sisters Are Doing It for Themselves," and the hit title track. During her time at Arista, Franklin branched out, recording songs for films and television, and duets with pop stars. Franklin also recorded several gospel albums on the Arista label. In 1998, Franklin returned to the top 40 with the Lauryn Hill-produced single "A Rose Is Still a Rose."

In 1987, Franklin was the first female performer to be inducted into the Rock and Roll Hall of Fame. In 2009, Franklin performed "My Country, 'Tis of Thee" at President Barack Obama's inauguration ceremony. Franklin remains one of the most successful and critically acclaimed performing artists ever, with more than 112 singles on the Billboard charts in both pop and rhythm and blues; landing at number nine for *Rolling Stone* magazine's 100 Greatest Artists of All Time; and first for the 100 Greatest Singers of All Time.

Ann M. Savage

See also: Carole King.

FURTHER READING

Bego, Mark. 2012. *Aretha Franklin: The Queen of Soul.* New York: Skyhorse Pub.
Jones, Hettie. 1995. *Big Star Fallin' Mama: Five Women in Black Music.* Rev. ed. New York: Viking.

Lordi, Emily J. 2013. *Black Resonance: Iconic Women Singers and African American Literature.* New Brunswick, NJ: Rutgers University Press.

Malawey V. 2014. "'Find Out What It Means to Me': Aretha Franklin's Gendered Re-Authoring of Otis Redding's Respect." *Popular Music*, 33(2): 185–207.

LORETTA LYNN (1932–)

Loretta Lynn's 1970 signature song, "Coal Miner's Daughter," details the story of her life, in which she overcame childhood poverty in rural Kentucky and an abusive marriage to become one of the most celebrated country-music artists of all time. Her 1976 best-selling autobiography (written with George Vecsey), sharing the same name as the song, was made into an Oscar-winning film in 1980.

With more than 15 number-one U.S. country music hits, ten number-one hit albums, and a successful career lasting more than 50 years, Lynn has made an indisputable mark on country music and has been recognized with an induction to the Country Music Hall of Fame, a Kennedy Center Honors Award, a Grammy Lifetime Achievement Award, and the Presidential Medal of Freedom.

Born into poverty as Loretta Webb in Butcher Holler, Kentucky, in 1932, she was the second oldest of eight children in a family that struggled to make ends meet. At the young age of 15, she met and married U.S. serviceman Oliver "Doolittle" Lynn. When she received a guitar as a gift from her husband, Lynn taught herself how to play. With encouragement and permission from her controlling husband, Lynn began performing at local bars and clubs. After appearing on local television performing in a talent show, she was signed by

Actress Sissy Spacek (right) with country singer-songwriter Loretta Lynn (left). Spacek won the Academy Award for Best Actress for her portrayal of Lynn in the 1980 film *Coal Miner's Daughter.* (Sbukley/Dreamstime.com)

upstart label Zero Records. After recording four songs, Lynn and her husband toured across the United States, and by the time they got to Nashville the single "I'm a Honky Tonk Girl" had climbed to number 14 on the country and western Charts. Soon Lynn and her husband moved to Nashville, where Lynn signed with Decca Records and began to work with producer Owen Bradley, who also produced country-music artist legend Patsy Cline. Though Kitty Wells was long an influence of Lynn's, she became even more influenced by her new friend Cline, who cultivated a more modern and pop sound. Lynn's first top-10 hit was the 1962 single "Success," written by Johnny Mullins.

Lynn's website describes her distinctive style as "a mature fusion of twang, grit, energy and libido." With much of her inspiration coming from her own life and her tumultuous marriage, Lynn's songs tell the stories of women, relationships, and temptations. Having developed a strong female point of view, which was unheard of for the time, her other early top-10 hits include threatening a hedonistic revenge toward a cheating husband in "Wine, Women and Song" and "Happy Birthday," as well as "Blue Kentucky Girl," which tells the story of a woman waiting at home for a gallivanting husband.

Lynn also began to write her own songs. Her first self-written song to hit the top 10 was 1966's "Dear Uncle Sam," which questioned whether the Vietnam conflict was worth the high cost of the human lives lost. Other strong women narratives written or cowritten by Lynn included "You Ain't Woman Enough (to Take My Man)," "Don't Come Home A'Drinking," and "Fist City." Lynn's music, considered radical for the time period, struck a chord with working-class wives and mothers who felt overwhelmed by their demanding lives without getting much in return. Even though country-music radio stations often banned her songs because of their controversial topics, Lynn kept her strong female point of view and continued on. In 1971's "One's on the Way," Lynn told the story of a worn-out mother with a husband at a bar. In "I Wanna Be Free," Lynn explored the bright side of divorce. Although Lynn stayed married to her husband, Oliver, until his death in 1996, Lynn challenged stereotypes about divorced women as being sexually "easy" in "Rated X." In "I Know How," she celebrated women's own sexual agency, and in one of Lynn's most controversial songs, "The Pill," she celebrated female empowerment through birth control.

Lynn remains one of the most successful female recording artists, in country music or otherwise, of all time. She was the first woman in country music to write a number-one hit and the first female recording artist to have more than 50 top-10 hits. Lynn was the first woman to be nominated for and win the Entertainer of the Year award at the Country Music Awards. In 2004, Lynn's career was revived, after a long slumber, when she worked with alternative rock guitarist Jack White. White produced Lynn's *Van Lear Rose* album, which won the Grammy Award for Best Country Album of the Year, Lynn's first Grammy win in more than 30 years. The two also sang a duet on the single "Portland, Oregon" from *Van Lear Rose*, which introduced Lynn to younger generations. In 2010, a wide variety of well-known country and pop artists including Kid Rock, Miranda Lambert, and Sheryl Crow celebrated Lynn's contributions to county music with the tribute album *Coal Miner's Daughter*.

Ann M. Savage

See also: Planned Parenthood; Women's Liberation Movement.

FURTHER READING

Lynn, Loretta, and George Vecsey. 1976. *Loretta Lynn: Coal Miner's Daughter*. Chicago: Regnery.

Lynn, Loretta, and Patsi Bale Cox. 2002. *Still Woman Enough: A Memoir*. New York: Hyperion.

Lynn, Loretta. 2012. *Honky Tonk Girl: My Life in Lyrics*. New York: Alfred A. Knopf.

Meier, Kenneth J. 2004. "Get Your Tongue Out of My Mouth 'Cause I'm Kissin' You Goodbye: The Politics of Ideas." *Policy Studies Journal*, 32(2): 225–33.

HELEN REDDY (1941–)

Singer-songwriter Helen Reddy is best known for her 1972 hit "I Am Woman," which came to be recognized as the anthem of the 1970s Women's Liberation Movement. When self-identified feminist Reddy wrote and recorded the song, she had no idea it would become so closely associated with the fight for women's rights. Reddy decided to pen the song after conducting an unsuccessful search for a song that was reflective of a woman's positive self-image. Cowritten with singer-songwriter Ray Buron, "I Am Woman" reached the number-one spot on Billboard's Hot 100 and made Reddy a star. Reddy was the first Australian to top the U.S. charts and to win a Grammy (for Best Female Artist). In her acceptance speech, Reddy challenged religious tradition and the assumption of God as male and thanked "God, because she makes everything possible" (Gaar, 1992). Reddy was also the first Australian to host a one-hour weekly primetime variety show on an American broadcast network.

Reddy was born in 1941 in Melbourne, Australia, into a show business family, as both of her parents were vaudeville performers. Reddy was encouraged to be a performer and at just four years old joined her parents onstage. As she entered her teenage years, Reddy was insistent on rebelling and rejected the performing life in favor of domesticity as a wife and mother. Marrying at 20 years old, Reddy's first marriage ended in divorce after just four years. Finding herself alone as a single mother, she returned to the stage in an effort to support herself and her daughter. In the mid-1960s, Reddy competed in a singing contest on Australia's musical television show *Bandstand* and won a trip to New York City to audition for Mercury Records. Although Mercury Records did not sign her, Reddy decided to stay in New York to pursue a musical career. Soon after, Reddy met and married Jeff Wald. Reddy and Wald struggled in New York and barely made enough money to survive. Eventually, the couple and Reddy's daughter moved to Chicago, where

Reddy was able to land a deal with Fontana Records, a division of Mercury Records. After Reddy achieved minor success with a number-83 hit in Australia, "One Way Ticket," the couple moved once again, this time to Los Angeles.

Reddy's husband, Wald, had success managing rock band Deep Purple and novelty act Tiny Tim, so Reddy challenged him to make her a success. Taking on the dare, Wald arranged a deal for Reddy to cut a single with Capitol Records in 1971. The track "I Believe in Music" failed, but the B-side, a cover of "I Don't Know How to Love Him" from the musical *Jesus Christ Superstar*, hit number 13 on the charts. One year later, Reddy released the song that would make her a star.

In a March 2013 *Chicago Tribune* article, Reddy indicated that she thought the runaway popularity of "I Am Woman" was due in large measure to the era in which it was released. "I think it came along at the right time. I'd gotten involved in the Women's Movement, and there were a lot of songs on the radio about being weak and being dainty and all those sort of things. All the women in my family, they were strong women . . . I certainly didn't see myself as being dainty."

Although most widely known for "I Am Woman," Reddy had 15 top-40 hits in the United States, including "Delta Dawn," "Leave Me Alone (Ruby Red Dress)," and "Angie Baby." Reddy also had success with the television variety show *The Helen Reddy Show*, and she became a regular host of the late-night variety show *The Midnight Special*. Reddy recorded a series of other albums with MCA and Capitol Records until the mid-1980s. She did some sporadic recording in the late 1980s and 1990s, but with no mainstream success she fell out of the spotlight. In 2002, Reddy gave a farewell performance and moved back to Australia soon thereafter. Despite her official retirement, though, Reddy has given occasional performances since 2012.

Ann M. Savage

See also: Women's Liberation Movement.

FURTHER READING

Arrow, Michelle. 2007. "'It Has Become My Personal Anthem': 'I Am Woman,' Popular Culture and 1970s Feminism." *Australian Feminist Studies*, 22(53): 213–30.

Gaar, Gillian G., and Seal Press. 1992. *She's a Rebel: The History of Women in Rock & Roll*. Seattle, WA: Seal Press.

Reddy, Helen. 2006. *The Woman I Am: A Memoir*. 1st American ed. New York: J.P. Tarcher/Penguin.

Rodnitzky, Jerome I. 1975. "Songs of Sisterhood: The Music of Women's Liberation." *Popular Music and Society*, 4(2), 77–85.

CAROLE KING (1942–)

A major influence in the development of pop music, Brooklyn-raised singer-songwriter Carole King is one of the greatest and most prolific songwriters of all time, with more than 100 hit songs to her credit. King's career spans over half a century, from the 1960s Brill Building era, where she cowrote hit after hit with her then-husband Gerry Goffin, to her record-breaking 1971 solo album, *Tapestry*, and a 2014 hit Broadway musical based on her life. King wrote or cowrote 118 hit pop songs, has won four Grammys, and has been inducted into the Rock and Roll Hall of Fame. She has toured as late as 2010 and performed at the 2016 Democratic National Convention. More than 1000 artists have recorded more than 400 of her compositions.

King learned to play piano as a child. As a teenager she dabbled with songwriting and singing. While taking classes at Queens College, she met Gerry Goffin, and the trajectory of both of their lives changed dramatically. King and Goffin not only married and had children, but they also became a successful and prolific songwriting duo.

King and Goffin were a part of what became known as the Brill Building Sound. In the 1960s, the music charts were ruled by girl groups like the Chiffons, the Chantels, and the Marvelettes, with the songs written in a sort of assembly-line fashion in several buildings—including the well-known Brill Building—near Broadway and 49th Street in Manhattan. With award-winning producers such as Don Kirschner, Phil Spector, and George "Shadow" Morton presiding over affairs, numerous chart-topping songs were generated by this formula. King and Goffin worked with Kirschner, writing more than 20 hits, with Goffin as the lyricist and King writing the music. Their first hit was the Shirelles' "Will You Still Love Me Tomorrow" (1960), the first number-one hit by a black girl group. Other big hits included "Take Good Care of My Baby" (recorded by Bobby Vee), "The Loco-Motion" (Little Eva), and "Go Away Little Girl" (Steve Lawrence). Goffin and King also cowrote one of superstar Aretha Franklin's signature songs, the hit "(You Make Me Feel Like) A Natural Woman" (1967).

In the late 1960s, King divorced Goffin and moved to Los Angeles with her two daughters. In California, she reinvented herself as a singer-songwriter. Her first solo release did not garner much attention, but in 1971 she released her second solo album, *Tapestry*. The album rocketed up to number one on the album charts, where it remained for 15 consecutive weeks, and the album sold more than 25 million copies worldwide. The album's popularity was driven by the inclusion of several major hit songs, including "It's Too Late," "You've Got a Friend," and "I Feel the Earth Move." With *Tapestry*, King became the first woman to win all three top Grammy Awards for Best Record, Best Song, and Best Album of the Year.

King went on to record 25 solo albums throughout her career, and in 2010 she launched a successful reunion tour with fellow singer-songwriter and longtime friend James Taylor. In 2012, she released her memoir *A Natural Woman*, which became a *New York Times* bestseller. King has been inducted into the Songwriters Hall of Fame and has been awarded the National Academy of Songwriters' Lifetime Achievement Award with Goffin. In 2013, she became the first woman to be honored with a Library of Congress Gershwin Prize for Popular Song. One year later, a musical about her life, *Beautiful: The Carole King Musical*, opened on Broadway to wide critical acclaim.

Ann M. Savage

See also: Aretha Franklin.

FURTHER READING

King, Carole. 2012. *A Natural Woman: A Memoir*. New York: Grand Central Publishing.
Warwick, Jacqueline C. 2007. *Girl Groups, Girl Culture: Popular Music and Identity in the 1960s*. New York: Routledge.
Weller, Sheila. 2008. *Girls Like Us: Carole King, Joni Mitchell, Carly Simon—and the Journey of a Generation*. New York: Atria Books.

THE RUNAWAYS (1975–1979)

One of the first all-female rock bands, the Runaways arrived on the music scene in 1976 with the self-titled album *The Runaways*. The band was founded by rock icon Joan Jett (1958–). Eager to be a rock star, Jett hung out on the now infamous Sunset Strip in Los Angeles, looking for band members. Inspired by rocker Suzi Quattro, Jett was particularly interested in starting an all-girl band, which at the time was an almost unheard-of proposition. Jett eventually met manager Kim Fowley (1939–2015), an eccentric and controversial strip mainstay, who saw gimmicky marketing potential in a teenage all-female rock band. Fowley put Jett in touch with drummer Sandy West, and soon they found three other bandmates: singer Cherie Currie and guitarists Lita Ford and Jackie Fox. Currie was born into a Hollywood family in the San Fernando Valley. With David Bowie as an idol, Currie began to sport a glam look and was a regular at popular club Rodney Bingenheimer's English Disco, where she met both Jett and Fowley.

Although the band lasted only three years, never developed a big hit song in America (although "Cherry Bomb" was a chart-topper in Japan), and never won a Grammy Award, it made an indelible mark on rock and roll by paving the way for other female rock bands to follow, including the likes of L7 and the Donnas. The band also launched the far more successful solo careers of Joan Jett and master guitarist Lita Ford, who is often cited as one of the greatest guitarists, male or female, of all time.

Under the abusive management of Kim Fowley, the young performers burned out quickly, recording five studio albums in just three years. During these same three years, with a revolving lineup, they toured Japan, and toured the United States and Europe twice. After Fowley's death in January 2015, Jackie Fuchs (Fox was her stage name) revealed that she had been drugged and raped by Fowley at a New Year's Eve party in 1975. Fuchs alleges that many witnessed the assault, including bandmates Jett and Currie. There are disputed accounts of the incident, with Jett and Currie denying being present while others say that there have been rumors about the incident for decades.

Frequently dismissed at the time by the almost exclusively male rock music press, these talented teenage female rockers have had a long-lasting impact on the genre. Joan Jett and Lita Ford went on to have the most successful solo careers. Jett has eight platinum and gold albums and nine top-40 singles, including "Bad Reputation," "I Love Rock 'n' Roll," and "I Hate Myself for Loving You." Jett has toured as late as 2016. After several disappointing album releases, Ford landed a number-eight hit on the *Billboard Hot 100* with "Close My Eyes Forever," a duet with metal rock performer Ozzy Osbourne. In 2016, Ford released the autobiography *Living Like a Runaway*.

Ann M. Savage

FURTHER READING

Cherkis, Jason. 2015. "The Lost Girls." *The Huffington Post*, July 10. http://high line.huffingtonpost.com/articles/en/the-lost-girls.

Edgeplay: A Film about the Runaways. Film. 2005. Directed/written by Victory Tischler-Blue. Image Entertainment.

Ford, Lita. 2016. *Living Like a Runaway*. New York: Dey Street Books.

McDonnell, Evelyn. 2013. *Queens of Noise: The Real Story of the Runaways*. Boston: Da Capo Press.

The Runaways. Film. 2010. Directed/written by Floria Sigismundi. Culver City, CA: Pictures Home Entertainment.

QUEEN LATIFAH (1970–)

A successful rapper, producer, actor, and talk show host, Queen Latifah (Dana Owens) made her mark bringing a feminist perspective to rap music with the release of her first studio album, *All Hail the Queen,* in 1989. The single "Ladies First," featuring female rapper Monie Love, celebrates the strength of women, challenges gender stereotypes—including the notion that women can't rap—and pays homage to important African American women throughout history. The video for the song underscores this message. As images transition from Harriet Tubman and Sojourner Truth to Angela Davis, Queen Latifah dons Afrocentric attire as she looks down on an apartheid-era map of South Africa. As the video continues, Latifah determines strategy on the map like a general, even as film of anti-apartheid black protestors is displayed.

Born into a middle-class family in 1970 in Newark, New Jersey, Dana Owens was given the nickname Latifah, an Arabic word for "delicate and sensitive," as a child. Owens later added "Queen" to her professional name to illustrate her demand for respect as an African American woman.

Owens showed an interest in performance as a child, regularly participating in school plays and performances. With the support of her mother, who was actively involved in Latifah's early career, she also joined with two female friends to form a rap group called Ladies Fresh. Her mother then put her daughter in contact with local DJ Mark James, who helped her record a demo that eventually came to the attention of Fred Braithwaite (professionally known as Fab 5 Freddy). Soon signed to independent music label Tommy Boy Music, she released her first single, "Wrath of My Madness," in 1988. One year later, she released her debut album, *All Hail the Queen*, which sold more than 1 million copies and established her as a star.

In 1994, Latifah released her third studio album, *Black Reign*, with Motown Records. That album included her biggest chart hit, "U.N.I.T.Y.," which reached number 23 on the Hot 100 and number seven on the Hot Rhythm and Blues/Hip-Hop Chart. This powerful song, which won the Grammy for Best Rap Solo Performance, addresses domestic abuse and directly challenges the use of demeaning terms like "bitch" and "ho" when referencing women. Queen Latifah went on to release several other studio albums, but none of them reached the heights that her earlier releases did.

Beyond being a musical artist, Queen Latifah demonstrated a keen interest in the business side of the entertainment industry. In 1991, while still early in her professional career, Latifah founded Flavor Unit Records and Management (now Florida-based Flavor Unit Entertainment) in Jersey City, New Jersey, with producer Shakim Compere. The entertainment production company has produced both television and film projects, some of which have been star vehicles for Queen Latifah. Latifah's first dramatic roles were small parts in several Spike Lee films, and from 1993 to 1998 she was a regular on the Fox television sitcom *Living Single*, which had strong ratings with black audiences. In 1999, she launched the short-lived talk show *The Queen Latifah Show*, which lasted for two years. She reintroduced the show in 2013, but again the show was short lived. Latifah's later notable film work included her Oscar-nominated role in the 2002 film *Chicago*; 2003's box office hit *Bringing Down the House*; the 2007 biopic *Life Support*, in which she played the leading role as an HIV-positive woman; and her performance as blues icon Bessie Smith in the 2015 HBO film *Bessie*, a film she also produced. The film won the Primetime Emmy Award for Outstanding Television Movie in 2016.

Ann M. Savage

See also: Bessie Smith; *Set It Off*.

FURTHER READING

Childress, Cindy. 2005. "Glamour's Portrayal of Queen Latifa: Another Unreal Ideal." *Feminist Media Studies*, 5(1): 84–87.

Queen Latifah, and Karen Hunter. 1999. *Ladies First: Revelations of a Strong Woman*. New York: William Morrow.

Roberts, Robin. 1994. "'Ladies First': Queen Latifah's Afrocentric Feminist Music Video." *African American Review*, 28: 245–57.

Rose, Tricia. 1994. *Black Noise: Rap Music and Black Culture in Contemporary America*. Hanover, NH: University Press of New England.

ANI DIFRANCO (1970–)

Born in Buffalo, New York, in 1970, singer, songwriter, and activist Ani DiFranco took a stand early in her career against the profit-motivated music industry and succeeded on her own terms. When major record labels came courting her, the self-identified and outspoken feminist DiFranco defiantly took the independent route in order to retain creative control over her music. At the young age of 19, DiFranco launched her own record label, Righteous Babe Records, based out of her economically depressed hometown. Despite this decision, which made it almost impossible for her songs to reach radio audiences, DiFranco developed a strong fan following through relentless touring and regular album releases. Her music, both personal and political, connected with young people as she sang about abortion, racism, poverty, and many other social justice issues.

DiFranco also demonstrated her commitment to the revitalization of her hometown by rescuing a Gothic Revival–style church in downtown Buffalo from destruction. She remodeled the building into a multiuse art facility called Babeville. DiFranco also chose to keep production of artist merchandise and albums in Buffalo.

DiFranco began performing publicly at a young age. After gaining emancipation at just 15 years old because she did not want to follow her mother to Connecticut, she began playing her guitar regularly at clubs, street corners, and dives. After her record label was established, she released a self-titled album at the young age of 20. A politically conscious artist from the start, DiFranco's songs often address inequality and injustice. Although frequently referred to as "the little folk singer," DiFranco's musical influences are broad and include jazz, punk, and funk. Throughout her multi-decade career, during which time she has released 24 studio albums, DiFranco has written and recorded songs about numerous political topics including women's reproductive rights, gender and sexuality, war, corporate greed, sexual assault, and gun control. In the "Lost Woman Song" (1990), DiFranco discusses attacks on women's reproductive rights while she simultaneously shares the experience of passing antichoice protestors while walking into a woman's health clinic for an abortion. In "In or Out" (1992), DiFranco declares and defends her bisexuality. In "Self Evident" (2002), she sings about the poor quality of media coverage and the failure of news media to question the U.S. presidential administration in the lead-up to the Iraq War. DiFranco sings again about the threat to women's reproductive rights, the murder of abortion provider Dr. George Tiller, and the bombing of an abortion clinic in the haunting "Hello Birmingham" (1999).

A resident of New Orleans, DiFranco wrote "Red Letter Year" (2008) as a critique of President George W. Bush's handling of 2005's Hurricane Katrina. In 2012, DiFranco reworked the lyrics of folk-singing icon Pete Seeger's labor song "Which Side Are You On" (2012), questioning the value of "free market trade." In 2016, DiFranco joined artists Tom Morella and Ryan Harvey in a remake of a newly discovered 60-year-old Woody Guthrie song, "Old Man Trump," which criticizes the racialized landlord policies of New York developer Fred C. Trump, father of then-presidential candidate Donald J. Trump.

Although not a mainstream artist or a chart topper, DiFranco's artistry has been recognized with multiple Grammy nominations and a win in 2004 for Best Recording Package for *Evolve*. DiFranco has also been bestowed with several Gay/Lesbian American Music Awards, a Planned Parenthood Maggie Award for Media Excellence, and a Woodie Guthrie Award in 2009. Her Righteous Babe label, meanwhile, has expanded to include more than a dozen artists.

Ann M. Savage

FURTHER READING

DiFranco, Ani, Mike Dillon, Allison Miller, and Todd Sickafoose. 2008. *Ani DiFranco—Live at Babeville*. Buffalo, NY: Righteous Babe Records.
Feigenbaum, Anna. 2005. "'Some Guy Designed This Room I'm Standing In': Marking Gender in Press Coverage of Ani DiFranco." *Popular Music*, 24(1): 37–56.
Goldberg, Hilary, Ani DiFranco, Scott Fisher, Commi Fag Film, and Righteous Babe Records. 2002. *Render*. Buffalo, NY: Righteous Babe Records.
Perea, Elizabeth. 1999. "Re-Articulation of Subjectivities in Popular Culture: Language and Gender Discourses in the Works of Ani DiFranco." *Women & Language*, 22(2).
Righteous Babe Records. "Ani DiFranco News." http://www.righteousbabe.com/blogs/ani-difranco-news.

RIOT GRRRL (EARLY 1990s)

Riot Grrrl was a feminist punk music scene that originated on the West Coast of the United States and Canada in the late 1980s and early 1990s. Riot Grrrl soon spread nationally and internationally, with groups establishing Riot Grrrl chapters in major cities. Those involved in the subculture made their own independently produced zines, started bands, organized workshops, and started consciousness-raising (CR) groups. One of the signature elements of Riot Grrrl was its do-it-yourself approach to organizing. Riot Grrrls encouraged other girls to start bands, make zines, and start chapters in their own communities. The scene was an outlet for young women and girls to express frustration with—and value feeling angry about—sexism and other forms of injustice.

The term "Riot Grrrl" came out of a zine publication called *Jigsaw* by Tobi Vail, a key figure in the Riot Grrrl scene of Olympia, Washington, and member of the band Bikini Kill. Other significant Riot Grrrl bands during the early 1990s included Bratmobile, Heavens to Betsy, Huggy Bear, Mecca Normal, and Sleater Kinney. Riot Grrrl punk music often contains lyrics that speak about sexism, sexual abuse, harassment, feminism, and revolution. Kathleen Hanna of Bikini Kill often performed on stage with words like "incest" and "slut" written on her body. Many members of these "first-generation" bands continue to be involved with other musical and artistic feminist projects.

Zine culture was a significant part of Riot Grrrl. Riot Grrrl zines often contain manifesto-like statements that describe the meaning of Riot Grrrl from the perspective of the zine makers. These zines often include discussions of sexism, racism, homophobia, and other forms of social injustice; body shaming and fat positivity; mental illness; and political revolution. Notable Riot Grrrl zines from the early 1990s were *Bikini Kill*, *Riot Grrrl*, *Action Girl*, and *Girl Germs*. Zines helped Riot Grrrl spread across the United States, Canada, and worldwide. Girls sent Riot Grrrl zines to each other in the mail or ordered zines after reading about them in *Sassy* magazine, which reviewed a zine in every issue, beginning in 1991.

The International Pop Underground Convention, held by K Records in Olympia, Washington, in 1991, is considered a significant moment in Riot Grrrl history. The first night of the event featured a musical lineup of all-women bands called "Love Rock Revolution Girl Style Now." The night brought together many participants in Riot Grrrl who had not previously met each other.

Riot Grrrl gained national media attention in the United States in the early 1990s, though much of this early coverage was patronizing. A 1992 *Newsweek* article called the more "extreme" Riot Grrrls "sanctimoniously committed" to the subculture. Many Riot Grrrls participated in a media blackout in response to the negative and biased coverage and refused to speak to mainstream media news outlets.

Riot Grrrl is widely considered part of third-wave feminism, in part because they both emerged during the time period of the late 1980s and early 1990s. But Riot Grrrl is also influenced by second-wave feminism. The manifestos, CR groups, and self-defense workshops of Riot Grrrls draw from second-wave activisms. Riot Grrrl aesthetics also draw upon avant-garde feminist artists, such as Kathy Acker and Nancy Spero.

Riot Grrrl is critiqued for being unable to adequately address issues pertaining to race and class, as well as racism and classism within the movement itself. Although there were women of color who participated in Riot Grrrl, the scene's normative subject was young, white, and female.

By the mid-1990s, the heyday of Riot Grrrl was over. However, there are newly formed Riot Grrrl chapters beginning in the 2000s with still-active music and zine cultures. Riot Grrrl and zine archives have been established at the Fales Library, the Sallie Bingham Center for Women's History and Culture, and Barnard College.

Elizabeth Groeneveld

See also: *Bitch* Magazine.

FURTHER READING

Darms, Lisa, ed. 2013. *The Riot Grrrl Collection*. New York: The Feminist Press.

Marcus, Sara. 2010. *Girls to the Front: The True Story of the Riot Grrrl Revolution*. New York: Harper Perennial.

Monem, Nadine, ed. 2007. *Riot Grrrl: Revolution Girl Style Now!* London: Black Dog Publishing.

MISSY ELLIOTT (1971–)

Missy "Misdemeanor" Elliott has sold more than seven million records in the United States and has won five Grammy awards since her rap career began in the early 1990s. As one critic said, "No female rap artist paralleled the success of Missy Elliott, neither during her reign nor before" (Birchmeier, 2016). Elliott rose to fame attracting a diverse fan base of varied ages, races, genders and cultural backgrounds. Her bold form of confident sexuality and self-acceptance, coupled with a strong will, musical talent, and hard work, challenged the status quo and accomplished the unexpected in the formerly male-dominated rap music industry. Consequently, many claim that Elliott has been a pioneer in bringing feminism into both the rap genre and mainstream pop music. As her talent and unapologetic feminism have consistently redefined the stereotypes of women and the expected role of female performers in rap music, Elliott has "established herself as queen of the freshest beats . . . [and the] hip-hop Madonna" (Lorraine and Ordonez, 2013: 100).

Born Melissa Arnette Elliott in 1971 in Portsmouth, Virginia, Elliott was witness to domestic violence and a victim of sexual violence throughout much of her childhood. Despite growing up in a mobile home where family dysfunction and poverty typified her early life, young Elliott was known in school as a class clown with a passion for singing. While still a teenager, she joined the R&B group Fayze, which after signing with Elektra Records was renamed Sista. However, the group's debut album was shelved by Elektra due to the lackluster performance of the single "Brand New." Nonetheless, during this time period, Elliott contributed lyrics and vocals to several hit tracks for other well-known artists in the hip-hop community, including Aaliyah, MC Lyte, Sean "Puffy" Combs, and Destiny's Child. As these connections and songwriting successes accumulated, Elliott was able to use them to springboard into a solo rap career.

Elliott's first solo album, *Supa Dupa Fly*, was released in 1997. A commercial and

Grammy Award–winning musical artist and producer Missy Elliott. Elliott became one of hip-hop's first female moguls with her record label The Goldmine Inc. (Carrienelson1/Dreamstime.com)

critical triumph, it brought her widespread acceptance and legitimacy as a female rap artist. Elliott then released a succession of other solo albums, including *Da Real World* (1999), *Miss E . . .* (2001), *Under Construction* (2002), *This Is Not a Test!* (2003), *The Cookbook* (2005), and a compilation album titled *Respect M.E.* (2006).

The majority of Elliott's song lyrics and music videos, including "Get Your Freak On" and "Work It," challenge industry and societal expectations in regards to body shape, size, age, sexuality, and/or gender. It has been argued that in contrast to many other female rap artists, Elliott "has always favoured personal style and self-confidence over male-dictated beauty ideals"; additionally, Elliott is known for having developed a musical resume that staunchly advocates for respect, empowerment, and sexual autonomy for all women (George, 2016). Over the span of her career, Elliott has composed, produced, engineered, provided vocals, and appeared as the feature artist on dozens of hit albums and songs.

Angeline Davis

FURTHER READING

Ali, Lorraine, and Jennifer Ordonez. 2003. "The Marketing of Missy." *Newsweek*, 142(23): 100.

Birchmeier, Jason. "Missy Elliott." ALLMUSIC. http://www.allmusic.com/artist/missy-elliott-mn0000502371.

George, Kat. 2016. "Why Missy Elliott's Feminist Legacy Is Criminally Underrated." *Dazed*. http://www.dazeddigital.com/music/article/29353/1/why-missy-elliott-s-feminist-legacy-is-criminally-underrated.

Morgan, Joan. March 2000. "The Making of Miss Thang!" *Essence*, 30(11): 92.

LAURA JANE GRACE (1980–)

Laura Jane Grace is an American musician and song writer best known as the founding member of Florida punk band Against Me!. In May 2012, Grace came out as transgender and announced her plan to release an album about her experiences. Grace's coming out helped initiate conversations about issues facing transgender people, as well as misogyny in punk music. The response to Grace's identity helps to demonstrate the limits of how gender is perceived and the way that gender went unquestioned in even the most rebellious movements.

Grace was born in 1980 in Fort Benning, Georgia. The child of Major Thomas Gabel, Grace grew up moving from one army base to another, including a NATO post in Italy during the first Gulf War. Her parents divorced when she was 11 years old, after which she and her mother moved to Naples, Florida. Constantly bullied at school, Grace began experimenting with drugs and alcohol at age 13 and continues to speak of her struggles with addiction. In 1995, she experienced a brutal arrest, which she later described as marking the beginning of her political consciousness. Grace formed Against Me! in 1997 to express her anarchist and anticapitalist politics. Gender was also a theme throughout her work, with songs about her gender dysphoria appearing on albums as early as 2002.

On Against Me!'s 2007 album *New Wave*, "The Ocean" includes lyrics in which Grace wishes she'd been born a woman. In May 2012, *Rolling Stone* magazine published an interview in which she came out as transgender and talked about the experience of being gender dysphoric in a hypermasculine music scene. The album she announced, *Transgender Dysphoria Blues*, was released in January 2014, debuting at number 23 on the *Billboard 200* (Caulfield, 2014). While touring over the next two years, Grace used her platform to speak about her experiences, the issues specific to transpeople, and how her experience of gender had always been present in her work. To this end, she produced an Emmy-nominated documentary series and spoke widely in both punk and mainstream media. Grace's visibility increased the exposure of other punk bands that have transgender members. She used her public position to promote groups such as HIRS, G.L.O.S.S, and the Worriers, even helping to produce the Worriers' 2015 album *Imaginary Life*.

Grace received an outpouring of support from a number of figures in the punk industry as well as from various LGBT organizations and feminist publications. Punk news sites produced articles on supporting transpeople, GLAAD voiced its support, and more than a few articles used her decision to come out to examine the issue of misogyny in punk. She was met with more reserved support by some members of the transgender community. Trans author Julia Serano, for example, expressed concern that the public conversation would only be about Grace's physical transition. She argued that the excessive focus on transgender bodies dehumanized transpeople (Serano, 2012).

In many of the interviews Grace has given, she has been asked intrusive questions about what she planned to do with her body and whether she would change her voice. She has received harassment from fans as well as radical feminists, many of whom argue that her gender is not valid because her sex cannot be "really" changed. These reactions reflect biological determinism of gender, the idea that sex assigned at birth determines gender, and a belief that the body has sexed characteristics that can never be changed "enough." Grace has responded to these challenges by demonstrating the fluidity of gender characteristics. When asked why she hadn't made her voice "like a woman's," she reminded interviewers that she didn't need to make her voice "like" a woman because she is a woman who is also transgender. Supporters have claimed that Grace's response, which resisted the idea that womanhood was defined by gendered stereotypes, illustrates how limited her challengers' notions of woman are.

Dorian Adams

FURTHER READING

Caulfield, Keith. 2014. "Chart Moves: Against Me!'s Highest Charting Album, Sara Bareilles' Grammy Gain." *Billboard*, January 31. http://www.billboard

.com/biz/articles/news/5893807/chart-moves-against-mes-highest-charting
-album-sara-bareilles-grammy-gain.

Eells, Josh. 2012. "The Secret Life of Transgender Rocker Tom Gabel." *Rolling Stone*, May 31. http://www.rollingstone.com/music/news/the-secret-life-of
-transgender-rocker-tom-gabel-20120531.

Serano, Julia. 2012. "Laura Jane Grace and Coming out as Trans in the Public Eye." *Whipping Girl*, May 30. http://juliaserano.blogspot.com/2012/05/laura
-jane-grace-and-coming-out-as.html.

Wisniewski, Kira. 2012. "Punk Community Reactions to Laura Jane Grace News." Punknews.org, May 12. https://www.punknews.org/article/47292/punk
-community-reactions-to-laura-jane-grace-news.

JANELLE MONÁE
(1985–)

Singer, songwriter, and activist Janelle Monáe sporting her trademark bouffant, and a black and white suit, which serves as an homage to domestic and service workers—a labor force that has been historically, and is still today, dominated by African Americans. (Featureflash/Dreamstime.com)

It wasn't until Atlanta-based singer-songwriter Janelle Monáe's (1985–) second album, but first on a major label, that Monáe had success on the charts as well as gained accolades from critics. *The Arch-Android* (2010), on her own Wondaland Arts Society/Bad Boy Records label, debuted at number 17 on the U.S. Billboard 200. Mixing African and futuristic aesthetics, her second album explored love, identity, and self-realization, and was part of a multipart concept series titled Metropolis. Monáe is a politically conscious artist who celebrates diversity and feels a responsibility to the underclass.

The release of the single "Tightrope" garnered attention from critics and audiences alike. With a funky fast-paced sound, the lyrics consider the balancing act and emotional ups and downs of life. The song's music video spotlights Monáe's dancing talent as she dons her signature black and white tuxedo-like suit, with her hair perfectly coiffed in a bouffant-like pouf. She often refers to her clothing choice as her uniform, which she wears in part as a dedication to the working class and her own working class roots. In 2013, Monáe released her second studio album, *The Electric Lady*, with the Wondaland label, to wide critical acclaim.

Monáe founded Wondaland Records in cooperation with Epic Records, a division of Sony Music Entertainment. Wondaland is more of an artists' collective than a traditional label. With musical artists Deep Cotton, Jidenna, and St. Beauty, Monáe seeks to start a movement to transform music and popular culture with an interdisciplinary approach to creativity—while simultaneously maintaining political consciousness. In 2015, Monáe participated in Black Lives Matter marches and released the bonus track "Hell You Talmbout" in collaboration with other Wondaland artists. Along with chants of "say his/her name," the names of victims of police brutality are recited over a deep, pounding drumbeat. In addition to her voice over work in the animated film *Rio 2*, Monáe has an acting role in two 2016 films, *Moonlight* and *Hidden Figures*. Moonlight centers on the coming-of-age story of an African American boy as he becomes a man. In *Hidden Figures*, Monáe has a starring role as one of the women at the center of the untold story of African American women's contributions to the United States space program.

Monáe has been nominated for numerous awards, including several Grammy nominations, and has won the 2010 Black Women in Music Award from Essence Awards, the 2014 Rising Star Award from Billboard's Women in Music, the 2014 Outstanding Music Video for Q.U.E.E.N. from the NAACP Image Awards, and the 2016 Hollywood Spotlight Award from the 20th Hollywood Film Awards, among others.

Ann M. Savage

FURTHER READING

Callahan, Yesha. n.d. "Janelle Monáe Reveals Why She Wears Black & White." *Clutch Magazine Online*. Accessed November 18, 2016. http://www.clutchm agonline.com/2013/04/janelle-monae-reveals-why-she-wears-black-white/.

Harris, Aisha. 2015. "Janelle Monáe Brings a Powerful New Protest Song to the Black Lives Matter Movement." *Slate*. August 14. http://www.slate.com/blogs/browbeat/2015/08/14/janelle_mon_e_s_hell_you_talmbout_is_a_rallying_cry_against_police_brutality.html.

Mock, Brentin. 2010. "The Joyful Noise of Janelle Monáe." *The Atlantic*, May 18. http://www.theatlantic.com/entertainment/archive/2010/05/the-joyful-noise-of-janelle-monae/56897/.

ANGEL HAZE (1992–)

Angel Haze, reported as being born Raykeea or Raeen Roes Wilson in 1992, is a rapper and singer from Detroit. Using they/them/their as a personal pronoun,

Haze gained popular recognition after mix-tape releases beginning in 2008, and has gone on to release two studio albums: *Dirty Gold* (2013) and *Back to the Woods* (2015). Haze's works have been critically acclaimed for their skill and lyricism, as well as for confronting issues of gender, sexuality, and abuse. Angel Haze identifies as agender (a trans identity that rejects the male/female binary and the construct of gender itself) and pansexual (able to experience attraction to a person of any gender), and has been lauded for bringing awareness to these identities. Of Native American descent, Haze has also used the Indian term "two-spirit" to describe their gender variant identity.

Many of Haze's songs have been critically praised for their frank discussion of difficult issues. Haze's 2012 song "Cleaning Out My Closet," a reworked version of fellow Detroit native Eminem's song of the same name, brought attention to childhood sexual abuse. Haze's personally revealing lyrics detail years of serial rape at the hands of a family friend. During a childhood spent living in what Haze described as a cult, their mother ignored the abuse, and Haze struggled with its effects on their psyche for years. The track received praise in *The Atlantic* for its honesty and critique of rape culture. In 2013, Haze released a remake of the artist Macklemore's straight ally song "Same Love." Over the song's backing track, Haze freestyles about the pain and rejection that LGBT young people face and about Haze's own experience in coming out to their mother.

Haze's gender-conscious rap challenges the genre's reputation as a bastion of sexism and homophobia. Haze has been outspoken about misogyny and homophobia, describing the rap and hip-hop music scene as a men's club that excludes women and queers.

Grace Lidinsky-Smith

FURTHER READING

Alexander, Ella. 2014. "Angel Haze interview: Lesbians, marriage, rap and depression—inside the mind of hip-hop's irrepressible female artist." *The Independent*, June 27. http://www.independent.co.uk/news/people/angel-haze-inter view-lesbians-marriage-rap-and-depression-inside-the-mind-of-hip-hop-s-irre pressible-9566207.html.

Haze, Angel. 2012. "Cleaning Out My Closet." *Classick*. Produced by LeRoy Ben-ros and Angel Haze. *Soundcloud*, October. https://soundcloud.com/noizycricket /cleaningoutmycloset.

Jeffries, Michael P. 2012. "How Rap Can Help End Rape Culture." *The Atlantic*, October 30. http://www.theatlantic.com/entertainment/archive/2012/10/how -rap-can-help-end-rape-culture/264258.

Keating, Shannon. 2015. "The Evolution of Angel Haze." *BuzzFeed LGBT*, May 27. http://www.buzzfeed.com/shannonkeating/the-evolution-of-angel-haze# .mizGxga1J.

LILITH FAIR (1997–1999 and 2010)

The Lilith Fair tour charged onto the U.S./Canadian music scene in 1997 with a roster of female-fronted bands. Organized by singer-songwriter Sarah McLachlan (1968–), the tour was revived in the summers of both 1998 and 1999, and it had a reprise in 2010. McLachlan said that she started the tour because "there's such a great diversity of music being made by women and very few places where you can see that kind of music." For many music fans, Lilith Fair marked an unprecedented opportunity to see many talented women performers at one event. Celebrated by many for bringing feminist consciousness to popular music and the broader culture, Lilith Fair's fans as well as critics have reveled in the celebration of women in music. At the same time, some mainstream media outlets have dismissed the festival with sexist-laden markers, calling the festival an "estrogen-fest," "breast-fest," or "lesbopalooza," and other media commentators all too often have referenced the appearance or marital status of the female artists.

The 1997 tour drew 600,000 fans, mostly women, in 37 cities. Although many celebrated the motivation of the fair, others criticized it for its heavy reliance on white singer-songwriters like Indigo Girls, Jewel, Paula Cole, and McLachlan; in subsequent years, the festival purposely diversified the lineup to include blues rocker Bonnie Raitt, pop/soul performer Erykah Badu, indie rocker Liz Phair, and rapper Missy Elliott, among others. Like Lollapalooza and similar tours, Lilith also offered a booth area for like-minded progressive organizations such as Planned Parenthood, domestic abuse shelters, and animal rights organizations. When right-wing groups complained about Planned Parenthood's presence, McLachlan insisted, "It's my festival and I believe in pro-choice." Additionally, the festival donated money from each ticket sale and raised over $10 million for charity. Although at first resistant to the label "feminist," McLachlan and others slowly began to warm up to the term.

McLachlan has often touted the fair as the first all-woman festival. However, many critics rightfully have pointed out that other festivals, such as the Michigan Womyn's Music Festival and the National Women's Music Festival, actually predated Lilith Fair. Lilith Fair also faced criticism from some feminists for its lack of a more women-centered atmosphere. Unlike Lilith Fair, the Michigan and National music festivals have been exclusively female, including stage crews and lighting and sound engineering technicians. There was another difference too. As a mainstream music festival, Lilith Fair was also plagued with corporate sponsorships and high-cost food, water, and merchandise. Despite these shortcomings, Lilith Fair represented a significant moment in women's pop music history.

Jamie Anderson

FURTHER READING

Childerhose, Buffy. 1998. *From Lilith to Lilith Fair: The Authorized Story*. New York: St. Martin's Press.

Iannacci, Elio. 2010. "Defending Lilith Fair" *Macleans,* May 10. 2016. http://www
.macleans.ca/culture/defending-lilith-fair/.

Lilith Fair: A Celebration of Women in Music. DVD. 1997. Directed by Buffy Childerhose and Alex Jamison. Brainchild Productions/High Five Entertainment/
Lilith Fair Productions.

Morris, Bonnie J. 2009. "Mainstreaming the 'Women's Music' Scene: Issues of Lesbian Visibility." In *Sapphists and Sexologists; Histories of Sexualities: Volume 2,*
191–207. Edited by Sonia Tiernan and Mary McAuliffe. UK: Cambridge Scholars Publishing.

PUSSY RIOT (2011–)

Pussy Riot is a Russian feminist punk-rock activist group of women who stage
unsanctioned protests against state-sponsored sexism and homophobia. Its provocative and illegal concerts, performed in various public spaces, are video recorded
and edited into music videos and released by the group on YouTube. The group first
formed in 2011 to protest the reelection campaign of Russian President Vladimir
Putin and to criticize the Russian Orthodox Church for supporting the Putin
regime and its consistent undermining of women's and gay rights. Pussy Riot's protest strategy is to shock and inform people through art and metaphor. The group
wears balaclava masks and brightly colored dresses and tights, and shows up to
public places unannounced and armed with electric guitars and microphones. In
unison, they shout anti-Putinist, feminist, and LGBTQ-positive lyrics while punching and kicking the air, creating an unavoidable public disturbance.

Pussy Riot gained international media attention in 2012 when three of its members were arrested and detained without bail for performing lyrics from the group's
song "Punk Prayer," also titled "Mother of God, Chase Putin Away," at the high altar
in the Cathedral of Christ the Savior in Moscow. The three arrested members,
Nadezhda Tolokonnikova (also known as Nadya or Nadia) (1989–), Maria Alyokhina (also known as Masha) (1988–) and Yekaterina Samutsevich (also known as
Katia) (1982–), were convicted for "hooliganism motivated by religious hatred" and
sentenced to serve two years in prison. The Russian government rejected Pussy
Riot's claim that their protest in the Church was a form of performance art, which
intended to cause political awareness rather than social harm. The Russian Courts
and media depoliticized the protest by characterizing Pussy Riot as a blasphemous
group that sought to infringe upon the human right to practice religion freely and
safely (*Pussy Riot: A Punk Prayer*, 2013).

Despite the West's overwhelming support for the women and political pressure
from human rights groups including Amnesty International, which named the
women "prisoners of conscience" (a person who is imprisoned for holding political or religious views that oppose those of the state), the Russian courts upheld the
women's sentences. The verdict was reportedly supported by the majority of Russian citizens, but it also resulted in mass protests across Europe, the United States,
and Canada, drawing hundreds of supporters out to public demonstrations. One

year after the women's sentencing, Amnesty International declared August 17th as Pussy Riot Global Day of Solidarity, and more than 60 cities around the world took part in protests against the group's continued imprisonment (Morris, 2012).

After serving their prison sentences, Tolokonnikova and Alyokhina travelled to the United States, where North American media outlets interviewed the women about their activism, the trial, and their experiences in prison. Their willingness to talk to Western media and forge political alliances with the West created tensions with some of their Russian activist allies, who accused them of "selling out" to American culture for fame and profit. One group of Russian feminists publicly criticized Pussy Riot's guerilla-style activism for causing too much backlash against feminism, which they felt jeopardized future gains for women's rights in Russia (Gessen, 2014). However, with international support and news coverage, Pussy Riot successfully tested and exposed the boundaries of Russian liberalism and its intolerance for political artistic expression and feminist activism. Pussy Riot continues to protest sexism and homophobia in Russia despite ongoing state persecution.

Andie Shabbar

FURTHER READING

The First Supper Symposium. Video. 2014. *Pussy Riot Meets Judith Butler and Rosi Braidotti.* https://www.youtube.com/watch?v=BXbx_P7UVtE.

Gessen, Masha. 2014. *Words Will Break Cement.* New York: Riverhead Books.

Morris, Harvey. 2012. "We're All Pussy Riot Now." *The New York Times*, August 17. http://rendezvous.blogs.nytimes.com/2012/08/17/were-all-pussy-riot-now/?_r =1. *Pussy Riot: A Punk Prayer.* Film. 2013. Directed by Mike Lerner and Maxim Pozdorovkin. Russia and United Kingdom: Roast Beef Productions.

Steinholt, Yngvar B. 2013. "Kitten Heresy: Lost Contexts of Pussy Riot's Punk Prayer." *Popular Music and Society*, 36(1): 120–24.

THREE

Film

Motion pictures have long held the public's imagination because of their power to give audiences a peek into worlds and experiences they would never experience otherwise. Films take us into the past, help us imagine the future, and can challenge us to think differently about the present. Like other forms of popular culture, films are not only reflections of real life or depictions of the unreal, but they also have the potential to play a role in pushing us to more progressive futures. This is certainly the case with women's rights, which have been championed in a wide range of films over the past half-century.

MOROCCO (1930)

Based on the 1927 novel *Amy Jolly* by Benno Vigny, Josef von Sternberg's first Hollywood film detailed the complicated romance between a womanizing legionnaire and an alluring nightclub entertainer. Though Sternberg is considered one of the great film auteurs, *Morocco* achieved popularity primarily because it introduced German actress Marlene Dietrich (1901–1992) to the United States. Dietrich plays Amy Jolly, a performer faced with a difficult decision: to live prosperously with Monsieur La Bessiere (Adolphe Menjou, 1890–1963), a man she does not love, or to choose romance with Legionnaire Tom Brown (Gary Cooper, 1901–1961) despite the uncertainties of their future together. This familiar romance plot provided the structure for a film that examined and unraveled traditional gender roles and representations. This task was already in motion at the turn of the century, with discourses on the "New Woman," a feminist ideal that was dangerous to the patriarchal status quo because of the woman's self-sufficiency, intellect, and sexual agency. Dietrich invokes this figure in her opening scene. Upon Amy's arrival to Morocco, Monsieur La Bessiere offers his assistance to her; she firmly replies, "I won't need any help." She destroys his business card and brazenly flicks the pieces

Marlene Dietrich (pictured) starred with Gary Cooper in the 1930 film *Morocco*. The film includes a scandalous scene where Dietrich dons a man's tailcoat suit, and kisses another woman. (Library of Congress)

into the sea, asserting her independence and rejecting male authority.

Likewise, in the film's most famous scene, Amy dons a tuxedo and top hat to give a radically androgynous cabaret performance that attracts both of her male suitors and undermines the notion of a gender binary (i.e., a distinct, mutually exclusive perspective of maleness and femaleness). Dietrich further challenged the producers' censorship in this iconic scene by sharing a kiss with a female audience member, a "Lesbian accent" (Sternberg, 1965: 247) that Sternberg desired for the film. In fact, *Morocco* was advertised by Paramount as the film that introduced "the Woman All Women Want to See," exploiting the scene's bisexual elements for increased sales (Baxter, 2010: 132).

Throughout the film, Amy consistently challenges Tom's limited, objectifying views of women, reminding him that "[t]here's a foreign legion of women, too." *Morocco*'s controversial conclusion finds Amy leaving her wealthy suitor to follow Tom into the Saharan desert. Although this ending disappointed some viewers who admired her earlier independence, others argued that her decision to risk everything for love showed bravery and contributed meaningfully to the romantic nature of the film overall.

Morocco was faulted by some for its thin characterization and plot, and a few critics even found Dietrich's performance lacking spark. The film also provoked public interest in Dietrich and Sternberg's strange off-screen relationship. Though each spoke admirably of their time together in their self-authored works, others described their relationship as masochistic and domineering. Despite these controversies, the film achieved remarkable success in 1930, including high box office sales and four Academy Award nominations in 1931. Dietrich, who was nominated for Best Actress, catapulted to celebrity status following its release and enjoyed continued success working alongside Sternberg on six other films. *Morocco* remains an enduring work that subverts conventions of gender and sexuality and infuses a queer sensibility into Depression-era film.

Jayda Coons

FURTHER READING

Bach, Steven. 2011. *Marlene Dietrich: Life and Legend.* Minneapolis: University of Minnesota Press.
Baxter, John. 2010. *Von Sternberg.* Lexington, KY: University Press of Kentucky.
Dietrich, Marlene. 1989. *Marlene.* Translated by Salvator Attanasio. New York: Grove Press.

CHRISTOPHER STRONG (1933)

The film *Christopher Strong* detailed adventurous aviator Lady Cynthia Darrington's move from strong, independent woman to politician's mistress. It was also the first major star vehicle for a young Katharine Hepburn (1907–2003), who would become the model for strong-minded, independent women in Hollywood from the 1930s until her death. In many ways, the film followed the conventions of typical "women's films" or melodramas at the time. These stories often featured women's downfalls through tragic love affairs and unrequited desires for things beyond their reach, be it status or romance. Although at first *Christopher Strong* appears to reaffirm the tragedy of being a married man's mistress, the film included a critique of marriage as an institution that supported male privilege and restricted women's freedoms.

The film's director, Dorothy Arzner (1897–1979), was already an established filmmaker by the release of the film in 1933. Her specialty was women's pictures, typically featuring working women. In *Christopher Strong*, Lady Cynthia (Hepburn) is a famous aviator who balks at the idea of love. She asserts her independence and willingness to pursue her career over men, making her a novelty among the upper class, who make light of fidelity throughout the film. The titular character, Sir Christopher Strong (Colin Clive), is a politician. At the beginning of the film, he is used as part of a scavenger hunt challenge to find a man who has been married for more than five years, has remained faithful to his wife, and is proud of the fact. Sir Christopher and Lady Cynthia's affair starts innocently enough as admiration for each person's strength of character and conviction. She respects his devotion to his wife (Billie Burke), and he respects her independent strength. Their affair leads to a host of contradictions and places their convictions regarding fidelity and freedom under the spotlight.

The film ends dramatically with Lady Cynthia driving her plane to beat the elevation record and passing out in the cockpit (seemingly on purpose). Critics at the time considered the ending to be a warning to those looking to start an affair and an example of the "fallen woman" receiving what she deserved. Looking back, however, scholars have found examples of the film being more critical toward the ways in which patriarchal institutions reinforce male privilege. The men in *Christopher Strong* have more flexibility and options, whereas women are forced to compete for eligible men and become each other's nemesis.

The film demonstrated the ways in which directors can abide by generic conventions, but also provided quite a bit of subtext to undermine dominant meanings. The film itself questioned the validity of the "rules" placed on these couplings and especially the double standards placed on women. As mistresses they are the villains, for example, whereas their male counterparts are depicted as being under spells. Arzner framed Lady Cynthia's move from staunch independent woman to submissive mistress as a tragedy. Though at first Christopher is enamored of Lady Cynthia's shirking of norms and promises to respect her choices, by the end of the film he treats her in the same way he betrays his wife. Arzner's film can thus be understood as a presentation of women's struggle to live freely in a patriarchal system that encourages women's subjugation to men.

Melinda Lewis

See also: *Adam's Rib.*

FURTHER READING

Casella, Donna. 2009. "What Women Want: The Complex World of Dorothy Arzner and Her Cinematic Women." *Framework: The Journal of Cinema & Media*, 50: 235–70.

Durham, Carolyn. 2001. "Missing Masculinity or Cherchez L'Homme: Re-Reading Dorothy Arzner's *Christopher Strong.*" *Quarterly Review of Film and Video*, 18: 63–70.

ADAM'S RIB (1950)

Released in 1950, George Cukor's *Adam's Rib* represented a growing struggle for equal rights in post–World War II America. The film opens with a woman following a man, who we soon find out is her husband. She then shoots him at his mistress's home. The case creates a stir at the home of Assistant District Attorney Adam Bonner (Spencer Tracy, 1900–1967) and his lawyer wife, Amanda (Katharine Hepburn, 1907–2003). As they discuss the merits of the case, Amanda sees it as an opportunity to expose double standards between the sexes. Adam is assigned to prosecute while Amanda volunteers to defend the wife and fight in the courtroom against her husband. The film thus takes on a "battle of the sexes" aspect, both in the nature of the case these two lawyers are fighting and within their own marriage.

The film is a classic screwball comedy with Tracy and Hepburn expertly snapping quick quips at each other throughout the film, poking and prodding each other, and acting as representatives in the battle of the sexes. In proving her case, Amanda insists on arguing that the issue is not about a woman shooting her husband, but one of motivation. She argues against ideologies that justify men's behaviors, but not women's. She seeks jurors who are not opposed to women's equality. She provides examples of women who are just as, if not more, capable in their occupations than men, and encourages the jury to look past their own biases and judge her client not as a woman, but as a man. The arguments she makes become those made by the film. The man who was shot (Tom Ewell, 1909–1994) is callous, cruel, and casual about domestic violence, cheating, and emotional abuse. But when asked if he is a good husband, he surprisingly declares, "Yes." The film highlights the hypocrisy of such double standards. Amanda wins the case, which demonstrates her ability to take on a seemingly unwinnable case and defeat her husband.

The film was daringly progressive for 1950, particularly in its representation of women workers. The film had to navigate post-war anxieties of men returning from war to their wives who had been working and experiencing financial independence through their own labor. However, Amanda's activism throughout the film pushes her husband away and interferes with their marriage. Instead of Adam being an ally, he declares his disinterest in the "new woman," arguing that he wants "a wife, not a competitor." His legal argument against Amanda's search for equality in their mutual case is not about human rights, but a citizen committing a crime. When Adam recreates the incident, finds Amanda alone with their lecherous neighbor and pretends to shoot, Amanda declares that he has "no right" to enact violence and realizes she has made his argument. Despite the fact that he felt as if she were a competitor as opposed to his wife, Adam and Amanda are able to mend their marriage, prioritizing the success of the marriage over Amanda's success in the courtroom. Hence, the film positioned itself in such a way as to make points about gender equality without alienating 1950s audiences.

Melinda Lewis

See also: *Christopher Strong.*

FURTHER READING

Glitre, Kathrina. 2013. *Hollywood Romantic Comedy: States of the Union, 1934–65.* Manchester: Manchester University Press.

Grindon, Leger. 2011. *The Hollywood Romantic Comedy: Conventions, History, and Controversies.* Oxford: Blackwell-Wiley.

JOHNNY GUITAR (1954)

Released by Republic Pictures in 1954, *Johnny Guitar* starred Joan Crawford (1904–1977) as Vienna, a saloon owner, and Mercedes McCambridge (1916–2004) as her rival, Emma Small. The film was notable for its casting of women as the main characters in positions of power in a Western film.

Joan Crawford was an accomplished movie star by the 1950s. She began her career in 1925 in the silent film era and went on to win the Academy Award for Best Actress in *Mildred Pierce* in 1945. Film roles for women in the 1950s were perhaps

HERBERT J. YATES presents
JOAN CRAWFORD
JOHNNY GUITAR
TRUCOLOR
STERLING HAYDEN SCOTT BRADY
MERCEDES McCAMBRIDGE
NOT SUITABLE FOR CHILDREN
A REPUBLIC PICTURE RELEASED THRU 20ᵀᴴ CENTURY FOX

Joan Crawford stars as Vienna in the 1954 western drama *Johnny Guitar*. Crawford's Vienna is a self-made woman who lives life on her own terms. (Republic Pictures/Photofest)

more varied than in previous decades, but they still primarily depicted women in either traditional gender roles or as sex symbols. The genre of Westerns in particular was also completely male dominated. When women did make appearances in these films, it was usually in the supporting role of the love interest. *Johnny Guitar* almost followed this formula as well; in the original script, the title character was supposed to play the lead role.

In fact, it was Crawford who, after expressing dissatisfaction with the original script, pushed for her character to be the focus of the film. The film's title actually refers to the character who arrives to help Vienna defend her saloon against Emma and the townspeople, who want Vienna to leave. Unlike many of Crawford's earlier film roles as dancers, shop girls, or women who had to work their way up in society, her role in *Johnny Guitar* portrayed her as already in control of and ready to defend the situation. This characterization "bluntly presented gender reversals, as gritty women tough it out with gentler male characters" (Chandler, 2008: 224).

Johnny Guitar is often described as one of the strangest and most unconventional films in the genre of Westerns, perhaps because it so blatantly subverted traditional gender roles. In many of her films, including *Mildred Pierce*, Crawford was recognized for her costumes as much as for her acting ability. Her naturally broad shoulders, further accentuated by shoulder pads in gowns designed for her by the costume designer Adrian, became a trademark for Crawford. Her appearance in a button-down shirt, pants, and boots in *Johnny Guitar* therefore further emphasized the film's forward-thinking depiction of women in Westerns.

The French film director François Truffaut was perhaps the film's biggest champion, praising it as "a Western that is dream-like [and] magical" (Peterson, 1996: 3). It was for these reasons that *Johnny Guitar* was chosen in 2008 by the Library of Congress for preservation in the United States National Film Registry. Today *Johnny Guitar* is often called a "cult classic," but its powerful depictions of women in a Western continue to stand the test of time.

Jeanette Sewell

FURTHER READING

Chandler, Charlotte. 2008. *Not the Girl Next Door: Joan Crawford, A Personal Biography.* New York: Applause Theatre & Cinema Books.

Peterson, Jennifer. 1996. "The Competing Tunes of 'Johnny Guitar': Liberalism, Sexuality, Masquerade." *Cinema Journal*, 35: 3–18.

IMITATION OF LIFE (1959)

The 1933 novel *Imitation of Life* by Fannie Hurst (1885–1968) dealt with issues of race, class, and gender through the narrative of mothers and daughters navigating a world in which the "one-drop rule" applied. This rule, enforced in some Southern states, classified anyone born with some African descent as black. In the two cinematic adaptations of the novel from 1934 (directed by John M. Stahl for Universal Pictures) and 1959 (directed by Douglas Sirk, also for Universal Pictures), a young, light-skinned woman grows to resent and reject her dark-skinned black mother. The novelist Hurst was a Jewish woman who was heavily involved in the nascent feminist movement and invested in the Harlem Renaissance.

The narrative follows an unusual family of two women, one black and one white, and their two young daughters. When a white widow—played by Claudette Colbert (1903–1996) in 1934 and Lana Turner (1921–1995) in 1959—and her child take in a black maid—played by Louise Beavers (1902–1962) in 1934 and Juanita Moore (1914–2014) in 1959—and her light-skinned daughter, the four become exceedingly close. In the 1934 version, the two mothers become business partners in a pancake flour and syrup business, with Louise Beavers becoming an Aunt Jemima–like figure. Though Beavers's character appears to do more work and becomes more crucial to the company's success, she appears complacent in her second-tier status, working as a maid even as Claudette Colbert's character becomes a wealthy woman of independent means. In the 1959 remake, the two women's business interests remain more codified into classist and racial separation; Juanita Moore's character remains simply as a maid while Lana Turner's character becomes a Broadway star.

The 1959 film, while retaining the general storyline, changed several aspects of the plot. The biracial daughter, played by Susan Kohner (1936–), begins dating a white man, who beats her up in an alleyway when he discovers that she has a black mother. Another significant difference between the two films is the casting of the light-skinned biracial daughter. The 1934 film cast actor Fredi Washington (1903–1994), who was of both African and European descent, whereas the 1959 film cast Kohner, who was of Mexican and Czech Jewish descent.

In addition to covering issues of independent, working women who must provide for their children, the films also included instances of adult and maternal romance. Colbert's and Turner's romantic aspirations are thwarted, however, by their daughters. The young girls develop crushes on their mothers' boyfriends, complicating family dynamics. Though given an opportunity to engage in a romantic relationship, the widowed mothers decide to hold off on pursuing matrimony until their teenage and young adult daughters "get over" these young crushes.

The United States National Film Registry cemented the 1934 film's iconic status when it was selected for preservation in 2005. The novel and the two film adaptations remain controversial, however, because of accusations that they engaged in racial stereotyping and improper casting (including a non-black actor as a light-skinned black woman).

Eleanor M. Huntington

FURTHER READING

Butler, Jeremy. 1987. "*Imitation of Life*: Style and the Domestic Melodrama." *Jump Cut*, 32: 25–28.

Everett, Anna. 1996. " 'I Want the Same Things Other People Enjoy': The Black Press and the Classic Hollywood Studio System, 1930–40." *Spectator*, 17(1): 40–53.

Heung, Marina. 1987. " 'What's the Matter with Sara Jane?': Daughters and Mothers in Douglas Sirk's *Imitation of Life*." *Cinema*, 26(3): 21–43.

Hiro, Molly. 2010. " 'Tain't No Tragedy Unless You Make It One': *Imitation of Life*, Melodrama, and the Mulatta." *Arizona Quarterly: A Journal of American Literature, Culture, and Theory*, 66(4): 93–110.

THE RAIN PEOPLE (1969)

"She. Me. The Wife." This is how Natalie Ravenna, the main character in the 1969 feminist-themed road film *The Rain People* describes herself to her husband Vinny. At the time of its release, the film, which was directed by Francis Ford Coppola (1939–), was reviewed coolly. Film critic Pauline Kael characterized Natalie (played by Shirley Knight, 1936–) as a pregnant woman who was "atrociously mannered." Roger Greenspun of *The New York Times* described her as "mixed-up." The subtle hostility toward Natalie reflected a dismissal of feminist-drawn characters in the late 1960s.

Natalie's story starts on a rainy morning while Vinny (Robert Modica, 1931– 2015) sleeps. She dutifully lays out his breakfast and then writes him a goodbye note. Later she calls him from a phone booth and meekly answers his angry question as to why she left. "I'm pregnant," she says. Vinny asks, "Who?" Natalie answers, "She. Me. The Wife," and then admits she is not sure she would make a good mother. Sensing that she might seek an illegal abortion, he furiously tells her not to "do anything."

Who are the three Natalies? The "me" is Natalie herself, a woman she does not know. The "she" is the "other" who lives to please men. The "wife" is the woman Natalie left behind that morning, a woman who lives for her husband and children.

Coppola reveals them cinematically as three separate mirror reflections of Natalie.

Natalie encounters several men on her trip. One is a rejected college football hero named Killer Gannon, played by James Caan (1940–), who has suffered a debilitating brain injury and is wandering the country alone. Her attempts to seduce him fail. Despite her attempts to separate from him, Killer stays with her throughout the film. Later, Natalie has a date with a cop, played by Robert Duvall (1931–), that ends tragically when he attempts to rape her. Watching from the window, Killer breaks in to save her, only to be shot dead by the cop's daughter, Rosalie, who wields her father's gun. Rosalie, played by Marya Zimmet (1957–), brazenly wears a bra for fun and is referred to as a "little bitch" by her father. Although Killer is dead, Natalie desperately tries to resurrect him by telling him that Vinny will take her back and all three of them will live together as a family. Who are the three? The individual, the other, and the wife.

Although the film eventually developed a cult following, *The Rain People* was overshadowed by the male-driven, critically acclaimed *Easy Rider*, which was released just one month later. If it had been made at a later time, when feminist ideas were more well known, Natalie's journey could have been completed, but as it stands *The Rain People* is an unfinished feminist journey.

Jennifer Hall Lee

FURTHER READING

Ebert, Roger. 1969. "The Rain People." http://www.rogerebert.com/reviews/the -rain-people-1969.

Greenspun, Roger. 1969. "The Rain People." *The New York Times*, August 28.

Kael, Pauline. 1991. *5001 Nights at The Movies*. New York: Henry Holt and Company.

ALICE DOESN'T LIVE HERE ANYMORE (1974)

Alice Doesn't Live Here Anymore (1974) was a film about a suddenly widowed woman who travels across the American Southwest to make a better life for herself and her preteen son. The production was the result of a collaboration by its star, Ellen Burstyn (1932–), who won an Academy Award for her performance; writer Robert Getchell (1936–); and director Martin Scorsese (1942–). A commercially successful and critically acclaimed film, it was later spun off into a long-running sitcom, called *Alice*, which aired from 1976–1985 on CBS. *Alice Doesn't Live Here Anymore* emerged during a decade when women were increasingly moving into the workforce, so the interest in female independence was at the forefront of social and political discussion.

During the 1970s, the United States underwent a dramatic shift in the demographic makeup of suburbia. American suburbanization began at the end of the Second World War, when housing and population expanded away from cities, and the suburbs became idealized in the American public consciousness as a desirable locale for white upper-/middle-class nuclear families with conservative values. By the early 1970s, this image was challenged as women's roles changed from homemakers and wives to heads of households and independent homeowners (Francescato, 2011: 10–13). Women's movement from domesticity into the workforce was an integral element of women's liberation and was increasingly reflected in films like *Alice Doesn't Live Here Anymore* that featured women as primary characters seeking independence and emancipation from traditional female roles. However, such feminist ventures in film often failed or were shown with great ambivalence. Although perhaps antithetical to the need for positive on-screen representations of female characters, such portrayals illustrated a sympathy with public anxiety about female emancipation as a difficult process with which the female character— and audience—learned to come to terms. While conservative values were gaining more traction, public opinion became more critical about dominant cultural norms and U.S. institutions, paralleling a prevailing cynicism born of the Vietnam War and the Watergate scandal (Francescato, 2011: 24–25).

Popular film critic Roger Ebert noted that the film was both "attacked and defended on feminist grounds" (Ebert, 2008: 36–37). Burstyn's Alice is not a glamorous Hollywood star or a liberated heroine, and this atypical film character received both praise (Davis, 1975) and criticism for what detractors called an unconvincing representation of lower-middle-class life (Webb and Martens, 1975). The plot predominantly revolves around Alice's relationships with others. In particular, her relationship with her son, Tommy (Alfred Lutter III, 1962–), is central to the story. Although motherhood is still showcased with overriding importance, the mother–son bonding has been praised for its frankness (Webb and Martens, 1975). Her confounding relationships with men have been particularly critiqued, especially her relationship with her boyfriend David (Kris Kristofferson, 1936–) as the allegorical Prince Charming. This classic Hollywood happy ending has been disparaged for backpedaling on Alice's statement about not needing a man in her life, a message important for the women's movement at the time. Indeed, the film's overall focus on interpersonal relationships has been critiqued by feminists for not depicting the women's movement, thereby obscuring feminist messages (Wood, 1990: 337). Nevertheless, the movie is regarded as a classic, and the character Alice achieved status as a feminist cult figure.

Monica Murtaugh

FURTHER READING

Davis, Russell E. 1975. *"Alice Doesn't Live Here Anymore*: Under the Comic Frosting." *Jump Cut*, 7. http://www.ejumpcut.org/archive/onlinessays/JC07folder/aliceDavis.html.

Ebert, Roger. 2008. *Scorsese by Ebert.* Chicago: University of Chicago Press.

Francescato, Simone. 2011. *La Donna È Mobile: Portraits of Suburban Women in 1970s American Cinema.* Palo Alto, CA: Academica Press.

Webb, Teena, and Betsy Martens. 1975. *"Alice Doesn't Live Here Anymore*: A Hollywood Liberation." *Jump Cut*, 7. http://www.ejumpcut.org/archive/onlinessays/JC07folder/aliceWebb.html.

Wood, Robin. 1990. "Images and Women." In *Issues in Feminist Film Criticism*, 337–52. Edited by Patricia Erens. Bloomington, IN: Indiana University Press.

FOXY BROWN (1974)

Foxy Brown, a 1974 film directed by Jack Hill (1933–) and starring Pam Grier (1949–), was both celebrated and despised upon its release. After her boyfriend is murdered by the mob, the title character, Foxy Brown, seeks to avenge his death by developing a plot that requires her to become a high-class prostitute. As a "blaxploitation" film, known for its raw footage, low budget, urban setting, and gritty plot, *Foxy Brown* challenged the way African American women were represented in film.

The social climate during the 1970s was one of rapid change. For women especially, the Women's Liberation Movement embraced female independence and increased the fight against sexism. Women were fighting for their visibility and their civil rights by increasingly making decisions for themselves regarding employment, education, politics, and what it meant to be a woman. As African American women shared in the fight to end sexism, they pointed out that they had to carry on the crusade for equality on multiple fronts; they not only had to combat sexism, but also racism, classism, and more. The film *Foxy Brown* not only challenged traditional gender roles but also views on women's sexuality.

In the decades before *Foxy Brown*, African American women were usually cast in American cinema in supporting roles such as poverty-stricken servants, drug addicts, or single mothers. These stereotypes, or controlling images, as scholar Patricia Hill Collins called them, proved damaging to African American women's identity. *Foxy Brown* was met with mixed reviews from feminists and African American activists. On one hand, many applauded the strong female lead and used

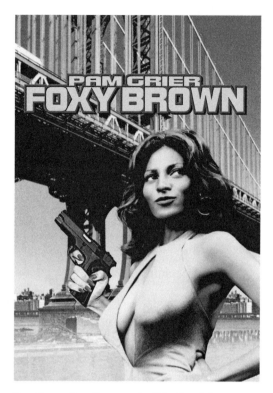

Pam Grier as Foxy Brown in the 1974 film of the same name. Directed by Jack Hill, *Foxy Brown* remains a significant film in popular culture despite its stereotypical depiction of black womanhood. (AIP/Photofest)

the film to expand acting roles for African American women from inferior servants to independent women, unafraid to be sexy and take charge. According to black studies professor Ingrid Banks, "Black women as action heroines ... [were] willing to protect family and community by any means necessary, [portraying Black women as strong and invincible]" (Knight, 2010: 127). On the other hand, some viewers saw *Foxy Brown* as a dangerous film because it furthered negative stereotypes of African American women as hypersexual or as just "ghetto smart black heroes" (Dunn, 2008: 108).

Foxy was an example of a woman embracing the ideals of sexual revolution prominent in the 1970s, characterized by women claiming power over their own bodies. As Grier later explained, "We redefined sexuality in America" (Dunn, 2008: 115). Because Foxy had agency, or free will over her own body, she, in keeping with feminist tradition, could be considered sexually liberated. On a large scale, Foxy was able to use her sexuality not as a weakness, but as a weapon to fight claims of inferiority and promote a more complex understanding of feminine power.

Erica Horhn

See also: Women's Liberation Movement.

FURTHER READING

Collins, Patricia Hill. 2009. *Black Feminist Thought*. New York: Routledge.

Dunn, Stephane. 2008. *"Baad Bitches" and Sassy Supermamas: Black Power Action Films*. Urbana, IL: University of Illinois Press.

King, Deborah K. 1988. "Multiple Jeopardy, Multiple Consciousness: The Context of a Black Feminist Ideology." *Signs: Journal of Women in Culture and Society*, 14: 42–72.

Knight, Gladys L. 2010. *Female Action Heroes: A Guide to Women in Comics, Video Games, Film, and Television*. Santa Barbara, CA: Greenwood.

Sims, Yvonne D. 2006. *Women of Blaxploitation: How the Black Action Film Heroine Changed American Popular Culture*. Jefferson, NC: McFarland.

NORMA RAE (1979)

Norma Rae was a 1979 film about a single mother with three young children who fights for unionization at the textile factory where she works in a small Southern town. The film was a critical success, gaining an Oscar win for Sally Field (1946–), who played the lead character, and a nomination for Best Picture. Its director, Martin Ritt (1914–1990), was an accomplished filmmaker despite being blacklisted in the 1950s during the height of anticommunist sentiment, and was known for his socially conscious movies. Based on the real-life experiences of labor activist Crystal Lee Sutton (1940–2009), the translation of this woman's life into film was significant for its revelations of social attitudes toward feminism and unionism.

The film's pro-unionist message was atypical at that time for a Hollywood film, which had historically portrayed organized labor as corrupt and criminal, as in the classic *On the Waterfront* (1954). This opposition to unions reflected the attitudes of studio executives who were concerned about their own workers, as well as rising conservative sentiment against the ongoing Civil Rights Movement, which would eventually culminate in the U.S. presidential election of Ronald Reagan. Indeed, although the movie itself was centered more on labor issues than feminist issues, *Norma Rae* was advertised for its feminist themes, with the protagonist promoted as a "female Rocky" who uses her independence and self-assertiveness to obtain her goals, even at great risk to her own livelihood (Toplin, 1996: 207–10). U.S. culture in the 1970s was increasingly more responsive to women's issues, with strong female characters reflecting a period of second-wave feminist activity that, in turn, inspired Hollywood's interest in dramatizing the lives of women.

Norma Rae did adhere to a standard Hollywood narrative structured around an individual. Concentrating on one character and her relationships with others does have shortcomings, especially with respect to overemphasizing Norma's role as an activist while oversimplifying the factors that bring about social change (Kuhn, 1994; Leonard, 2007). This focus on the individual has been criticized for being too personal rather than offering a more grounded political statement (Leonard, 2007: 130). However, centering the plot on Norma and her social circle has been applauded by some scholars for showcasing the lived experiences of a blue-collar worker in a manner that is still class conscious (Giroux, 2002: 21). Additionally, Norma's relationship with another primary character, a male labor organizer played by Ron Leibman (1937–), has been hailed as progressive for challenging traditional and sexist male–female relationship models (Giroux, 2002: 24). This personal tale is furthermore complemented by the setting, which scholars praised for its gritty depiction of the poor working conditions and health hazards at the factory, as well as overtones of racial disparity at the workplace and in the surrounding community (Zieger and Zieger, 1982: 70–72). In 2011, *Norma Rae* was included in the United States Film Registry by the Library of Congress for its enduring significance to U.S. culture.

Monica Murtaugh

FURTHER READING

Giroux, Henry A. 2002. *Breaking in to the Movies: Film and the Culture of Politics.* Malden, MA: Blackwell Publishers.

Kuhn, Annette. 1994. *Women's Pictures: Feminism and Cinema*, 2nd ed. London: Verso.

Leonard, Suzanne. 2007. "'I Hate My Job, I Hate Everybody Here': Adultery, Boredom, and the 'Working Girl' in Twenty-First-Century American Cinema." In *Interrogating Postfeminism: Gender and the Politics of Popular Culture*, 100–131. Edited by Yvonne Tasker and Diane Negra. Durham, NC: Duke University Press.

Toplin, Robert Brent. 1996. *History by Hollywood: The Use and Abuse of the American Past.* Urbana, IL: University of Illinois Press.

Zieger, Gary P., and Robert H. Zieger. 1982. "Unions on the Silver Screen: A Review Essay of F.I.S.T., Blue Collar, and Norma Rae." *Labor History*, 23(1): 67–78.

THE COLOR PURPLE (1985)

In 1985, the film *The Color Purple* was released to both popular and critical acclaim. Directed by Steven Spielberg (1946–) and featuring a score composed by celebrated musician Quincy Jones (1933–), the film was based on the Pulitzer Prize–winning novel of the same name written by Alice Walker (1944–), one of the most prolific contemporary American writers. Highly visible actors such as Danny Glover (1946–), Whoopi Goldberg (1955–), and Oprah Winfrey (1954–) were given prominent roles in this controversial film, which focused on the oppressive conditions under which many black women suffered at the hands of family members in the 1930s post-Reconstruction U.S. South. That a black woman's voice of intraracial and familial violence, self-doubt, and then ultimately love found through intimacy in sisterhood could be presented with such a universality through an epistolary novel was certainly ripe for film consideration, but the interest of Steven Spielberg, who had directed seven blockbuster films to that date, made it that much more popular.

The authenticity of the main character, Celie (played by Goldberg), whose story was representational of Walker's family history in rural Georgia in the 1930s, resonated with many people across various cultural and economic backgrounds. Controversy surrounded the film because there was a heightened public critique of how black men were negatively represented in popular culture and media generally and in Walker's text specifically. And there was justifiably a particular sensitivity to how minority groups were stereotyped when the images that represented them in American popular culture were so limited and marginal.

Spielberg's access to a large production budget afforded him a significant degree of creative latitude that the film seemed to require. Spielberg's résumé at that time included blockbuster films such as *Close Encounters of the Third Kind* (1977), *Jaws* (1975), *Poltergeist* (1982), and *E.T.—the Extra-Terrestrial* (1982), and he had a reputation for speaking to the deep emotions of the viewing public by focusing on themes of redemption and happy endings. So one can imagine the challenges presented to Spielberg with *The Color Purple*, steeped as it was in controversy for allegedly being antagonistic toward black men. *The Color Purple* received 11 Academy Award nominations, including Best Picture and Best Actress for Whoopi Goldberg, but did not win any awards. Many expected that Steven Spielberg would win for Best Director, but he surprisingly never even received a nomination.

Alice Walker has always been clear that her writing is more representational of the black woman's voice from a feminist perspective, which she calls "womanist" to distinguish it from traditional white middle-class feminism. In many of her writings, as well as in the film version of *The Color Purple*, the audience is provided the particular and historical lens of rural black women in struggles with family and love; these personal struggles, in concert with cultural and systemic barriers, are represented as challenges that black women navigate and ultimately survive, even moving forward toward some level of success.

Walker documented her tumultuous experiences after the publication of *The Color Purple* and the release of the film adaptation in the book *The Same River Twice: Honoring the Difficult* (1996). In it she wrote that she had been asked numerous times about her reaction to Spielberg's film. After noting that the first time she saw the film she ended up with a headache, she went on to state that she sometimes expressed mixed feelings or that she loved it. However, her most affirming moment took place when her mother went to a viewing of the film, "carried there in an ambulance," and stated that she "liked it very much because it reminded her of her mother" (Walker, 1996).

Terri Jett

See also: *The Color Purple* by Alice Walker.

FURTHER READING

Alice Walker: The Official Website. http://alicewalkersgarden.com.

Donnelly, Mary. 2010. *Alice Walker: The Color Purple and Other Works*. New York: Marshall Cavendish Benchmark.

Walker, Alice. 1996. *The Same River Twice: Honoring the Difficult: A Meditation on Life, Spirit, Art, and the Making of the Film, the Color Purple, Ten Years Later*. New York: Scribner.

White, Evelyn C. 2004. *Alice Walker: A Life*. New York: Norton.

Daughters of the Dust (1991) is the first feature film to be written, directed, and produced by an African American woman, Julie Dash. Pictured from left are Alva Rogers, Barbara O. Jones, and Cora Lee Day. (Kino International Corp./Photofest)

DAUGHTERS OF THE DUST (1991)

Daughters of the Dust (1991), an independent film written, produced, and directed by Julie Dash (1951–), was the first full-length film helmed by an African American woman to receive a general theatrical release in the United States. The film is also significant because it introduced viewers to a lesser-known aspect of African American history and to a new style of storytelling in film. Through her characters, Dash demonstrated the value of women as the caretakers and interpreters of cultural heritage. Although the film addressed the damage caused by institutional racism and white men's violence, the story was told entirely from the point of view of African American women.

Daughters of the Dust is the story of the Peazant family, African Americans living on one of the Gullah Islands, a string of islands off the coast of South Carolina and Georgia where formerly enslaved people formed a unique language and culture. The film follows the events of one day in 1902, when a large number of family members are making plans to migrate from the island where they have lived for many generations to the North. Through multiple vantage points, the film provides various aspects of the family's history and reveals the circumstances of the tension between those who want to stay and those who want to go. Nana Peazant (Cora Lee Day, 1914–1996), the family matriarch, is the guardian of the West African religious and cultural heritage. She is fearful that a move to the mainland will mean that her family will become disconnected from its African roots. Viola Peazant (Cheryl Lynn Bruce, 1957–) rejects the African spirituality of Nana and hopes that by moving to the mainland she can protect her children by raising them as Christians. Nana is able to convince a few family members to remain with her on the island, but most decide to relocate. In a ritual, Nana gives her departing family members some of the things they will need to remember their heritage.

Julie Dash was part of the "L.A. Rebellion," a group of African and African American independent filmmakers who attended the UCLA Film School from 1960 until 1980. Together with Charles Burnett and Haile Gerima, Dash was influenced by foreign films and used ethnographic methods to depict aspects of African American life not being portrayed in Hollywood cinema. Her films provide a commentary on the gender-race relations of the post–Civil Rights era by addressing the theme of African American women's sexual agency. One main theme within *Daughters of the Dust* is the struggle for self-determination on the part of women who are routinely subjected to sexual assault and the exploitation of their labor. In this and other films, Dash also addressed some of the challenges within African American women's communities, like skin color discrimination and the stigma associated with rape.

Dash had a difficult time producing her film because many felt there would be no audience for a story focused on African American women. *Daughters of the Dust* was considered inaccessible to some among American audiences; however, international audiences seemed to be more receptive to becoming fully engrossed in a different language and culture. In general, *Daughters of the Dust* received positive acclaim; however, the success of the film did not translate into more work for Dash.

Gabrie'l J. Atchison

FURTHER READING

Bambara, Toni Cade. 1996. "Reading the Signs, Empowering the Eye: *Daughters of the Dust* and the Black Independent Cinema Movement." In *Deep Sightings and Rescue Missions: Fiction, Essays and Conversations*, 89–138. Edited by Toni Cade Bambara. New York: Vintage.

Dash, Julie. 1992. *Daughters of the Dust: The Making of an African American Woman's Film*. New York: The New Press.

Diawara, Manthia. 1993. *Black American Cinema*. New York: Routledge.

Hellencamp, Patricia. 1995. *A Fine Romance: Five Ages of Film Feminism*. Philadelphia: Temple University Press.

THELMA AND LOUISE (1991)

In the 1990s, discussions about women's rights, roles, and opportunities were being revisited in popular media from a postfeminist perspective, which emphasized individual choice and assumed an empowered female position, and thus seemed to render feminism and women's collective struggles for empowerment obsolete. The film *Thelma and Louise*, directed by Ridley Scott (1937–), found itself at the crossroads of these discourses as a road movie centered on two female leads who commit acts of violence as they escape their everyday lives.

The overarching debate raised by *Thelma and Louise* concerned the place of women within patriarchy. This entailed a number of things: women's role in the private and public spheres; women and crime; the continued objectification of women, both on the level of representation and in real life; and the lack of female agency or self-determination within a male-dominated system. The film's focus on a female friendship also challenged conventions of the road movie genre, which up to that point had been populated almost exclusively by men.

Questions about women's roles were raised particularly in relation to the character of Thelma (Geena Davis, 1956–). At the start of the film, she is a housewife who is terrified of her husband. Thelma's character development sees her increasingly gaining control of her own body and her own decision-making. Her choices and behavior are decidedly contrary to all the ways patriarchy systematically restricts women. The two main characters' existence outside prescribed domestic roles, or outside their association to a man, is represented as "criminal." The final sequence of the film has been analyzed precisely in these terms: they need to "keep going" (even if this means to their death) in order to maintain their freedom.

Another theme that has been extensively discussed in relation to *Thelma and Louise* is rape. It has been noted that Louise (Susan Sarandon, 1946–) does not shoot Thelma's rapist when he is in the act, but when he retorts to her with a sexist insult. In this sense, Louise's action has been read as a decided rejection of abusive attitudes toward women. This was criticized by another strand of feminism that views women as having a natural capacity as pacifist caregivers rather than violent agents. However, this stance was itself seen as problematic for reinforcing dominant portrayals of women as passive victims. Instead, the importance of more complex representations of women in relation to crime was noted.

In placing women at the center of the film and having their friendship supersede their heterosexual relationships, and in foregrounding debates about women's agency and rights, the film has established itself as a text that still challenges patriarchal orthodoxies.

Tonia Kazakopoulou

FURTHER READING

Dowell, Pat, Elayne Rapping, Alice Cross, Sarah Schulman, and Roy Grundmann. 1991. "Should We Go Along for the Ride?: A Critical Symposium on *Thelma & Louise*." *Cineaste*, 18(4): 28–36.

Lipsitz, Raina. 2011. "*Thelma & Louise*: The Last Great Film About Women." *The Atlantic*, August 31. https://www.theatlantic.com/entertainment/archive/2011/08/thelma-louise-the-last-great-film-about-women/244336.

Tarr, Carrie, with Brigitte Rollet. 2001. *Cinema and the Second Sex*. New York and London: Continuum.

Willis, Sharon. 1993. "Hardware and Hardbodies, What Do Women Want?: A Reading of *Thelma and Louise*." In *Film Theory Goes to the Movies*, 120–28. Edited by Jim Collins, Hilary Radner, and Ava Preacher Collins. New York and London: Routledge.

A LEAGUE OF THEIR OWN (1992)

A League of Their Own (1992) tells the story of Dottie (Geena Davis, 1956–) and Kit Hinson (Lori Petty, 1963–), two sisters recruited to play in a newly formed women's baseball league. Although fictional, the storyline was inspired by real events. As young men were called off to war during World War II, Minor League Baseball teams were being disbanded. Fearing that this trend would spread to Major League Baseball, team owners formed the All-American Girls Softball League (later renamed the All-American Girls Professional Baseball League).

The film, which was released to positive reviews from *The New York Times*, Siskel and Ebert, *Rolling Stone* magazine, and others, told the story of these players' struggle to reconcile traditional gender roles and values with changing desires and expectations. The film was directed by Penny Marshall (1943–) and featured celebrities like Madonna (1958–) and Rosie O'Donnell (1962–), with Tom Hanks (1956–) as the team's coach. The players prove to be pioneers not just in women's baseball but in challenging gender role expectations. As one marketing tagline for the film states, "This summer, Tom Hanks and the Rockford Peaches prove that a woman's place is at home . . . first, second & third."

With men off at war in the mid-20th century, women were encouraged to fill labor gaps as temporary workers by campaigns like Rosie the Riveter. Although women were being encouraged to work, social expectations to maintain popular standards of femininity did not change. Selected for their looks as much as their skills, the women's baseball players were, as film critic Roger Ebert explained, placed in a tug-of-war between old values and new desires. Scenes where players attended charm school and played in uniforms that included skirts instead of pants depicted this struggle between these conflicting roles. In one widely noted scene, a player begins to cry after she is reprimanded for making an error. The team's coach yells at her, "Are you crying? There's no crying in baseball." Here, being emotional is presented as a negative feminine quality that should be avoided, unlike other more acceptable qualities like proper manners and sex appeal.

In this struggle to reconcile new gender roles and expectations, there were also differing opinions about the permanence of these new roles. Were changes meant to be temporary, or were they indicative of a new status quo that would remain after the war? These questions were addressed through players who were shown as either enjoying their role as workers or merely waiting for their husbands or boyfriends to return home from the war.

The filmmakers included an important footnote to this conversation, pointing out that the experiences of these players were not meant to be representative of all women and all struggles. In one scene, an errant ball lands near some spectators. An African American woman retrieves the ball and shows great skill when she throws it back to a player on the field. This woman then looks at a player whose return gesture offers a quiet acknowledgment of the unfairness that minority players were excluded from the league and thus from the historical narrative.

Evan L. Kropp

FURTHER READING

Ebert, Roger. 2012. "A League of Their Own." July 1. http://www.rogerebert.com/reviews/a-league-of-their-own-1992.

Bonzel, Katharina. 2013. "A League of Their Own: The Impossibility of the Female Sports Hero." *Screening the Past: An International, Refereed, Electronic Journal of Visual Media & History*, 37: 10.

"League of Their Own/Unlawful Entry/Pinocchio." 1992. Siskel&Ebert.org. http://siskelandebert.org/video/RG8GSYH9WS3G/League-of-Their-Own-Unlawful-Entry-Pinocchio-1992.

THE JOY LUCK CLUB (1993)

The 1993 American film *The Joy Luck Club* explored the relationships among four Chinese mothers—Lindo (Tsai Chin, 1933–), Ying-Ying (France Nuyen, 1939–), An-Mei (Lisa Lu, 1927–), and Suyuan (Kieu Chinh, 1937–)—and their Chinese American daughters—Waverly (Tamlyn Tomita, 1966–), Lena (Lauren Tom, 1961–), Rose (Rosalind Chao, 1957–), and June (Ming-Na Wen, 1968–). Directed by Wayne Wang (1949–), the film was based on Amy Tan's (1952–) eponymous 1989 novel. Tan also cowrote the screenplay with Ronald Bass (1942–). Upon its release, critics praised *Joy Luck* for representing Asian American women and culture with nuance. Others, however, criticized the film for being saccharine, too dogmatic, and overtly moralizing.

Joy Luck underscored the power of mother–daughter relationships and storytelling. Ying-Ying, for example, tells Lena about her abusive marriage in China to warn against female passivity. The women also tell stories to help family members (and viewers through them) appreciate Chinese heritage and Chinese American culture. The film presented sexism as common to both Chinese and American women's lives. Lindo conforms to Chinese dictates of female obedience when she acts as servant to both her mother-in-law and her husband. After An-Mei's mother

Directed by Wayne Wang, *The Joy Luck Club* (1993) explores the clash of cultures and generations between Chinese mothers and their Chinese American daughters. Pictured from the left: Kieu Chinh (as Suyuan Woo), Ming-Na Wen (as Jing-Mei 'June' Woo), Tamlyn Tomita (as Waverly Jong), Tsai Chin (as Lindo Jong), France Nuyen (as Ying-Ying St. Clair), Lauren Tom (as Lena St. Clair), Lisa Lu (as An-Mei Hsu), Rosalind Chao (as Rose Hsu Jordan). (Buena Vista Pictures/Photofest)

is raped, she is forced to marry her rapist to preserve her honor. In America, Rose's submission to her husband is based on a stereotypical understanding of the man as head of the household. Lena's willingness to serve as a lower-level associate in the firm she helped found—and to make a fraction of her husband's salary there—is grounded in the sexist expectation that the man is the primary provider.

The depiction of antifemale sexism in *Joy Luck* led some critics to accuse the film of perpetuating "reverse sexism" against Asian men. Al Wong, for one, contended that the Chinese characters are predominately rapists, gangsters, and playboys (1997). The single Chinese American husband depicted controls and demeans his wife. Others, however, refuted Wong's claims, asserting that *Joy Luck* does not portray Asian men negatively, but focuses instead on how systemic patriarchal oppression—versus individual characters—affects (Asian) American women. Moreover, defenders claimed that the film demonstrated how women can also perpetuate sexism against other women: Lindo's mother-in-law abuses her; An-Mei's mother disowns her; Waverly competes with June for status instead of working with her to elevate them both. These examples suggest that the film does not critique individual men, but the patriarchy as a whole and the men *and* women who help maintain it. Overall, *Joy Luck* counters stereotypical presentations of Asian women as submissive and marginalized and celebrates instead their diversity, centrality, and strength.

Eden Elizabeth Wales Freedman

FURTHER READING

Chu, Patricia P. 2000. *Assimilating Asians: Gendered Strategies of Authorship in Asian America*. Durham, NC: Duke University Press.
Huntley, E. D. 1989. *Amy Tan: A Critical Companion*. Westport, CT: Greenwood.
Tan, Amy. 1989. *The Joy Luck Club*. New York: Penguin.
Wong, Al. 1997. "Why *The Joy Luck Club* Sucks." https://www.eskimo.com/~webguy/writings/joysucks.html.

IF THESE WALLS COULD TALK (1996)

If These Walls Could Talk was a 1996 HBO film told in segments dated 1952, 1974, and 1996, with all events taking place in the same house. *Walls* tells the story of three women in three different time periods who face an unplanned pregnancy. Two of the women choose abortion, and one decides to carry the pregnancy to term. Written, directed, and produced by women, the film is one of the few mainstream film productions wholly about a woman's right to choose.

Released 23 years after *Roe v. Wade* (the 1973 U.S. Supreme Court case that declared abortion a constitutional right), *If These Walls Could Talk* showed viewers what obtaining an abortion was like for some women in the 1950s, how the conversation briefly changed in the 1970s, and the backlash against abortion that occurred in the 1990s. Although Barbara Barrows (Sissy Spacek, 1949–) makes a fairly peaceful and private decision to remain pregnant in 1974, the 1952 and 1996 segments both end with a woman bleeding out on the floor (the patient in 1952 and the doctor in 1996).

Though reviews were mostly positive, some suggested that the reproductive rights message was too heavy-handed. The acting was generally the most praised aspect of the film, which was nominated for three Golden Globes and four Emmys. Demi Moore's (1962–) performance was especially noteworthy. Moore played Claire Donnelly, a newly widowed nurse in 1952. Claire finds herself pregnant after a grief-induced encounter with her brother-in-law.

Claire tries to access a safe abortion, but the high cost and her feelings of shame cause her to resort to unsafe and illegal methods. The film depicts both attempts somewhat graphically. In the first scene, a desperate Claire attempts to induce abortion herself. In the second, an abortionist terminates the pregnancy on her kitchen table. These scenes reportedly caused five people to faint at the New York City premiere (Newman, 1996).

Also controversial was the representation of the anti-choice stance. In the 1996 storyline, Anne Heche (1969–) plays Christine Cullen, a college student impregnated by a married professor. Just as her procedure is completed, a deranged young protestor storms in and shoots Claire's doctor (Cher, 1946–). Although many critics felt that Barbara's story and Christine's anti-choice roommate Patti (Jada Pinkett Smith, 1971–) provided balance, some argued that the depiction of the protestors in the 1996 segment mocked the stance of those who would call themselves "pro-life."

In 2000, HBO broadcast *If These Walls Could Talk 2*, which followed three lesbian couples, each at a different time period but in the same house, as they navigate their queer lives in a culture that privileges heterosexuality.

Michele Ren

See also: *The Handmaid's Tale*; *Our Bodies, Ourselves*; Planned Parenthood.

FURTHER READING

Dreifus, Claudia. 1996. "A Case for Abortion Rights. No Apologies." *The New York Times*, October 13. http://www.nytimes.com/1996/10/13/arts/a-case-for-abortion-rights-no-apologies.html.

Lewis, Judith. 1996. "The Movie That Dare Not Speak Its Name." *Elle*, October: 152–61.

Newman, Bruce. 1996. "Truth Behind 'These Walls'." *Los Angeles Times*, October 13. http://articles.latimes.com/1996-10-13/entertainment/ca-53251_1_abortion.

Press, Andrea Lee, and Elizabeth R. Cole. 1999. *Speaking of Abortion: Television and Authority in the Lives of Women*. Chicago: University of Chicago Press.

Shalit, Wendy D. 1997. "A Tale of Three Pregnancies." *First Things*, March: 10–12. ATLA Religion Database. http://www.firstthings.com/article/1997/03/003-a-tale-of-three-pregnancies.

SET IT OFF (1996)

Set It Off (1996) is an action-packed, star-studded film that focused on the lives of four African American female friends in a tough inner-city environment who are willing to go to any length, including bank robbery, to escape the limitations and struggles of their gender, race, and socioeconomic status. According to director Gary Gray (1969–), the film was "not so much about robbing banks as choices young sisters make when their backs are against the wall" (Gregory, 1996: 56). Although the film's depiction of urban youth struggles was similar to those found in many of the other "ghettocentric" films of the 1990s, such as Boyz n the Hood and Menace to Society, Set It Off distinguished itself in the genre with its all-star cast of African American actresses and for portraying themes that concentrated on the plight of African American women. The film explored single parenting, lesbianism, poverty, racism, crime, violence, and police brutality. The main characters included Cleo (Queen Latifah, 1970–), Frankie (Vivica A. Fox, 1964–), Stoney (Jada Pinkett Smith, 1971–), and T.T. (Kimberly Elise, 1967–).

The filmmakers intentionally grounded the film in the harsh realities faced by African American women in Los Angeles, California. Frankie is fired for having a personal connection to the man who robs the bank where she works, even though she clearly has no involvement in the heist. Stoney's younger brother is gunned down by police at his own high school graduation ceremony when he is mistakenly identified as the robber of Frankie's bank. And when T.T. is forced to bring her son to work because of a lack of affordable childcare, her son is taken away by Child Protective Services when he gets injured at her job. Each of these events lead the foursome, at the suggestion of Cleo, to form a pact to start a life of crime as a means to better their lives. As they embark on their mission to escape their cruel circumstances, all of the women except for Stoney pay the price with their lives.

The script was originally turned away by numerous film studios because of its utilization of black female lead characters, one of which is a lesbian. But once New Line Cinema finally bought the script, the film went on to become both a critical and box office hit. The film's soundtrack featured African American recording artists such as Bone Thugs-n-Harmony, Chaka Khan, Busta Rhymes, and En Vogue. Despite criticism that the plot lacked originality and stereotyped women as emotional, other critics argue that the film offered a rare glimpse into the lives of women of color in economic crisis.

Angeline Davis

See also: Queen Latifah.

FURTHER READING

Ascher-Walsh, Rebecca, and Kristen Baldwin. 1996. "Set It Off. (Cover story)." *Entertainment Weekly*, 341/342: 79.

Ebert, Roger. 1996. "Set It Off Movie Review & Film Summary." *Roger Ebert*. http://www.rogerebert.com/reviews/set-it-off-1996.

Gregory, Deborah. 1996. "Girlz 'n the 'hood: watch out! Four sisters are 'Setting it off' on the big screen." *Essence*, 27: 56.

Keeling, Kara. 2003. "'Ghetto Heaven': Set It Off and the Valorization of Black Lesbian Butch-Femme Sociality." *Black Scholar*, 33(1): 33.

REAL WOMEN HAVE CURVES (2002)

Real Women Have Curves (2002) was a film that demonstrated inclusive feminism by addressing issues of hybrid identities, gender roles, class position, immigration status, and hegemonic notions of beauty. Directed by Patricia Cardoso, it tells the coming-of-age story of an 18-year-old first-generation Chicana, Ana García, who lives with her family in a predominantly Latino community in Los Angeles. Ana has recently graduated from high school and dreams of going to college. Societal, economic, and familial pressures lead her to work at a garment factory owned by her older sister, Estella. However, at the urging of a caring teacher, she applies and gets admitted to a prestigious university. She leaves her ethnic roots in Latino East Lost Angeles to go to Columbia University in New York. Her experience is a journey of independence, of creating a unique identity from the several identities thrust on her by the conflicting cultural worlds she traverses, and a journey to self-actualization.

One of the key themes of the film was questioning hegemonic notions of beauty marketed by the glamour and media industries. The lead character and most of the supporting characters are overweight by conventional standards. Throughout the film, Ana's mother makes derogatory remarks about her physical appearance, insisting that she lose weight to find a suitable husband. Rejecting her mother's position, Ana maintains that her body is her own, meant to please her and not to fulfill someone else's expectations. The film also illustrated the interconnectedness of gender and race. As many scholars have pointed out, Latina culture has been accepting of a curvier, larger body size, and skinniness has been equated with unattractiveness and an unhealthy lifestyle. In accepting her body with all its "imperfections," Ana embraces her Latina roots and rejects an assimilationist (Euro-American identity that exalts thinness and signifies it with social mobility and success. At the same time, she also rejects her own community's association of women's bodies with home and marriage. In this way, she manages to forge a unique hybrid identity that is at the same time Latina and American.

A second theme in the film was class differences and the unjust economic conditions in which immigrants often find themselves. The garment factory, where most of the film is set, makes dresses for an upscale clothing store. Ana and her coworkers earn $18 to make a dress that retails for $600. When the corporation licensing the dress production refuses to give Estella and her coworkers an advance on what they are supposed to receive for the dresses, the factory almost shuts down. The oppressive and stifling heat in the factory becomes a metaphor for the oppressive and exploitative corporate system, and the dresses Ana helps to make become a metaphor for understanding her place in the class hierarchy of society.

Real Women Have Curves is a film about the rising feminist and class consciousness of a young woman. The "curves" in the title refer both to the contours of women's bodies and to the obstacles women must negotiate to find their place in society.

Sanjukta Ghosh

FURTHER READING

Braziel, Jana Evans. 2001. "Sex and Fat Chics: Deterritorializing the Fat Female Body." In *Bodies Out of Bounds: Fatness and Transgression*, 231–54. Edited by Jana Evans Braziel and Kathleen LeBesco. Berkeley, CA: University of California Press.

Figueroa, Maria P. 2003. "*Resisting 'Beauty'* and *Real Women Have Curves.*" *Velvet Barrios: Popular Culture and Chicana/o Sexualities* 265–82. Edited by Alicia Gaspar de Alba. New York: Palgrave Macmillan.

Rodríguez y Gibson, Eliza. 2009. "Crossing Over: Assimilation, Utopia and the Bildungsroman on Stage and Screen in Real Women Have Curves." *Camino Real*, 135–51.

IRON JAWED ANGELS (2004)

Home Box Office's film *Iron Jawed Angels* (2004) explored the issues surrounding the fight for women's suffrage in the United States from 1913 to the ratification of the 19th Amendment on August 18, 1920. The 19th Amendment reads, "The right of citizens of the United States shall not be denied or abridged by the United States or by any state on account of sex." The film covered the impact of Alice Paul (1885–1977; played by Hilary Swank, 1974–) and Lucy Burns (1879–1966; played by Frances O'Connor, 1967–) on suffrage and the formation of the National Women's Party in 1916. The film was significant in the history of women's rights because it detailed the extremes women such as Paul and Burns were willing to go to in order to achieve voting rights for women. Topics of generational differences, race, and worker's rights, and how these impacted suffrage, were all presented in the film. The film premiered at the Sundance Film Festival in January 2004 and received a standing ovation.

The struggles suffragettes endured are explicitly shown in the film. *Iron Jawed Angels* includes many historically accurate moments, including the 1913 march for suffrage on President Woodrow Wilson's inauguration day and the violent reactions to the parade by many in attendance; the ultimate ideological splits of Paul and Burns from the already established National American Woman Suffrage Association (NAWSA; in 1920 NAWSA became the League of Women Voters) led by Carrie Chapman Catt (1859–1947; played by Anjelica Huston, 1951–) and Reverend Anna Howard Shaw (1847–1919; played by Lois Smith, 1930–); the protests and pickets outside of the White House gates during World War I that led to the assault and arrest of many suffragettes; and the events in the jail surrounding the imprisoned suffragettes—including the hunger strike, the force-feeding of prisoners including Paul and Burns, and the suffragettes' insistence to be classified and thus treated as political prisoners.

Although there are many historically accurate aspects to the film, there are also elements added to the narrative in order to increase the romance, drama, and conflict. The character of Ben Weissman, who serves as a potential love interest of Alice Paul, is fictional. There are no reports of Alice Paul having a romantic relationship throughout her lifetime. The characters of Senator Thomas "Tom" Leighton and his wife, Emily, are also made up. Some viewers have argued that these two characters represented a combination of opinions on suffrage during the time period, and the creation of these characters allowed historical information to be presented from the time period.

The film was not without controversy in the portrayal of several key figures. The first is that President Wilson is made out to be a villain or an enemy of suffrage. Although President Wilson did not outright support suffrage throughout most of the movement, and some report that he verbally opposed it, he did eventually come out in support of the amendment in 1918. The second figure with a less than accurate portrayal is Carrie Chapman Catt from NAWSA. Catt played an integral role in the formation of several key factors that aided in the ratification of the 19th Amendment. Huston won the Golden Globe for best supporting actress for a miniseries or television movie for her portrayal of Catt in *Iron Jawed Angels*.

Andrea McClanahan

FURTHER READING

Adams, Katherine H., and Michael L. Keane. 2008. *Alice Paul and the American Suffrage Campaign.* Chicago: University of Illinois Press.

Gluck, Sharna Berger. 1976. *From Parlor to Prison: Five American Suffragists Talk about Their Lives.* New York: Vintage Books.

Iron Jawed Angels. DVD. Directed by Katja Von Gardner. 2004. New York: Home Box Office, 2005.

Nardo, Don. 2014. *A Split History of the Women's Suffrage Movement.* Mankato, MN: Compass Point Books.

PERSEPOLIS (2007)

The animated film *Persepolis* (2007) was based on a graphic novel of the same name by Marjane Satrapi (1969–), who also cowrote and codirected the film with Vincent Paronnaud (1970–). Based on Satrapi's own life, the film centered on Marjane, an Iranian young woman, before and after the Iranian Revolution in 1979. Marjane comes from a progressive family that refuses to subscribe to the country's post-revolution ultrareligious, conservative politics. Even though she struggles under the new, restrictive theocracy, she continues to challenge the preconceived notions of a submissive, voiceless, Iranian woman by resisting the structures that oppress her. Sexism, which is inherent in the Islamic fundamentalism adopted by the rulers, shapes all aspects of women's lives, including family relations, education, and work. Marjane confronts the university religious leaders on their strict female attire policy that unjustly targets women, and she argues that the suggested attire interferes with her work as an art student. *Persepolis* can also be seen as a coming-of-age story that connects the Western world to the mystified Middle East on common grounds such as teen angst and rock and roll. Young Marjane's resistance to an increasingly oppressive environment is at times reflected through her Western wardrobe (e.g., her T-shirt that states "Punk Is Not Ded [*sic*]") and choice of music (e.g., Iron Maiden and other hard-rock bands).

Concerned for her safety during the turmoil in Iran, Marjane's family sends her to Vienna. There she explores the world of alternative music and European philosophy while trying to relate to her new friends from different parts of the world. The move to Europe awards Marjane many freedoms, but being thrown into a foreign context without her loved ones causes her to feel alienated, and she longs for her home country. Following a debilitating heartbreak, Marjane turns back to Iran with hopes of recovery and finding her inner peace. But soon after her return she realizes that she is no longer an insider in that context either, but rather an "outsider within" (Collins, 1986: 14). That is, she has considerable insight into the Iranian culture and society, being born and raised there, but due to her family's minority status (leftist intellectuals) and experiences she had abroad, she no longer feels the same level of belonging. Her outsider-within status provides a unique standpoint from which she can see the power dynamics that shape women's lives in both Middle East and Western contexts.

Persepolis won various awards and was nominated for an Oscar and Golden Globe. It was banned from screening inside Iran, for the government perceived the film as a threat to the regime. *The New York Times* highlighted *Persepolis* for its "no-nonsense feminism" represented in the worldview of Ms. Satrapi, Marjane's grandmother, who has a big influence on Marjane's choices (Scott, 2007). The film succeeded in telling Marjane's journey to independence and belonging at the same time, without ignoring her multiple identities and reducing her experiences to a false, politically charged dichotomy of being oppressed in the Middle East and saved in the Western world.

Ebru Cayir
Suzan Neda Soltani

FURTHER READING

Collins, Patricia Hill. 1986. "Learning from the Outsider Within: The Sociological Significance of Black Feminist Thought." *Social Problems*, 33(6): 14–32.
Persepolis. DVD. 2007. Directed by Vincent Paronnaud and Marjane Satrapi. Performed by Chiara Mastroianni, Danielle Darrieux, Catherine Deneuve, and Simon Abkarian.
Scott, A. O. 2007. "In a Flat World, a Rebel with a Cause." *The New York Times*, December 25.

GRANDMA (2015)

Grandma, written and directed by Paul Weitz (1965–), was a 2015 drama-comedy about the personal dimension of abortion. The narrative followed the relationship between Elle Reid (Lily Tomlin, 1939–), a sardonic, lesbian poet in her 70s, recently bereft of her partner of 38 years and more recently separated from her much younger girlfriend, Olivia (Judy Greer, 1975–), and her granddaughter, Sage (Julia Garner, 1994–), a teenager with plans for college who is 10 weeks pregnant and financially broke. When Elle finds out that Sage needs $600 for an abortion, Elle is equally outraged at the price and chagrined that she has recently cut up her credit cards.

The film's opening words, "Things change; that's for sure," from American poet Eileen Myles (the basis for Elle's character) introduce the thematic question of how women's lives have changed since Elle's recollected heyday of 1970s feminist activism. Over the course of one day, Elle and Sage traverse Los Angeles, trying unsuccessfully to collect old debts and borrow cash. Along the way, Elle is shocked by signs of retrogression in women's lives: the demise of a free women's clinic and its replacement with a trendy coffee shop; her now nearly worthless first editions of classic feminist texts and her granddaughter's ignorance of them; and Sage's inability to confront her boyfriend, her anxiety that her girlfriends will call her a slut, and her fear that she has failed her demanding mother. However, Sage ultimately gets money from her driven, corporate mother (Marcia Gay Harden, 1959–) and obtains her safe termination at a supportive clinic. Elle, recalling her own painful and frightening illegal abortion decades earlier, reflects on this improvement. She ruefully realizes that, as much as the world has changed (abortion is legal and safe), much remains the same (male privilege, hostile female relationships, and constrained reproductive freedom). At the film's conclusion, Elle symbolically passes the torch to Olivia by giving her the feminist texts and walking home unburdened.

The setting of the film in California leaves out challenges to abortion rights in other states, such as waiting periods, parental consent or notification laws, and mandatory counseling or ultrasounds policies. Nor does *Grandma* directly address *Roe v. Wade* (1973), the U.S. Supreme Court decision legalizing abortion, and the subsequent backlash of decisions and policies that have curtailed women's access, including the Hyde Amendment (1976), *Webster v. Reproductive Health Services* (1989), *Planned Parenthood v. Casey* (1992), and recent Targeted Regulation of Abortion Providers ("TRAP") laws. Nevertheless, the film hints at how persistent sexism and political apathy erode support for women's reproductive rights. The uncertain future of abortion is left in the hands of Olivia, Sage, and the film's audience.

Mary Thompson

See also: Planned Parenthood.

FURTHER READING

Grandma. Film. Directed by Paul Weitz. 2015. Culver City, CA: SONY Pictures Classics.

Joffe, Carole. 2009. *Dispatches from the Abortion Wars: The Costs of Fanaticism to Doctors, Patients, and the Rest of Us*. Boston: Beacon Press.

Kaplan, Laura. 1995. *The Story of Jane: The Legendary Underground Feminist Abortion Service*. Chicago: The University of Chicago Press.

FOUR

Literature

Well before the electronic age of radio and television, dreams, ideas, and knowledge were shared through books. Throughout history and still today, literary texts have played an important role in telling the story of human experience while also preserving the ideals and ambitions of humanity. Although women have historically been restricted in their access to education and have been prohibited from contributing to the literary tradition, as roles changed and women experienced more personal freedom to self-actualization, books became an important part of women's lives and played a significant role in both reflecting culture and changing worldviews. This manuscript details select literary works by women and about women, with an eye toward inclusivity, acknowledging that literature about race is also about women, and writing about class is also about women because all of us, regardless of gender, embody these identity categories.

THE AWAKENING BY KATE CHOPIN (1899)

Published at a time when debates about the "New Woman" raged throughout American society, Kate Chopin's (1850–1904) *The Awakening* attracted a considerable amount of attention from both press and the public upon its 1899 publication. The novel told the story of Edna Pontellier, a young, white, affluent wife and mother who, at the beginning of the tale, begins to chafe against the numerous restrictions placed on her as a respectable matron in late 19th-century Southern society. Beginning to articulate a new sense of self and a desire for artistic and sexual expression outside of marriage and motherhood, Edna struggles throughout *The Awakening* to find a way to live as an independent, autonomous woman within a repressive culture. Having failed in this endeavor, the end of the novel finds Edna swimming out to sea, seemingly having chosen death over a life lived in conformity to society's confining expectations for women.

The Awakening was far from a popular success upon its initial publication. To the contrary, it was widely reviled by the American press, which condemned the novel as a vulgar, immoral exploration of a (allegedly silly) woman's sexual transgressions. So shocked were reviewers and readers by the novel's open acknowledgement of female sexual desire, and the reality of female sexual expression outside of marriage, that *The Awakening* largely ended Chopin's (previously very successful) career as an author.

After Chopin's premature death at the age of 54 in 1904, *The Awakening* remained out of print and largely unremembered for many decades thereafter. It was not until the rise of second-wave feminism (and of feminist literary scholarship within the academy) that *The Awakening* came back to scholarly and popular attention, and new editions of the novel began to appear. Since the 1960s and 1970s, *The Awakening* has been a key text in American literature and history courses and has been a vitally important one in ongoing debates about definitions of femininity and struggles for female independence and autonomy.

The Awakening tackled numerous issues that remain vital to discussions about gender oppression and women's efforts to achieve full selfhood within fundamentally sexist social systems. Edna challenges existing definitions of marriage, which define her sole role as self-effacing support to her husband. She insists on her fundamental right to sexual self-ownership, and rejects the efforts of the men around her to define or control her sexual expression. Though she loves her children, she resists a definition of motherhood that requires women's total self-sacrifice. Above all else, Edna consistently asserts the right to her own self—to have a home of her own, money of her own, time to pursue her artistic interests, and to be her own person, outside of her roles as wife and mother. Vibrantly entering into late 19th-century debates about the "New Woman" and serving as a touchstone for second-wave feminists, the questions that *The Awakening* raised about how women strive to be full people remain profoundly relevant to contemporary feminism.

Holly M. Kent

FURTHER READING

Chopin, Kate. 1997. *The Awakening.* Charlottesville, VA: University of Virginia Press.

Martin, Wendy, ed. 1988. *New Essays on The Awakening.* New York: Cambridge University Press.

THE HOUSE OF MIRTH BY EDITH WHARTON (1905)

Edith Wharton's (1862–1937) *The House of Mirth* (1905) was a novel of manners that followed the beautiful and well-bred but penniless Lily Bart as she negotiated a place for herself in upper-class New York society. The novel examined the particular bind women like Lily experienced: depending on men for their livelihoods, they had no choice but to shape their lives to make themselves suitable for marriage. Any deviation from proper decorum was likely to have disastrous results for the reputation and future of a young lady. Though Lily's social skills are honed to a fine point, her expensive tastes and the cost of keeping up with her wealthy social circle cause her to overextend her income before she is able to attain the security and acceptance marriage to a wealthy suitor would bring. Bad debt and social missteps eventually land Lily in a milliner's shop, where she tries to make a living for herself and repay her debts. The strain of her reduced circumstances leads Lily to a dependence on chloral, a medicinal sleep aid, which is the eventual cause of her death at the end of the novel.

The House of Mirth was an instant popular success, climbing the bestsellers' list a month after its release. Contemporary reviewers seemed to focus either on the novel's tragic elements (many readers were greatly drawn in and distressed by Lily's death) or on its gossip value, assuming that it shed light on the real lives of socialites in Wharton's New York social circle. The novel attracted a fair amount of serious academic attention as well; *The House of Mirth* launched Wharton's career as a serious writer and social commentator (Beer et al., 2007: 63).

Despite mixed critical opinion, all reviewers could agree that Wharton had achieved great mastery of language and treated her subject with uncompromising attention to detail. Where critics began to disagree was whether Wharton's subject—a young socialite grasping at the edges of a frivolous upper-class society—was worthy of literary attention. Those who praised the novel did so for its keen ability to capture an exact cultural moment in New York society when women were trapped in what feminists would later dub the "Madonna–whore complex," the contradictory cultural mandate to be at once virtuous and above moral reproach, but also physically beautiful and alluring to the opposite sex. Those who found fault with the novel

Novelist and short story writer Edith Wharton was the first woman to win a Pulitzer Prize for her novel *The Age of Innocence*. Wharton is also widely known for her novel *The House of Mirth*. (Library of Congress)

pointed to its alleged immorality, citing the excessive and casual destructiveness and self-absorption of the characters populating the novel.

Wharton mocked her reviewers' squeamishness about Lily's behavior. In her introduction to the 1936 edition of *The House of Mirth*, she wrote: "What picture did the writer offer to their horrified eyes? That of a young girl of their work who rouged, smoked, ran into debt, borrowed money, gambled, and—crowning horror!—went home with a bachelor friend to take tea in his flat!" (Wharton, 1936: 375). Wharton's sarcasm underscores the strict social parameters within which Lily, and the women who were reading her story and perhaps even Wharton herself, were expected to operate.

Erica Robak

FURTHER READING

Beer, Janet, Pamela Knights, and Elizabeth Nolan, eds. 2007. *Edith Wharton's The House of Mirth: A Routledge Study Guide*. New York: Routledge.

The Edith Wharton Society. 2016. https://edithwhartonsociety.wordpress.com.

Wharton, Edith. 1936. "Appendix A: Edith Wharton's Introduction to the 1936 Edition of *The House of Mirth*." In *The House of Mirth*, 371–76. Edited by Janet Beer, and Elizabeth Nolan. Ontario: Broadview Press.

Wolff, Cynthia Griffin. 1994. *A Feast of Words: The Triumph of Edith Wharton*. New York: Perseus.

THE SECRET GARDEN BY FRANCES HODGSON BURNETT (1911)

With a garden metaphor, Frances Hodgson Burnett (1849–1924) examined nature's healing power, described as Magic, throughout *The Secret Garden* (1911). Mary Lennox, the young protagonist, learns to care for herself and experience solitude in the garden. The secret garden becomes a room of her own, where Mary discovers how to enjoy her body, exercise her imagination, and expand her social circle.

The Secret Garden was published as a novel after being released as a serial in *The American Magazine*. During Burnett's life, *The Secret Garden* was an overlooked part of her work. It was not even mentioned in her obituary. With the rise of children's literature in the late 20th century, as well as an uptick in adaptations after the work's U.S. copyright expired in 1987, *The Secret Garden* is now one of Burnett's best-known works. Basing Mary on the popular English nursery rhyme "Mary, Mary Quite Contrary," Burnett created a girl who was brash, hurting, and real. Mary claims, "People never like me and I never like people." This is a stark difference from the Victorian notion that girls are quiet, polite, and unassuming.

We meet 10-year-old Mary in India during a cholera outbreak. As a spoiled, disagreeable, and sometimes violent child, she is unwanted by her parents and tyrannical to the Indian servants. During the crisis, her parents and nanny die. When she is discovered alone in the house, she is sent to live with her uncle in England. In contrast to other portrayals of girls of the time (Anne Shirley, Jane Eyre, Heidi), Mary Lennox is not a good-hearted orphan; she is willful and self-absorbed.

Upon her arrival in Yorkshire, Mary is lonely and far away from a life she understands. Though she is left alone by her uncle, Archibald Craven, to amuse herself in her rooms, Martha, a talkative maid, tells Mary a story of a locked garden, which piques the child's imagination. Boredom leads Mary to find the secret garden. In the process, she strengthens her body and softens her disposition. When she finds her way into the locked garden, she discovers life among the dead branches, mirroring the growth Mary experiences as she meets new people.

Along with the garden, another mystery consumes Mary's attention. She hears unexplained crying inside the manor. Following the sound, she finds her sickly cousin, Colin, living in a hidden room. Mary visits, distracting him with stories of the secret garden. Eventually, Mary admits she has access to the garden and invites Colin to join her for some fresh air. Spending every day in the garden, Colin gets stronger, even standing to prove he is not crippled. The transformation of Mary and Colin from lonely to well-adjusted children is attributed to Magic. Though Magic is not defined, the healing properties of nature and positive thinking reflect Burnett's interest in Christian Science theories.

Sarah E. Colonna

See also: *A Room of One's Own* by Virginia Woolf.

FURTHER READING

Gerzina, Gretchen H. 2004. *Frances Hodgson Burnett: The Unexpected Life of the Author of The Secret Garden*. New Brunswick, NJ: Rutgers University Press.
Lundin, Anne. 2006. "The Critical and Commercial Reception of *The Secret Garden*." In *In the Garden: Essays in Honour of Frances Hodgson Burnett*, 1911–2004. Edited by Angelica Shirley Carpenter. Toronto: Scarecrow Press.

ORLANDO BY VIRGINIA WOOLF (1928)

Virginia Woolf's (1882–1941) *Orlando* (1928) was constructed as a biography spanning three centuries. The novel chronicled Orlando, a wealthy British landowner, from young adulthood to middle age. He is first a confidant to the Queen, later a duke in Constantinople, and afterward a wife to Sheldermine in Britain. Perhaps the most notable aspect is Orlando's transformation—at the midpoint—from male to female, which occurs after he sleeps for seven days. Though many theories regarding the novel exist, its importance and influence are not to be doubted. This influence consists of two elements: an interrogation of the traditional concepts of sex, gender, and sexuality; and an exploration and challenge to literary conventions and patriarchal language.

Tradition dictates that sex, gender, and sexuality are stable, biological aspects, but *Orlando* offered readers the exact opposite conceptualization: they are fluid, morphing ideas. This portrayal fosters a disruption of the binary system (male/

female), thereby working toward parity. Orlando is male for the first half and female for the second; the alteration is accepted with little fretting. Orlando is aware of the element of gender, though she does not use that term. For example, Orlando ponders the perceived importance of dress, and once she returns to Britain, she embraces both male and female clothing styles: "From the probity of breeches she turned to the seductiveness of petticoats and enjoyed the love of both sexes equally" (Woolf, 1928: 161). While in these different clothes, her attractions shift, pointing to a sexual fluidity absent from early 20th-century ideas of sexuality. Whether this flexibility is an embrace of androgyny, bisexuality, or sapphism, the novel's characterization of Orlando broadened the concept of sexuality. Woolf's uncompromising portrayal of Orlando deconstructed these binaries, provoking a challenge to dominant understandings of sex, gender, and sexuality.

Dominant understandings of traditional literary conventions are also challenged throughout *Orlando*. By depicting the author characters as deeply flawed and parodying the genre of biography, Woolf denounced patriarchal language and the ideal of male narratives. For example, Nick Greene, a writer Orlando deeply admires, writes a scathing critique of his work. The incident forces Orlando to question the very purpose of writing and the intentionality of authors. A second moment occurs when Orlando (now female) tires of the sneer of Mr. Pope (18th-century poet) and the condescension of Mr. Addison (late 17th-/early 20th-century poet and essayist). In addition to this exposé of the literary tradition, the representation of the Biographer is similarly imperfect, as his reliability and truthfulness remain dubious. These incidences combined create a mockery of patriarchal language. That mockery fosters a space for women and their writing, which is realized in Orlando's publication of her life's work ("The Oak Tree"), once she returns to Britain as a woman. Together these aspects expanded readers' understanding of narrative, voice, and truth.

Orlando garnered varied responses, ranging from praise as a clever and radical romance to criticism as superficial and a departure from Woolf's previous works. Commenting on this contradictory reception, Maria DiBattista observed, "The combinatory magic of *Orlando*, in which fact and fancy, dream and history indiscriminately mix and alter each other, dismayed as many of its readers as it enchanted" (Woolf, 1928: xli). She also noted, however, that it immediately "[sold] six thousand copies and [went] into a third edition two months after its publication" (xl). Regardless of the response, the life of the protagonist, Orlando, captivated many.

Sarah E. Fryett

See also: *A Room of One's Own* by Virginia Woolf.

FURTHER READING

De Gay, Jane. 2007. *Virginia Woolf's Novels and the Literary Past*. Edinburgh: Edinburgh University Press.

Knopp, Sherron E. 1988. " 'If I Saw You Would You Kiss Me?': Sapphism and the Subversiveness of Virginia Woolf's *Orlando*." *Modern Language Association*, 103: 24–34.

Majumdar, Robin, and Allen McLaurin. 2003. *Virginia Woolf: The Critical Heritage*. London: Routledge.

Marcus, Jane. 1987. *Virginia Woolf and the Languages of Patriarchy*. Bloomington, IN: Indiana University Press

Woolf, Virginia. 1928. *Orlando*. Orlando: Harcourt, Inc.

"A ROOM OF ONE'S OWN" BY VIRGINIA WOOLF (1929)

Published in 1929, the essay "A Room of One's Own" by Virginia Woolf (1882–1941) remains a groundbreaking feminist text that continues to be read by high school and college students today. The fictional essay was a narrative account of Mary Benton's two days prior to her delivery of a lecture on the topic of women and fiction to young scholars at a women's college. The narrative account illuminated the negative effects that patriarchy has had on women and their ability to write fiction.

During the first day, Mary visits a men's college, where she is shooed off the grass by a professor and then denied entry into the library because she is a woman. She has a most lovely and lavish lunch at the college, in which the wine flows freely. She notes the benefit of good food and wine on the ability to think and write well. That evening Mary visits her academic friend at the women's college. In contrast to the meal at lunch, Mary and her friend have a bland, boring dinner that lacks flavor and wine. Mary and her friend discuss why it is that women's colleges are so poor and men's are so wealthy. In their discussion, they note that men have historically controlled the money, and women have had the babies. They observe that men give their money to support their institutions, whereas it was not until recently that women were even legally allowed to keep the money they earned.

The next day, Mary goes to the British Library in London. She finds that although there is much written about women, most of it is written by men. She notes that many famous women had to write in secret or write under a male pseudonym in order to get published. She contends that in reading women's writing, the reader can feel the woman's anger about being placed in a lower position in society solely because of her gender. This thinking of one's gender while writing hinders their ability to write. Woolf theorizes that good writers have unified the masculine with the feminine part of their brain, like William Shakespeare (1564–1616). If Shakespeare had had a sister named Judith, and she too had been an artistic genius, Mary inquires what would have become of her. The answer that Woolf provides is that Judith's life would end tragically if she were to pursue her craft, because of her limited role and rights in society. She concludes that women need to have a room of their own in which to write and their own financial means to support themselves.

The essay is filled with allusions and comments on political and social issues of the time. Scholars continue to write and comment on Woolf's text and the concepts and phrases she coined. One such concept is her use of "androgyny" to describe the unification of the masculine and feminine in a good writer's mind. Some critics argue that this concept disregards Woolf's own ambitions, whereas others found the idea liberating, and still others contend that androgyny was a trope congruent with Woolf's time. Scholars play on Woolf's phraseology in their own work. Alice Walker borrows from Woolf the notion of thinking through our mothers and inquires into thinking about one's mothers and grandmothers if they were slaves. The phrase "a room of one's own" remains synonymous with the desire for privacy and freedom to write.

Kristin A. Swenson

See also: *Orlando* by Virginia Woolf.

FURTHER READING

Lemaster, Tracy. 2012. "Girl with a Pen": Girls' Studies and Third-Wave Feminism in *A Room of One's Own* and "Professions for Women." *Feminist Formations*, 24(2) (Summer): 77–99.

Moi, Toril. 2008. "'I Am Not a Woman Writer': About Women, Literature and Feminist Theory Today." *Feminist Theory*, 9(3): 259–71.

Showalter, Elaine. 1982. "Feminist Criticism in the Wilderness." In *Writing and Sexual Difference*. Edited by Elizabeth Abel. Chicago: University of Chicago Press.

Walker, Alice. 1983. *In Search of Our Mother's Gardens: Womanist Prose*. San Diego: Harcourt Brace Jovanovich.

THEIR EYES WERE WATCHING GOD BY ZORA NEALE HURSTON (1937)

Zora Neale Hurston (1891–1960) was an African American writer, folklorist, and anthropologist. She is remembered as a major figure of the cultural movement known as the Harlem Renaissance, which took place during the 1920s and 1930s. *Their Eyes Were Watching God*, which was published in 1937, was her second novel. Scholars commonly describe the novel as the story of an African American woman's quest for independence and self-knowledge. Throughout most of the novel, the protagonist, Janie Crawford, struggles with gender-based and class-based oppression.

Janie's narrative, as told to her best friend, Phoeby, is the basis of the novel, which is set in Florida and contains much dialogue written in a black vernacular. When Janie is 16, her aging grandmother forces her to marry Logan Killicks. Janie's assumption that love will follow marriage proves incorrect. After receiving threats of violence from Logan, she leaves him in order to marry Joe Starks, who offers her lofty dreams. The two move to Eatonville, Florida, where Joe becomes mayor and provides Janie with social standing. However, he is a restrictive husband throughout their 20-year marriage, and Janie discovers that a leisurely middle-class lifestyle is not satisfying. By suppressing her own voice, she survives her marriage, which becomes loveless and involves occasional domestic violence. After Joe's death, Janie inherits financial independence and meets a younger man named Vergible

Zora Neale Hurston, anthropologist, author, and prominent figure of the Harlem Renaissance. She is considered one of the premiere twentieth-century African American writers and is best known for her 1937 novel *Their Eyes Were Watching God*. (Library of Congress)

"Tea Cake" Wood. Contrary to Joe, Tea Cake is working-class and invites Janie into many male-dominated activities. The two marry and live in the Everglades, where Tea Cake insists on being the breadwinner. Janie idealizes the relationship, even though it contains incidents of domestic violence. After Tea Cake contracts rabies from a dog he encounters during a hurricane, Janie shoots him in an act of self-preservation. Following a brief murder trial, she is acquitted. Despite the lack of a happy ending, she attains a sense of empowerment and returns to her house in Eatonville, where she tells her best friend, Phoeby, her story of personal transformation.

In the first year after its publication, *Their Eyes Were Watching God* received mixed reviews. Prominent figures of the Harlem Renaissance, of which Richard Wright is the most notable, were critical of the novel. Early 20th-century African American intellectuals believed that literature written by African Americans should improve the status of the race, and guidelines were published for African American writers. Hurston's resistance to the guidelines was subversive. Ultimately, *Their Eyes Were Watching God* went out of print, and Hurston fell into obscurity in the 1950s.

Feminist literary theory—and, more specifically, black feminist thought—both of which are products of second-wave feminism of the 1960s and 1970s, created space for analysis of gender-based power imbalances in literature. *Their Eyes Were Watching God* was reissued during this time period, and a new generation of readers was receptive to the novel. In 1975, Alice Walker published "In Search of Zora Neale Hurston," which played a key role in resurrecting Hurston from obscurity. Today a rich body of diverse scholarship exists on *Their Eyes Were Watching God*, which is considered a classic. The novel occupies a central position in the canons of American literature, African American literature, and feminist literature. It has influenced many other African American writers, including Alice Walker, Toni Morrison, Gloria Naylor, and Toni Cade Bambara.

Christine DeCleene

FURTHER READING

Corse, Sarah M., and Monica D. Griffin. 1977. "Cultural Valorization and African American Literary History: Reconstructing the Canon." *Sociological Forum*, 12(2): 173–203.

Gates, Henry Louis, Jr. 1993. "*Their Eyes Were Watching God:* Hurston and the Speakerly Text." In *Zora Neale Hurston: Critical Perspectives Past and Present*, 154–203. Edited by Henry Louis Gates Jr. and K. A. Appiah. New York: Harper.

Hemenway, Robert E. 1980. *Zora Neale Hurston: A Literary Biography.* Champaign, IL: University of Illinois Press.

Walker, Alice. March 1975. "In Search of Zora Neale Hurston." *Ms.*

A TREE GROWS IN BROOKLYN BY BETTY SMITH (1943)

Betty Smith (1896–1972) published her first novel, *A Tree Grows in Brooklyn*, in 1943. Although Smith did not speak explicitly of feminism and women's rights in the novel, she presented several issues that disrupted perceptions of women and made clear the realities of growing up female in the early 1900s.

A Tree Grows in Brooklyn is the coming-of-age story of Francie Nolan and how her relationships with her family, teachers, and neighbors impact her life. The Nolans live in a tenement building in Williamsburg, Brooklyn. The intersectionality of gender and class informs Francie's narrative and portrays the veracity of the time period. Francie is a voracious reader who demonstrates a commitment to challenging the expectations of others.

Class and gender are intricately tied together as Francie's mother provides the only steady income to the family through cleaning tenement buildings. Francie's father is an alcoholic, who has shift work from the Waiters' Union. Francie learns at an early age that women are treated differently. In the beginning of the novel, when Francie and Neeley go to the junker to earn money for the trash they collected for the week, Francie allows the junker to pinch her cheek, knowing it will earn her an extra penny—something not offered to the boys in the neighborhood. Francie also witnesses the way people speak of women who do not follow the expectations of marriage before having children. Francie is told by her mother to let Joanna, a neighbor who had a child out of wedlock, be a lesson to her in life. Through Francie, Smith questions a variety of cultural perceptions surrounding women and provides a critical lens in which to view the world and a belief that determination can change the outcome of one's life. Similar to the tree outside of Francie's tenement building that keeps growing back after being cut down, Francie continues to persevere and work toward achieving her goals of becoming a writer despite her environment.

A Tree Grows in Brooklyn was received positively by the public. The Literary Guild selected Smith's novel for their selection in September 1943. The first printing of the novel sold out quickly, which led to an almost immediate second printing upon the novel's release. A bestseller in the United States, Smith's novel was selected as one to be published as an Armed Services Edition during World War II. The book was so popular among servicemen that a second printing of the book was ordered, which was the first for an Armed Services Edition selection (Newman, 2011). Many soldiers subsequently wrote to Smith to relate the impact of her novel on their lives. She estimated that she received 1500 letters a year, and she responded personally to almost all of them.

Andrea McClanahan

FURTHER READING

Manning, Molly G. 2014. *When Books Went to War: The Stories That Helped Us Win World War II.* Boston: Houghton Mifflin.

Newman, Caitlin. 2011. "Armed Services Editions: A Few Square Inches of Home." November 27. http://www.historynet.com/armed-services-editions-a-few-square-inches-of-home.htm.

Smith, Betty. 1943. *A Tree Grows in Brooklyn.* New York: HarperCollins.

Weidman, Katharine. n.d. "Smith, Betty: *A Tree Grows in Brooklyn.*" 20th Century American Bestsellers. http://bestsellers.lib.virginia.edu/submissions/144.

PEYTON PLACE BY GRACE METALIOUS (1956)

Peyton Place was a 1956 novel by Grace Metalious (1924–1964) set in the 1930s in a fictional, seemingly quiet New England town. The novel focused on the lives of three women: Constance MacKenzie; her daughter, Allison; and Allison's friend, Selena Cross. Through the characters' lives, *Peyton Place* explored issues of class, murder, rape, abortion, and female sexuality.

When *Peyton Place* was published in 1956, it caused a literary and social firestorm due to its controversial themes. Constance is a single mother who had an affair with a married man, Allison's father, when she left Peyton Place as a young woman. Such a situation was not openly discussed in the 1930s, nor was it socially accepted. This plot device also mirrored 1950s morals in the United States. The other, more controversial storyline focuses on Selena, a girl "from the wrong side of the tracks." Selena struggles to help provide for her family, as well as escape the sexual abuse of her stepfather. She becomes pregnant by him and eventually kills him after undergoing an abortion. Meanwhile, Allison explores her own desires as a teenage girl and dreams of becoming a writer while her mother begins a relationship with the new high school principal. Despite the drama, *Peyton Place* ends happily for the three women. Metalious also wrote a sequel, *Return to Peyton Place*, with Allison as the main character.

The provocative themes in *Peyton Place* made the novel extremely popular. It sold 60,000 copies in the first 10 days of its release and stayed on *The New York Times* bestseller list for 59 weeks. Although the book was very successful, it was also criticized as "the decline and fall of the American novel" (Brier, 2005: 51). Metalious made a conscious decision to feature women as the main characters of her novel, exploring their inner struggles rather than simply presenting them as secondary to men in more socially acceptable roles. That the author was a woman who featured women as the main characters, shown to be imperfect, resilient, and largely escaping punishment for their transgressions, contributed to concerns that the book was trashy and without literary merit.

Peyton Place was made into a film in 1957 and later adapted into a television soap opera that aired from 1964 to 1969. The novel and its themes have continued to influence television in particular. Many sitcoms and even reality TV shows of today are built on the premise of exposing the same kinds of secrets popularized in *Peyton Place*.

Jeanette Sewell

FURTHER READING

Ardis, Cameron. 2015. *Unbuttoning of America: A Biography of Peyton Place.* Ithaca, NY: Cornell University Press.

Brier, Evan. 2005. "The Accidental Blockbuster: "Peyton Place" in Literary and Institutional Context." *Women's Studies Quarterly*, 33: 48–65.

Toth, Emily. 1981. *Inside Peyton Place: The Life of Grace Metalious.* New York: Doubleday.

A RAISIN IN THE SUN BY LORRAINE HANSBERRY (1959)

Lorraine Hansberry's (1930–1965) *A Raisin in the Sun* (1959) was a protest play focusing on the emotional conflicts within a black working-class family in Southside Chicago. The three-act play was set sometime between World War II and 1959, with most of the action taking place in the Younger family's living room. When Mama, the head of the family, uses life insurance money received after the death of her husband to make a down payment for a home in Clybourne Park, it appears that the family's dream of a better future has finally come true. Although Mama's son, Walter Younger, may be the central figure of the play, the cultural conflicts are expressed through the female characters, making women's rights an important part of the play. As one of the first black women writers, Hansberry openly questioned whether black women should be loyal to black men and put their personal aspirations behind those of the men, while also addressing reproductive rights issues such as abortion. Hansberry also critiqued black chauvinism by demonstrating that it "transcends cultural, national, educational and economic boundaries" (Lester, 2003: 247). The play initially struggled for financial support and recognition, but upon moving to Broadway, it garnered considerable attention, and in 1959 Hansberry received the prestigious New York Drama Critic's Circle Award for Best Play of the Year. At the age of 29, Lorraine Hansberry became the youngest American, the fifth woman, and the first black to win the award.

Early critics tended to misinterpret the play by regarding the Youngers as a typical American middle-class family and ignoring the importance of racism as a crucial influence on the family's life. Hansberry distanced herself from this perspective by claiming that her characters "transcend category" and that "in order to create the universal, you must pay very great attention to the specific" (Hansberry, 1969: 128). Race, however, was just one category that Hansberry used to describe the life of the Youngers. One of Hansberry's central concerns was that race intersects with gender and social class, a perspective that also influenced her take on women's rights. Some critics also argued that Hansberry's dramatic strategy seems to support the notion that black men were the key victims of white American racism and that strong black women were potentially seen to undermine the struggles of black men for self-respect. The play's conclusion "reinstates the black man as the center of family authority and as a heroic figure" (Keyssar, 1989: 229), which supports this perspective and highlights some of the tensions that Hansberry as a black female writer had to face.

Daniela Hrzán

FURTHER READING

Hansberry, Lorraine. 1959/1994. *A Raisin in the Sun*. New York: Vintage Books.

Hansberry, Lorraine. 1969. *To Be Young, Gifted and Black. Lorraine Hansberry in Her Own Words*. Adapted by Robert Nemiroff. New York: New American Library.

Keyssar, Helene. 1989. "Rites and Responsibilities: The Drama of Black American Women." In *Feminine Focus: The New Women Playwrights*, 226–40. Edited by Enoch Brater. New York and Oxford: Oxford University Press.

Lester, Neal A. 2003. "Seasonal with Quiet Strength: Black Womanhood in Lorraine Hansberry's *A Raisin in the Sun* (1959)." In *Women in Literature: Reading through the Lens of Gender*, 246–49. Edited by Jerilyn Fisher and Ellen S. Silber. Westport, CT, and London: Greenwood Press.

THE BELL JAR BY SYLVIA PLATH (1963)

The Bell Jar, considered a quasi-autobiographical novel, was initially published under the pseudonym Victoria Lucas in 1963. It was published in 1971 in the United States under Sylvia Plath's (1932–1963) name. In the foreword to the 1988 edition of the book, editor Frances McCullough, regarding its reception, noted: "[It] sailed right onto the bestseller list and despite some complaining reviews, it quickly established itself as a female rite-of-passage novel" (Plath, 1988: xii). The novel, known for its confessional, deeply personal style of writing, presents the internal struggles and the external societal pressures that Esther Greenwood—the perceptive, darkly humorous protagonist—confronts in 1950s Boston. The first half of the novel chronicles Esther's internship with the *Ladies' Day* magazine in Manhattan; the second half follows her journey home to the suburbs of Boston before returning to college. While home, Esther's depression climaxes in her suicide attempt. The remainder of the novel is situated in two mental health facilities, where she is treated and eventually released. This popular and political novel offered a critical examination of Cold War America, focusing on issues of patriarchal dominance, normative femininity, identity, and mental illness.

Two images—the bell jar (a bell-shaped glass often used in a laboratory to contain sensitive objects) and the fig tree—reverberated throughout the novel and illuminated Esther's confinement within patriarchy (a system where men hold the power). The bell jar metaphor signified her profound loneliness and her feelings of being trapped within a normative feminine identity. This quintessential identity, represented by Mrs. Greenwood, Mrs. Willard, and Dodo Conway, adhered to a strict guideline: women are wives and mothers. Though Esther encounters a number of her own contemporaries (Doreen, her risk-taking internship pal; Betsy, a happy and plain girl from the Midwest; and Jody, her close friend from home), they are unable to provide satisfactory alternatives. Her feelings of being trapped are extended within the fig tree image: "One fig was a husband and happy home and children, and another fig was a famous poet [. . .]" (Plath, 1988: 77). Each option comes at the exclusion of the other possibilities; it is clear which option is the cultural norm. Buddy Willard, Esther's dwindling romantic interest, reminds her repeatedly that marriage and family will bring her happiness. Buddy, along with the other male characters (Dr. Gordon, Constantin, Marco, and Irwin), represent diverse elements of male oppression that range from the unobtrusive but decidedly sexist asides of Buddy to the violent misogyny of Marco. The machinations of patriarchy are transparent throughout the novel, exposing the falsehood of the 1950s housewife ideal and the suffering of those unable to conform to that model.

The critical perspective created through the novel's treatment of patriarchy extends to its examination of mental illness, which Plath tackles with sensitivity and honesty. Many theories exist regarding Esther's illness (depression, schizophrenia, and bipolar disorder), but the novel makes it clear that Esther's increasing inability to reconcile society's pressures with her own desires prompts her to swallow a handful of pills. Once found, she is whisked off to a mental health facility. Plath critically analyzes the state of mental health services: the conditions of the facilities, the role of the doctors, and the questionable treatment methods. Although Esther appears to benefit from these treatments, the novel ends on an ambivalent note. Leaving the facility and wanting to feel hopeful, she observes, "Instead, all I could see were question marks" (Plath, 1988: 243). This ambivalence, combined with the critique of patriarchy and the illumination of the dismal state of America's mental health services system, renders *The Bell Jar* a powerful and provocative coming-of-age novel.

Sarah E. Fryett

FURTHER READING

Perloff, Marjorie G. 1972. "'A Ritual for Being Born Twice': Sylvia Plath's *The Bell Jar*." *Contemporary Literature*, 13: 507–22.
Plath, Sylvia. 1971. *The Bell Jar*. New York: First Perennial Classics.
Wagner-Martin, Linda. 1992. *The Bell Jar, A Novel of the Fifties*. New York: Twayne.
Wagner-Martin, Linda, ed. 1988. *Sylvia Plath: The Critical Heritage*. New York: Routledge.

I KNOW WHY THE CAGED BIRD SINGS BY
MAYA ANGELOU (1969)

Maya Angelou's (1928–2014) 1969 autobiography, *I Know Why the Caged Bird Sings*, detailed her transition from childhood to adulthood in the 1930s American South. The narrative begins when three-year-old Maya is sent to live with her grandmother in Stamps, Arkansas, and ends when she gives birth to a son at age 16. *Caged Bird* derives its title from the third stanza of Paul Laurence Dunbar's poem "Sympathy":

> I know why the caged bird sings, ah me,
> When his wing is bruised and his bosom sore,—
> When he beats his bars and he would be free;
> It is not a carol of joy or glee,
> But a plea, that upward to Heaven he flings—
> I know why the caged bird sings!" (1993: 334).

The poem and title suggested that, even when one feels trapped, through singing—or speaking or writing—one's trauma, one can prevail over it. *Caged Bird* was nominated for a National Book Award and appeared on *Time* Magazine's list of the 100 Best Books Written in English. Despite its successes, however, the autobiography has also been banned in many cities in the United States because of its explicit portrayal of racism, sexism, and sexual assault.

Angelou portrayed Stamps, Arkansas, as a racist and sexist town. Young Maya grows up believing that, as an African American girl, she will never achieve the beauty and status of white women. This internalized oppression is reinforced by a white dentist who refuses to extract her rotten tooth, claiming he would rather place his hand in a dog's mouth, and by her mother's boyfriend, Mr. Freeman, who rapes Maya when she is eight years old. After Maya lies during Freeman's trial, claiming (falsely) that there were no other sexual abusive incidents before her rape, Freeman is murdered, and Maya—believing her words can kill—resolves not to speak again. The narrator's silence denotes traumatic construction, what psychiatrist Judith Herman calls the "numbing response of surrender" associated with post-traumatic stress (Herman, 1992: 23). Maya's refusal to speak, however, also underscores the power of language: words can both slay and resurrect, particularly when one speaks or writes through trauma to surmount it. Indeed, Maya regains both her voice and her well-being when she begins to read literature out loud. Likewise, the adult Angelou writes through her trauma in *Caged Bird*. In doing so, like the bruised bird that sings while sore, Angelou underscores the capacity of language to help one prevail. Maya's discovery of freedom in both the spoken and the written word also parallels the theme of literacy as liberty in the African American autobiographical tradition (found in the writings of Frederick Douglass, Harriet Jacobs, and Malcolm X).

Although *Caged Bird* detailed the pain Maya suffered as a black girl growing up in the racist and sexist South, Angelou's autobiography ultimately celebrated the beauty and power of black women in general and the centrality of African Americans to the American South. Although Maya initially struggles to locate her own self-worth, she also has noteworthy African American role models to guide her way: her grandmother, "Momma;" her mother, Vivian; and her mentor, Bertha Flowers, who prompts Maya to read out loud in order to heal. These formidable women

Acclaimed poet and civil rights activist Maya Angelou. Angelou penned as many as seven biographies with her first one, *I Know Why the Caged Bird Sings*, bringing her international attention and accolades. (National Archives)

have different struggles of their own, but each maintains her dignity and agency in a hostile world. Perhaps informed by their example, by the end of *Caged Bird*, Maya herself has become a paradigm of black and female strength: while still a teenager, she has overcome prejudice, rape, silence, and childbirth to become the first African American streetcar conductor in San Francisco.

Eden Elizabeth Wales Freedman

FURTHER READING

Braxton, Joanne. 1999. *I Know Why the Caged Bird Sings: A Casebook*. New York: Oxford.

Dunbar, Paul. 1993. "Sympathy." *The Collected Poetry of Paul Laurence Dunbar*. Edited by Joanne Braxton. Charlottesville, VA: University of Virginia Press.

Hagen, Lyman. 1996. *Heart of a Woman, Mind of a Writer, and Soul of a Poet: A Critical Analysis of the Writings of Maya Angelou*. Lanham, MD: UP of America.

Herman, Judith. 1992. *Trauma and Recovery*. New York: Basic Books.

Lupton, Mary Jane. 1998. *Maya Angelou: A Critical Companion*. Westport, CT: Greenwood.

THE BLUEST EYE BY TONI MORRISON (1970)

Toni Morrison's (1931–) first novel, *The Bluest Eye* (1970), addressed the imposition of white American beauty ideals on the development of young African American women's identity. Morrison explored women's issues through a close examination of the coming of age and psychological destruction of Pecola Breedlove, an African American girl in Lorain, Ohio, in the early 1940s. Through the narration of a now-adult childhood friend of Pecola, the narration of an omniscient narrator, and the use of a children's primer from that period, Morrison described Pecola's desire for and obsession with typical American standards of beauty as portrayed in movies, books, advertisements, and merchandise. Pecola believes that if she has the bluest eyes, she will be beautiful and loved by her parents and the rest of her community, which will in turn ultimately result in a better life.

In a nonchronological, fragmented narrative, *The Bluest Eye* recounts the memories and stories surrounding Pecola Breedlove during one year in the Midwest post-Depression era. The primary narrator, Claudia MacTeer, recounts the events of the year as related to the main character. In the opening pages of the novel, Claudia reveals that Pecola becomes pregnant with her father's child; that the child and Pecola's father, Cholly Breedlove, die; and innocence and faith are lost. Claudia also talks of her own transformation from a child who despises the white idealization of beauty embodied in Shirley Temple and white dolls to a girl with "fraudulent love" of the beauty myth (Morrison, 1994: 23). Claudia tells of this change in herself before ever mentioning Pecola's prayer for blue eyes, thus showing that Pecola's obsession is not an anomaly but the norm of girls at the time. Hated for her dark skin and eyes, Pecola pines for blue eyes: "It had occurred to Pecola some time ago that if . . . those eyes of hers were different, that is to say, beautiful, she herself would be different. . . . If she looked different, beautiful, maybe Cholly would be different, and Mrs. Breedlove too. . . . Each night, without fail, she prayed for blue eyes" (46). As the events of the novel unfold, the narrator relates that Pecola's obsession becomes her insanity. In the final chapter, Pecola's voice illustrates her psychological break as she speaks of the bluest eyes she now possesses, the most beautiful and bluest of any eyes in the world (203). The fragmented voice of Pecola at the end of the novel depicts the broken, fragmented identity of the young American girl who reaps the fruits of a society poisoned by the beauty myth to which all women are held.

This novel shed light on the painful reality of how the white beauty standard affected an African American community, especially its girls and women. Morrison portrayed the internalized racism of this community through characters that devalued themselves in favor of lighter skin and eyes, and women's growing self-hatred via a continuous cultural consumption of white beauty.

The Bluest Eye received modest reviews when first published, then faded into relative obscurity for a number of years. However, as Toni Morrison gained increasing literary recognition, her first novel also garnered praise from literary scholars and has become a standard in many high school and college classes. In the past decade, *The Bluest Eye* received backlash as well. It has been placed on the top 10 list of most highly contested/banned books in the United States for its graphic depictions of sex, incest, rape, and pedophilia.

Rachel R. Martin

FURTHER READING

McKay, Nellie Y., ed. 1988. *Critical Essays on Toni Morrison.* Boston: G.K. Hall & Co.

Miner, Madonne M. 1985. "Lady No Longer Sings the Blues: Rape, Madness, and Silence in *The Bluest Eye.*" In *Conjuring: Black Women, Fiction, and Literary Tradition*, 176–91. Edited by Marjorie Pryse and Hortense J. Spillers. Bloomington, IN: Indiana University Press.

Morrison, Toni. 1994. *The Bluest Eye.* New York: Plume Printing.

Peach, Linden, ed. 1998. *Toni Morrison: Contemporary Critical Essays (New Casebooks).* London: Palgrave Macmillan.

RUBYFRUIT JUNGLE BY RITA MAE BROWN (1973)

Rita Mae Brown (1944–) is an American novelist and political activist best known for the publication of *Rubyfruit Jungle* (1973), one of the most significant contemporary American novels to include lesbian characters and themes. Known for her political convictions and her outspokenness, Brown's contributions to lesbian writing have bolstered the visibility and representation of queer characters in American literature and popular culture.

Since her youth, Brown has been involved with the feminist movement and with LGBTQ (lesbian, gay, bisexual, transgender, queer) activism. Her activist roots trace back to her time spent at the University of Florida at Gainesville. Due to her participation in the Civil Rights Movement and her identification with lesbian social circles, one of the university's deans threatened to revoke her scholarship if she did not undergo psychological counseling and "straighten up and fly right" (Brown, 1997: 184). After Brown was expelled from the University of Florida in 1964, she moved to New York City, where she attended New York University (NYU) and the New York School of Visual Arts. Brown helped establish a women's center on the Lower East Side of New York and the Student Homophile League at NYU and Brown University. She also addressed homophobic, racist, and sexist attitudes present in activist groups such as the National Organization for Women (NOW). During the 1970s, Brown moved to Washington, D.C., where she lectured at Federal City College and the Institute for Policy Studies, and published essays on political philosophy and feminism.

Brown blossomed as a writer during her time in Washington, D.C., where she published various critical essays and poetry collections. During the same year in which she published a collection of erotic poetry titled *Songs to a Handsome Woman* (1973), Brown also published her celebrated novel *Rubyfruit Jungle*—her first work of fiction, which was partially inspired by her childhood and early adulthood. Critics approach this novel as one of the earliest American works to explicitly and unapologetically deal with lesbian and queer themes. Brown's novel is often categorized as an archetypal lesbian bildungsroman (novel of development). *Rubyfruit Jungle* depicted Molly Bolt's struggles to deal with the prejudice present in her family and her surrounding social institutions. The novel focused on the discrimination that Molly faced while attempting to complete an undergraduate degree at the University of Florida and a degree in filmmaking in New York. Although *Rubyfruit Jungle* has remained widely popular throughout the years, critical and scholarly work on the novel has varied: the novel "has been examined both as a lesbian feminist manifesto and as not being feminist or lesbian enough" (Harde, 2002: 43).

Although Brown has written a number of other novels, none of her later works have been as culturally or historically significant as *Rubyfruit Jungle*. Readers, scholars, and institutions still celebrate Brown's legacy and her classic lesbian novel today. In 2015, Brown received two accolades that recognized her novel's influence and impact: the Lee Lynch Classic Award for groundbreaking LGBTQ literary works, and the Lambda Literary Pioneer Award for authors who have significantly altered the landscape of LGBTQ writing and publishing. *Rubyfruit Jungle* continues to be in print four decades after its initial publication.

Angel Daniel Matos

FURTHER READING

AOL. 2015 "Makers Profile: Rita Mae Brown, Author & Activist." *Makers* video series. http://www.makers.com/rita-mae-brown.

Brown, Rita Mae. 1997. *Rita Will: Memoir of a Literary Rabble-Rouser.* New York: Bantam Books.

Harde, Roxanne. 2002. "Rita Mae Brown (1944–)." In *Contemporary American Women Fiction Writers*, 40–45. Edited by Laurie Champion and Rhonda Austin. Westport, CT: Greenwood Press.

Ward, Carol M. 1993. *Rita Mae Brown.* New York: Twayne Publishers.

THE DREAM OF A COMMON LANGUAGE: POEMS 1974–1977 BY ADRIENNE RICH (1978)

The Dream of a Common Language: Poems 1974–1977 (1978) appeared early in Adrienne Rich's (1929–2012) long career and solidified her position as a leader who articulated the central ideas of the second-wave U.S. feminist movement. These poems, about and for women, envisioned an alternative to a patriarchal system in which men control the avenues of power and the definitions of female existence. They established the primary concerns of Rich's life's work to promote (1) solidarity among women and the power that emerges from their collaboration; (2) the legitimacy of lesbian existence within a homophobic world; (3) a reconceptualization of motherhood as institution; (4) the mind's relation to the body; and (5) the destructive nature of a dominant culture that renders its marginalized members invisible and silent. Rich refused any division between the artistic and political aspects of her poetry as she used both to explore social relations in a world hostile to female identity and creativity.

In the poem "Origins and History of Consciousness," Rich equated "[t]he drive to connect" with "[t]he dream of a common language." Rich's notion of a *common language* stressed a desire for the direct communication of care and concern within a community of speakers, and the power that ensues from this achievement. At this point in Rich's evolving process—separatist, radical feminist—she reserved dialogue for the shared experience of women. Although they may remain only *dreams*, such creative acts can bring forth new realities in the face of a damaging, male-dominated culture where women are not full participants.

The critics' varied response to *The Dream of a Common Language* sparked debates that increased Rich's popularity and notoriety in the public sphere. Many celebrated her attention to women's history, her rhetorical talent, and her outspoken approach to taboo topics. Others warned against her generalized category of womanhood and condemned what they saw as the continuation of an obsessively anti-male focus on patriarchal power. Sensing this backlash, Rich shifted her lens from the world of men to that of women in both *Of Woman Born: Motherhood as Experience and Institution* (1976) and *Dream of a Common Language.* Nevertheless, several critics rejected her incorporation of poetry and politics: some declared her work overtly propagandistic, didactic, and dogmatic.

At the time of her death, Rich enjoyed an international following. Rich, who was white, won the 1974 National Book Award for *Diving into the Wreck*. In a characteristic move, she refused the award as an individual but accepted it with fellow nominees Alice Walker and Audre Lorde, who are black, "in the name of all women whose voices have gone and still go unheard in a patriarchal world." Rich leaves her mark on today's popular culture as an innovative, antiracist feminist who maintained her commitment to dialogue as an instrument for change in the world.

Sarah Wyman

FURTHER READING

Gelpi, Barbara Charlesworth, and Albert Gelpi, eds. 1993. *Adrienne Rich's Poetry and Prose: Poems, Prose, Reviews and Criticism.* New York: Norton.

Keyes, Claire. 1986. *The Aesthetics of Power: The Poetry of Adrienne Rich.* Athens, GA: University of Georgia Press.

Langdell, Cheri Colby. 2004. *Adrienne Rich: The Moment of Change.* Westport, CT: Praeger.

Rich, Adrienne. 1974. "Statement to Be Read by Adrienne Rich at National Book Award Ceremony." http://www.nationalbook.org/graphics/2011_nba_poetry/1974/rich_accept_speech_74.pdf.

Rich, Adrienne. 1979. "When We Dead Awaken: Writing as Re-Vision 1971." In *On Lies, Secrets, and Silence: Selected Prose 1966–1978.* New York: Norton.

Werner, Craig. 1988. *Adrienne Rich: The Poet and Her Critics.* Chicago: American Library Association.

FOR COLORED GIRLS WHO HAVE CONSIDERED SUICIDE WHEN THE RAINBOW IS ENUF BY NTOZAKE SHANGE (1975)

Ntozake Shange's (1948–) choreopoem *For Colored Girls Who Have Considered Suicide When the Rainbow Is Enuf* was published in 1975, which she stated, "began in the middle of itself " (Shange, 1997). Writers often speak of that moment when their own lives or those of communities with which they identify are going through significant political and cultural shifts, and for Shange this was a time of awakening of the black feminist voice. In a remarkably short time from its creation, it became only the second play by a black woman to reach Broadway (the first being Lorraine Hansberry's *A Raisin in the Sun* in 1959). The "rainbow" in the play consists of the following: "A Lady in Red," "A Lady in Blue," "A Lady in Purple," "A Lady in Yellow," "A Lady in Brown," "A Lady in Green," and "A Lady in Orange." Each of the poems represents a woman in a different urban center in the United States, which is learned early on in the play: the lady in brown represents Chicago; the lady in yellow, Detroit; the lady in purple, Houston; the lady in red, Baltimore; the lady in green,

San Francisco; the lady in blue, Manhattan; and the lady in orange, St. Louis. The location of each story is secondary to the fact that they are expressing the very real struggles of black women from a collective standpoint that transcends both space and time.

Originally written in 1974 as separate poems, Shange premiered her work in 1976 as a choreopoem production at the Bacchanal in Berkeley, California. It was groundbreaking because as Shange wrote these separate poems toward the development of a collective body, she was also considering the role of movement—specifically how dancers were vital to her artistic expression of the black women's voice. The timing of her efforts was key, as they occurred at the same time as the Black Power movement and the second-wave feminist movement in the 1970s. In 1974, a black feminist and lesbian group came to the forefront—the Combahee River Collective—and released a statement that drew attention to their doubly oppressed status because of the intersection of racism and heterosexism that had previously gone unspoken. The Combahee River Collective served as a critical opening for the reception of Shange's "For Colored Girls" work. "The synthesis of these oppressions creates the conditions of our lives. As Black Women we see Black feminism as the logical political movement to combat the manifold and simultaneous oppressions that all women of color face" (*Women's Studies Quarterly*, 2014).

Noting the cultural context and time period of her work, Shange stated:

There was a sense of optimism in the feminist community throughout the country. We felt many things were going to change. We were going to have shelters, we were going to stop battery, we were going to inhibit and suppress rapists, we were going to change attitudes about child molestation, we were going to have free and legal abortions, we were going to be able to trust men we invited into our house! Our dreams were going to be respected and not negated every time we turn around. (Blount, 1995)

The fact that "For Colored Girls . . ." was made into an acclaimed 2010 film by Tyler Perry demonstrates the ongoing relevance of the perspective presented.

When one considers the "why" of using a rainbow with regard to the emotional state of "colored girls" in the title of this play, recall that a rainbow is seen when there is both sun and rain appearing. In addition, the colors of the rainbow, though seen separately, all must blend together and appear in the same formation for completion. Finally, the rainbow image is symbolically associated with the possibility of fortune—for example, the "pot of gold at the end of a rainbow." Therefore, in the title much is stated about the intent of Shange in that she is writing about a collective state of being through individual sufferings of women of color, where hope lies in communal as well as individual understanding and the determination to overcome oppressive conditions—even ones that intimately involve loved ones.

Terri Jett

FURTHER READING

Bilowit, Ira J. 1995. "20 Years Later, Shange's 'Colored Girls' Take a New Look at Life." *Back Stage*, 36(26): 15.

Colbert, Soyica Diggs. 2014. "Black Feminist Collectivity in Ntozake Shange's "For Colored Girls Who Have Considered Suicide/When the Rainbow Is Enuf." *The Scholar & Feminist online*, 12.3–13.1 (Summer/Fall). http://sfonline.barnard.edu/worlds-of-ntozake-shange/black-feminist-collectivity-in-ntozake-shanges-for-colored-girls-who-have-considered-suicide-when-the-rainbow-is-enuf.

The Combahee River Collective. 2014. "A Black Feminist Statement." *Women's Studies Quarterly*, 42(3/4): 271–80.

THE COLOR PURPLE BY ALICE WALKER (1982)

The Color Purple (1982) is considered the seminal novel written by author, poet, and essayist Alice Walker (1944–). Walker's coming-of-age novel about Southern life at the beginning of the 20th century is significant because the lives of African American women were placed at the center of analysis. *The Color Purple* provided an unprecedented platform for African American women writers and scholars to discuss the double oppression experienced by African American women who not only face racism in society but also abuse and subjugation at the hands of African American men. *The Color Purple* is an enduring story because it celebrates black women's resilience and the healing power of the bonds between women.

The protagonist in *The Color Purple* is Celie, a young African American girl who is being sexually abused by the man she believes to be her father (but later learns is her stepfather). Alice Walker uses an epistolary form (a novel written as a series of letters) to give the reader a sense of the rich inner life of a silenced and abused girl. Celie addresses her letters to God in hopes that God can be a witness to her suffering. Two children, born of incest, are given away. Celie endures many hardships as she is married off to a violent man who expects her to raise his unruly children and who also drives her sister Nettie out of her life. As time passes, however, Celie finds strong kinship relationships with the women connected to her husband, Albert (most often referenced as Mr._____ in the novel)—including his sisters; his daughter-in-law, Sofia; and his lover, a woman named Shug Avery. The emotional and physical intimacy Celie shares with Shug helps her heal from her past sexual abuse. Further, Shug's audacious views on God help Celie grow in her own spirituality and gain a sense of self-sufficiency. With Shug's help, Celie also discovers that her sister, Nettie, has been writing her letters since their separation that have been kept hidden by Albert. Through letters, Celie learns that Nettie has traveled with a couple doing missionary work, and has been living in Africa with Celie's two children. By the end of the novel, Celie has grown into a self-actualized, whole woman who has forgiven those who have caused her harm, and she runs a successful small business. Finally, she is reunited with Nettie and her two children.

The Color Purple received both the National Book Award and a Pulitzer Prize in 1983, and was later made into both a film (1985) and a musical (2005). Walker's story of the resilience of black womanhood continues to speak to readers of new generations. By addressing incest, domestic violence, and patriarchy in the African American community, Alice Walker's novel gave a voice to many women who had been silenced in their suffering. Further, Walker's novels and essays aided the next generation of artists, scholars, theologians, and critics to articulate an African American woman's feminism. Both the book and the movie version of *The Color Purple* experienced significant backlash within the African American community. Critics of the novel felt uncomfortable with the themes of lesbianism and black female sexual agency. Others believed that Walker's portrayal of African American men was too negative and that the novel supported stereotypes of black men as violent.

Gabrie'l J. Atchison

See also: *The Color Purple* (film).

FURTHER READING

Fifer, Elizabeth. 1985. "The Dialect and Letters of *The Color Purple*." In *Contemporary American Women Writer: Narrative Strategies*, 155–71. Edited by Catherine Rainwater and William J. Scheick. Lexington, KY: University Press of Kentucky.

hooks, bell. 1990. "Writing the Subject: Reading *The Color Purple*." In *Reading Black, Reading Feminist: A Critical Anthology*, 454–70. Edited by Henry Louis Gates, Jr. New York: Meridian.

LaGrone, Kheven, and Michael Meyer, eds. 2009. *Alice Walker's* The Color Purple. Amsterdam: Rodopi.

White, Evelyn. 2004. *Alice Walker: A Life*. New York: W.W. Norton.

ZAMI: A NEW SPELLING OF MY NAME BY AUDRE LORDE (1982)

Zami: A New Spelling of My Name (1982) is renowned poet, critic, and writer Audre Lorde's (1934–1992) feminist telling of her story not as autobiography, but as a form she called "biomythography." For Lorde, biomythography functioned as both biography and history of myth; it was a way of expanding what we already see as having constructed each individual's identity. It did that through acknowledging multiple voices that aid in telling one's story. In other words, no one person's identity is formed from one set of experiences; rather, who we are is derived from our ancestors (and, in her case, her Afro-Caribbean roots), our families, and other communities in which we live. Biomythography disrupted a singular "master" narrative and made explicit the intersectionalities of race, sexuality, gender, class, and citizenship that are at the heart of *Zami*. Adopting this mode of storytelling enabled

Lorde to work within the autobiographical tradition even while distancing herself from it. The book picked up on these ideas and pulled them together into a lesbian bildungsroman (a coming-of-age story) that was at once Lorde's story as well as the story of her ancestors and of her adopted home of New York.

The critically acclaimed and celebrated novel opens with a chronicling of her black, working-class family's life in New York City, particularly after the stock market crash in 1929. Her parents, West Indian immigrants, struggle to find a way to take care of their growing family. In particular, Lorde focuses on her mother, Linda, whose homesickness and feeling out of place in the United States causes her much stress and is central to the conflicts she has with her daughter. For Lorde, Linda symbolizes that home where she does not belong, both in her family and in Grenada. The result of this is a haunting loneliness that permeates the pages of the book and is palpable in all the different life experiences she chronicles. In the early chapters of the book, it is the ritual of cooking that captures for her a linking to her West Indian ancestors and which she tries to use to link to her mother. In Chapter 11, for example, she describes in painstaking details her pounding of spices for her mother's *souse*. The *souse* serves as a reminder of a home she never knew and a mother for whom she ached. These early chapters reinforce, as Barbara DiBernard has argued, that "[f]or black women in the United States the mother-daughter relationship is complicated by racism and the history of blacks here" (Lorde, 1982: 202).

The search for belonging is a running theme throughout the rest of the book, and is most present in her relationships with various women including Gennie, her "first true friend" (87); Ginger, her first lover; Muriel, the white woman with whom Lorde considered herself married; and to Kitty/Afrekete, who ultimately helps Lorde to come to a new spelling of her name: Zami. Along the way, Lorde also moves to Mexico, explores the place of the black lesbian within the predominantly white lesbian culture in New York City during the 1950s, and eventually goes to Hunter College. Murie's affair with a friend serves as an impetus for Lorde to find her own way, and her meeting and brief tryst with Kitty/Afrekete paves the way for her to claim all different parts of herself. At the end of the book, she claims the name Zami: "Zami. A Carriacou name for women who work together as friends and lovers" (Lorde, 1982: 255). By the end, she makes a complete full circle to her mother, whose blood, she claims, brings about the desire to "lie with other women." The book ultimately asks us to "recognize and celebrate those before us and around us who survived and who gave us the tools for survival" and also pleads with us to "do our work to ensure the survival of others" (DiBernard, 1991: 211). It is by centralizing our lives in these ways that we can then form our communities and make our home within ourselves.

Priya Jha

FURTHER READING

DiBernard, Barbara. 1991. "Zami: A Portrait of an Artist as a Black Lesbian." *Kenyon Review*, S13: 195–213.

Gillan, Jennifer. 1996. "Relocating Home and Identity in Zami: A New Spelling of My Name." In *Homemaking: Women Writers and the Politics and Poetics of Home*, 207–219. Edited by Catherine Wiley and Fiona R. Barnes. New York: Garland.

Kader, Cheryl. 1993. " 'The Very House of Difference': Zami, Audre Lorde's Lesbian-Centered Text." *Journal of homosexuality*, 26(2–3): 181–94.

Keating, AnnLouise. 1992. "Making" Our Shattered Faces Whole": The Black Goddess and Audre Lorde's Revision of Patriarchal Myth." *Frontiers: A Journal of Women Studies*, 13(1): 20–33.

THE HANDMAID'S TALE BY MARGARET ATWOOD (1985)

The Handmaid's Tale (1985), by Canadian author Margaret Atwood (1939–), was set in a dystopic, near-future North America. Frequently compared to George Orwell's dystopian novel *1984*, Atwood's novel also projected a totalitarian future. *The Handmaid's Tale* focused on the role of women in a military theocracy called the Republic of Gilead. Although it received a mixed reception, most positive analyses consider the novel a complex, multifaceted critique of both radical feminism and religious fundamentalism. Scholarly analysis and critique of the novel have focused on themes of patriarchal domination, gender role enforcement, unstable identity, and sexuality.

The Handmaid's Tale begins after the eventual Republic of Gilead overthrows the United States government. The protagonist, Offred, has just begun her third assignment as a Handmaid. Toxic waste has rendered much of the population infertile, and a caste system with rigid gender roles structures Gilead's white supremacist, patriarchal society. Black people have been wholly relocated to an area outside Gilead; other "non-persons," including most infertile women as well as infants born with physical or other abnormalities, are sent to die in the polluted "colonies." Fertile women who violate gender rules become Handmaids, expected to produce children for the infertile Wives of Commanders, a task justified by Biblical reinterpretation. Handmaids are valued solely for their ability to procreate; infertility or insubordination dooms them to the colonies. The narrative revolves around Offred's recollections of her previous life as she attempts to cope with her assigned role as a Handmaid, its constrictions, and its complications.

Atwood's novel was nominated for several awards, including the Nebula Award, Booker Prize, and Prometheus Award. *The Handmaid's Tale* received the Governor General's Award in 1985 and the inaugural Arthur C. Clarke Award in 1987. Critical reception of the novel has varied, ranging from declarations that it "has no satiric bite" and is so unrealistic that it is "powerless to scare" (McCarthy, 1986) to assertions that it is "gripping in its horrendous details" while it "predicts what future women in the United States can expect" (Grumbach, 1986). As assigned reading in some high school and college classrooms, *The Handmaid's Tale* has sparked significant controversy, placing 37th in the American Library Association's 1990–1999 list of most frequently challenged books and 88th in the 2000–2009 list; complaints about its contents included sexuality, profanity, and/or anti-Christian themes.

The narrative has been adapted into various other media forms, including film (1990), radio (BBC-4, 2000), opera (2000), audiobook (2012), ballet (2013), and stage play (2002, 2015). "Handmaid's Tale" is used as shorthand for women's reproductive and social subjugation. One of its most popular quotations is *"Nolite te bastardes carborundorum,"* a mock-Latin saying translated as "Don't let the bastards grind you down."

Jessica E. Birch

FURTHER READING

Atwood, Margaret. 2005. "Aliens Have Taken the Place of Angels." *The Guardian*, June 16. https://www.theguardian.com/film/2005/jun/17/sciencefictionfantasyandhorror.margaretatwood.

Grumbach, Doris. 1986. "Handmaid's Tale Offers a Grim View of Loveless Future." *Chicago Tribune*, January 26. http://articles.chicagotribune.com/1986-01-26/entertainment/8601070476_1_offred-handmaid-margaret-atwood.

Hammer, Stephanie Barbé. 1990. "The World as It Will Be? Female Satire and the Technology of Power in *The Handmaid's Tale*." *Modern Language Studies*, 20(2): 39–49.

McCarthy, Mary. 1986. "Book Review." *The New York Times*, February 9. https://www.nytimes.com/books/00/03/26/specials/mccarthy-atwood.html.

Tomc, Sandra. 1993. "'The Missionary Position': Feminism and Nationalism in Margaret Atwood's *The Handmaid's Tale*." *Canadian Literature*, 138–9: 73–87.

ORANGES ARE NOT THE ONLY FRUIT BY JEANETTE WINTERSON (1985)

Jeanette Winterson's (1959–) first novel, *Oranges Are Not the Only Fruit*, told the coming-of-age story of a young woman (Jeanette), her relationship with her adopted mother, her love of and expulsion from her church, and her self-exploration and sexual realization in Northern England in the 1960s. Winterson's work addressed women's rights through an exploration of a woman's power to define herself, women's relationships, and gender within the institutions of religious and familial patriarchy abundant in contemporary culture.

Although this novel closely parallels Winterson's life, *Oranges* is fiction. The fragmented narrative uses texts such as the Bible, *Jane Eyre*, fairy tales, and myths to create stories within the main story (metafiction), depicting the narrator's own identity construction. Raised by her adopted mother to be a missionary, Jeanette "cannot recall a time when [she] did not know that [she] was special" (Winterson, 1985: 2). Her zealot mother and the Elim Pentecostal Church confirm Jeanette's uniqueness through praise and establishing her as the model of Christianity, and young Jeanette wholeheartedly believes in the word of her mother, the church, and the Bible. However, Jeanette begins to question her commitment to the church and its teachings as she recognizes her sexual attraction to women.

Award-winning author Jeanette Winterson garnered much attention with her first book *Oranges Are Not the Only Fruit*. A semi-autobiographical book, the novel follows a teenage girl who rebels against traditional norms. (AP Photo/Rick Maiman)

As her lesbianism clashes with her religious community, Jeanette's identity develops at odds with her mother's plan for Jeanette. Her mother thinks of the world in binary terms. At the beginning of the novel, the narrator shows her mother's binary, singular thinking through her mother's insistence that oranges are "the only fruit" (29). In all aspects of Jeanette's life, her mother presents Jeanette one option: one path, one truth, and one fruit. In this novel, oranges represent gender and sexuality norms, the limitations of traditional gender roles, and heteronormativity. Jeanette's mother selects a single fruit, gender, and sexual orientation for her daughter. Distinguishing herself from her mother, Jeanette identifies many fruits, many ways to live, and many ways to love.

After Jeanette's mother discovers her daughter's sexual relationship with a woman in the church's congregation for the second time, the narrator is forced to leave her church and her home. Jeanette forsakes the path laid out for her, and rather than accept her mother's black-and-white view of the world, Jeanette explores arenas of contradiction, ambiguity, and multiple truths. After several years on her own, Jeanette returns to her mother's home, and while they do not discuss Jeanette's sexual orientation, her mother now recognizes another fruit, pineapple, implying that her binary, judgmental view of the world is expanding.

The mainstream press, along with feminist, left-wing presses, greeted *Oranges Are Not the Only Fruit* with positive reviews. Winterson won the Whitbread Award for a First Novel in 1985, and in 1990 she adapted the book into a series for British television. Although *Oranges* has often been referred to as a "lesbian novel," Winterson objects to this categorization, saying she "never understood why straight fiction is supposed to be for everyone, but anything with a gay character or that includes gay experience is only for queers. That said, I'm really glad the book has made a difference to so many women" (Winterson, "Interview").

Rachel R. Martin

FURTHER READING

Beirne, Rebecca. 2008. *Lesbians in Television and Text after the Millennium*. New York: Palgrave Macmillan.

Winterson, Jeanette. "Interview on Jeanette Winterson's Official Site." http://www.jeanettewinterson.com/book/oranges-are-not-the-only-fruit.

Winterson, Jeanette. 1985. *Oranges Are Not the Only Fruit*. New York: Grove Press.

HOW THE GARCIA GIRLS LOST THEIR ACCENTS
BY JULIA ALVAREZ (2010)

How the Garcia Girls Lost Their Accents is a classic in Latina literature. It has been widely adopted in high schools and university curricula across the United States as a perfect example of the internal journey of a group of Dominican teenagers trying to fit in in 1960s New York. That term, "fit," is probably the keyword to frame Julia Alvarez's (1950–) work. *How the Garcia Girls Lost Their Accents* is, in sum, a reflection on ethnic identity in the development of the Garcia sisters as full-grown women. It is, moreover, a critique of Hispanicity in the context of late 20th-century American feminism and women's rights.

Unlike so many Latinos, Alvarez came from a very wealthy upbringing. She attended an American school in the Dominican Republic, where she learned English. When she was 10, her entire family pretended that they were traveling to the United States for summer break. But on arriving in New York City, they never returned to the Dominican Republic. It was the 1960s, but before the 1960s were really the 1960s as they have come to be engraved in our cultural imagination. It was before the Civil Rights Movements, before Martin Luther King Jr. and the Beatles and the Vietnam War, before second-wave feminism, and before Dolores Huerta and César Chávez shouted *Se, se puede* ("Yes, we can"). If the past, as L. P. Hartley would have it, is a foreign country, Julia Alvarez was twice an immigrant. She came from the Dominican Republic to *those* United States, trying so hard to fit in that she lost her accent and whatever cultural roots a 10-year-old with an American education might have preserved. And then the 1960s really came. And she had to migrate again—from trying to be white to trying to be Latina, from an America where differences were antipatriotic to an America where differences were celebrated, and from the melting pot to the mosaic.

How the Garcia Girls Lost Their Accents tells this double journey. Some people have argued that this double ambivalence toward her identity as an American and her identity as a Latina has often been neglected. The novel has too often been read as the story of a group of Latina girls trying to assimilate in the United States, but some experts think it's much more about a group of girls trying to assimilate in the United States as white, middle-class Americans who then try to assimilate as Latina, middle-class Americans. It's much more about the mythical utopian dream to assimilate rather than the process of assimilation itself.

As much as Alvarez critiques the social stereotypes Americans impose on Latinos, she also indulges in stereotyping Hispanic culture throughout the book: looking at the Dominican Republic with a colonizer's gaze, adopting the same proud ignorance Americans hold against ethnic minorities and immigrants. At the end, Alvarez's work is a fundamental work in Latina literature not so much for its presentation of the struggles of assimilation into Americanness and womanhood, but because of what it reveals: the radical impossibility of assimilation, the artificial construction of an ancestral identity, and the fears (and freedom) that the migrant experience entails.

Eduardo Gregori

FURTHER READING

Chandra, Sarika. 2008. "Re-Producing a Nationalist Literature in the Age of Globalization: Reading (Im)migration in Julia Alvarez's *How the Garcia Girls Lost Their Accents.*" *American Quarterly*, 60.3: 829–50.

Luis, William. 2000. "A Search for Identity in Julia Alvarez's *How the Garcia Girls Lost Their Accents.*" *Callaloo*, 23(3): 839–49.

Mitchell, David T. 1999. *Beyond the Binary: Reconstructing Cultural Identity in a Multicultural Context.* Rutgers, NJ: Rutgers University Press.

THE ROUND HOUSE BY LOUISE ERDRICH (2012)

The Round House (2012), the 14th novel by Ojibwe author Louise Erdrich (1954–), was awarded the 2012 National Book Award for Fiction. *The Round House* is narrated by Joe Coutts, whose world is irreparably changed two weeks after his 13th birthday when his mother, a tribal enrollment specialist in North Dakota, is brutally assaulted and raped. Joe's mother cannot identify the location of her assault (on tribal or nontribal lands) and will not identify her assailant (as an Indian or non-Indian)—information necessary to determine the jurisdiction of the crime. Erdrich called her work a suspense novel "masking a crusade" (Tharp, 2014: 25) against a loophole in conflicting tribal, state, and federal jurisdictions that leaves Native American women vulnerable. In "Rape on the Reservation," an essay Erdrich wrote for *The New York Times*, she described the higher rate of rape for Native women, the lower rate of reporting, the failure of federal authorities to prosecute sexual abuse cases, and the statistic that "more than 80 percent of sex crimes on reservations are committed by non-Indian men" (Erdrich, 2013). Tribal authorities were only empowered to prosecute non-Indians for abuses committed on tribal lands in 2013, when a landmark addition was made to the renewed Violence Against Women Act.

In *The Round House*, Joe's nascent interest in law is initially expressed as disappointment at his tribal judge father's seemingly trivial rulings. However, through reading his father's books—including Felix Cohen's *Handbook of Federal Indian Law* (1941)—Joe realizes that "our treaties with the government were like treaties with foreign nations" (Erdrich, 2012: 2). He surveys the 20th-century laws that preclude justice for his mother: the Major Crimes Act (1885), authorizing the U.S. federal government's intervention in restitution and punishment on reservations; Public Law 280 and House Concurrent Resolution 108 (1953), replacing federal jurisdiction with state jurisdiction and revoking tribal recognition; and *Oliphant v. Suquamish Indian Tribe* (1978), a ruling that tribal courts did not have the criminal jurisdiction to prosecute non-Indians. In 1988, the setting for Joe's narrative, both PL 280 and HCR 108, were formally abandoned. By the novel's conclusion, Joe exchanges his contempt for admiration at his father's lifelong, case-by-case assertion of tribal sovereignty.

Equally a suspense novel and coming-of-age story, *The Round House* links Joe's development to thematic explorations of justice. Joe's adolescent fantasy life, for instance, draws on the science fiction narratives of *Star Trek* and *Star Wars* for their metaphors of frontiers, justice, alien/Others, and revenge. In addition, Joe must reconsider his adolescent attitudes toward women. The attack on his mother at the sacred Round House (symbolic of grandmother buffalo's corporeal sacrifice and a space of tribal justice and restitution) compels Joe to assess the violation of lineal heritage through mothers by Western colonialism.

Mary Thompson

FURTHER READING

Erdrich, Louise. 2013. "Rape on the Reservation." *The New York Times*, February 27.

Goodman, Amy. 2013. "New Violence Against Women Act Includes Historic Protections for Native American and LGBT Survivors." *Democracy Now!* https://www.democracynow.org/2013/3/8/new_violence_against_women_act_includes.

Owens, Jasmine. 2012. "'Historic' in a Bad Way: How the Tribal Law and Order Act Continues the American Tradition of Providing Inadequate Protection to American Indian and Alaska Native Rape Victims." *Journal of Criminal Law & Criminology*, 102(2): 497–524.

Tharp, Julie. 2014. "Erdrich's Crusade: Sexual Violence in *The Round House*." *Studies in American Indian Literatures*, 26(3): 25–40.

BAD FEMINIST BY ROXANE GAY (2014)

Bad Feminist (2014) is a collection of political and personal essays by writer, professor, and blogger Roxane Gay (1974–). The book positively portrays feminism and accessibly presents basic feminist theory. Gay sets up a "good" feminist straw man in the image of longstanding feminist stereotypes: militant, man-hating women who won't wear pink and don't have a sense of humor. This distorted caricature relies heavily on the presumption that good feminists strictly adhere to feminist theory. Gay calls herself a bad feminist because she often falls short when trying to live feminist theory. Despite not always performing feminism "correctly," Gay is still a feminist. The overarching argument connecting the essays is that there are multiple feminisms: one size does not fit all. A flawed feminist is still a feminist.

Gay illustrates negotiating feminism in essays documenting her complicated relationship with popular culture. For instance, she enjoys rap music that sometimes disparages women and reads *Vogue* magazine despite the fashion industry's role in creating unattainable standards for female beauty. Gay, like many feminist women and men, enjoys and consumes media despite problematic content. Yet she does not blindly consume these texts. Gay critiques representations of race and gender in the movies *Django Unchained*, *Fifty Shades of Grey*, and *The Help*. Popular culture segues to bigger conversations about racism, sexism, privilege, violence, rape, and trigger warnings.

Bad Feminist spent a month on *The New York Times* Bestseller List in 2014. This is notable because a book that so candidly discusses feminism in a positive, proactive way rarely achieves widespread popular success. Praised for its candid, accessible tone, the book is lauded by many feminist scholars, who identify with the way Gay captures the sometimes contradictory negotiation of personal and political identities. Additionally, Gay's inclusive language creates a nonjudgmental space for readers to explore how a feminist framework might be employed in their own lives. Gay achieves this by plainly stating her standpoint as an upper-middle-class black woman. Her race, class, and gender inform her position as well as her view of the world, but these identities also affect how the world sees her.

Alternatively, some critics feel that *Bad Feminist* suffers from a lack of history or theoretical grounding. In an effort to avoid jargon and bogging down her cultural critique with a literature review, Gay skates over a rich past of feminist thought without acknowledging her feminist predecessors. Other critics are put off by the way *Bad Feminist* never offers a definition of what feminism is. Instead, the book focuses on what a bad feminist is not. This result is a loose definition of feminism despite Gay's attempt to avoid a rigid set of rules. By railing against the feminist stereotype, Gay both challenges and perpetuates the myths about feminism she is trying to dispel.

Katie Sullivan Barak

FURTHER READING

Cooper, Brittney. 2015. "Feminism for Badasses." *Short Takes: Roxane Gay's* Bad Feminist. June 12. http://signsjournal.org/bad-feminist.

Kaplan, Carla. 2015. "Feminism for Those Who Don't Like Feminists." *Short Takes: Roxane Gay's* Bad Feminist. June 12. http://signsjournal.org/bad -feminist.

Wessing, Emily. 2015. "Vulnerable, Human, & Flawed: Confessions of a Bad Feminist." *Feminist Collections*, 36: 4–5.

Wolf, Naomi. 2015. " 'Bad Feminist,' Great Rhetorician." *Short Takes: Roxane Gay's* Bad Feminist. June 12. http://signsjournal.org/bad-feminist.

CITIZEN: AN AMERICAN LYRIC BY CLAUDIA RANKINE (2014)

Citizen: An American Lyric is a 2014 book of poetry by American writer Claudia Rankine (1963–). Rankine, the Aerol Arnold Chair in the University of Southern California English Department, has published four other volumes of poetry (including the 2004 *Don't Let Me Be Lonely*, subtitled *An American Lyric*), as well as two plays and a variety of essays; she has also edited multiple anthologies. *Citizen*, described by some as a book-length poem and by others as a work that blends or blurs genre boundaries, explores identity, race, and racism in the United States. Images and vignettes spanning the range from personal to political, to public— described by some as "micro-aggressions" (commonplace, casual, and usually unintentional interactions that exclude, demean, and/or insult marginalized persons)—comprise the seven chapters of the book, which has won a wide variety of awards and general acclaim.

Nearly all of the book is written in the second person (you) present tense, a source of conflict and interest among both everyday readers and reviewers. One reviewer describes it as "a tense that implicates as it includes" (Laird, 2015), and Shockley (2016) notes that for African Americans, "the second-person speaker . . . tends to affirm [our] subjective experience," but points out that "white readers . . . will face quite a different psychic situation." Although many praise its accessibility in language and form, the book has also been critiqued for its binary presentation of race and racial dynamics.

Some of the text reads as intimately autobiographical, delineating the boundaries of a black American life lived in racism. Another section focuses on Serena Williams, using Hennessy Youngman's philosophy on "commodified anger" (Rankine, 2014: 23) to frame media coverage of Williams's blackness, tennis matches, and personality. The text also includes scripts for films about notable news events of both the recent and more distant past, including Hurricane Katrina, Trayvon Martin, James Craig Anderson, and the Jena Six. Much of the format consists of short paragraphs, with occasional pages nearly bare of text. One is a three-line poem: "because white men can't/police their imagination/black men are dying" (135). Opposite the poem is a memorial to black women and men killed.

The book has won multiple awards, including being named the Best Book of the Year by publications including *The New Yorker*, *Slate*, *National Public Radio*, the *Los Angeles Times*, and *Publishers Weekly*. *Citizen* was also a finalist for the National Book Award, the Forward Prize, and the Hurston/Wright Legacy Award in Poetry, among others, and winner of the NAACP Image Award for Outstanding Literary Work in Poetry and the PEN Open Book Award. A 2015 stage adaptation premiered at The Fountain Theatre in Los Angeles.

Jessica E. Birch

FURTHER READING

Laird, Nick. 2015. "A New Way of Writing about Race." *The New York Review of Books*, April 23. http://www.nybooks.com/articles/2015/04/23/claudia-rankine -new-way-writing-about-race.

Rankine, Claudia. 2014. *Citizen: An American Lyric.* Minneapolis: Gray Wolf Press.

Rankine, Claudia. 2015. "The Condition of Black Life Is One of Mourning." *The New York Times Magazine*, June 22. http://www.nytimes.com/2015/06/22/mag-azine/the-condition-of-black-life-is-one-of-mourning.html?emc=eta1&_r=1.

Shockley, Evie. 2016. "Reconsidering Claudia Rankine's *Citizen: An American Lyric.* A Symposium, Part I." *Los Angeles Review of Books*, January 6. https://lareviewof-books.org/essay/reconsidering-claudia-rankines-citizen-an-american-lyric -a-symposium-part-i.

FIVE

In the News

News disseminated through multiple mediated platforms, (print, television, online) is indeed a part of popular culture. Issues, people, and events brought to the public's attention through the media pervade a society and influence what we know and how we think. Journalism is a venue for the circulation of ideas and knowledge. Just like other channels of popular culture, such as literature and film, news media tell the stories of our lives as well as our dreams and desires. This anthology focuses on women who found themselves in news headlines and became important parts of the ongoing and evolving dialogue about women's roles and women's rights in the United States.

MARGARET SANGER (1879–1966)

Margaret Sanger fought for the most fundamental of women's rights—the right to one's body. For Sanger, control over reproduction was a revolutionary act, with the potential for women's personal and political liberation. However, it remains uncertain in whose interests this revolution was waged. Was Sanger pushing for a personal right of reproduction, or was she working for political population control? Controversy permeates Sanger's life, and despite the layers of complexities her life reveals, she continues to be a cultural icon of the feminist movement.

Sanger saw her personal experience as connected with a political cause that deeply impacted other women. Sanger's commitment to birth control—a term she coined—was influenced by her mother's early death following 18 pregnancies and 11 live births. Additionally, as a nurse, Sanger met women living in poverty who, recovering from multiple pregnancies, were desperate for contraceptive information. Her activism led to the opening of the nation's first birth control clinic in 1916, which drew a crowd of 400 women. But this action quickly resulted in her arrest for causing a public nuisance, and the closure of the clinic.

Activist Margaret Sanger popularized the term "birth control" as an advocate for women's health. The clinic she opened evolved into what is now known as Planned Parenthood. (Courtesy of the George Grantham Bain Collection, Library of Congress)

Sanger would later go on to establish the first legal birth control clinics in the United States. In 1921, she founded the American Birth Control League, which would later become the Planned Parenthood Federation. During World War II, Sanger focused her efforts on international birth control, helping to found the International Planned Parenthood Federation. Finally, in the 1950s she played an important role in the development of the birth control pill.

Sanger began her crusade for birth control by working closely with the Socialist party, militant working-class groups, and the anarchist movement. However, Sanger's alliance with radical feminist causes would not be long lasting. Influenced by population control advocates and eugenicists, her birth control movement was robbed of its progressive possibilities as Sanger repositioned her work to align with mainstream conservative efforts. Sanger linked the devastating effects of poverty to uncontrolled population growth, which led many to assume that birth control was the duty, rather than the right, of the poor.

The nuances of Sanger's life and her work are to be found in her letters, journals, articles, and speeches. These sources reveal her struggles to find balance within and without amid her all-consuming fight for women's freedom. Before Sanger's death in 1966, she saw the Supreme Court make birth control legal for married couples in *Griswold v. Connecticut*. The progressive possibilities of birth control ignited by Sanger remain, and she leaves a legacy that continues to be disputed today.

Stephanie Leo Hudson

See also: Planned Parenthood.

FURTHER READING

Davis, Angela. 1981. "Racism, Birth Control and Reproductive Rights." In *Women, Race and Class*, 202–21. New York: Random House.

The Margaret Sanger Papers Project. New York University, https://www.nyu.edu/projects/sanger/.

Sanger, Alexander. 2007. "Eugenics, Race, and Margaret Sanger Revisited: Reproductive Freedom for All?" *Hypatia*, 22: 210–17.

Sanger, Margaret. 2003. *The Selected Papers of Margaret Sanger, Volume 1: The Woman Rebel, 1900–1928*. Edited by Esther Katz. Chicago: University of Illinois Press.

Sanger, Margaret. 2006. *The Selected Papers of Margaret Sanger, Volume 2: Birth Control Comes of Age, 1928–1939*. Edited by Esther Katz. Chicago: University of Illinois Press.

Sanger, Margaret. 2010. *The Selected Papers of Margaret Sanger, Volume 3: The Politics of Planned Parenthood, 1939–1966*. Edited by Esther Katz. Chicago: University of Illinois Press.

Steinem, Gloria. 1998. "Margaret Sanger." *Time* Magazine, April 13.

FANNIE LOU HAMER (1917–1977)

Fannie Lou Hamer was the youngest of 20 children born to Mississippi share-croppers Jim and Ella Townsend. At age 44, she immersed herself in the Civil Rights Movement and quickly emerged as a leader. The model of the passionate layperson who lived the inequities that propelled the grassroots movement, Hamer became well known for saying, "All my life I've been sick and tired. Now I'm sick and tired of being sick and tired" (Mills, 1996: 93). She was a rhetorically savvy speaker who remains a symbol of the Civil Rights Movement.

Hamer lived in poverty in a racially segregated community, began picking cotton at the age of six, and left school after sixth grade to support her family. She married Perry Hamer in 1944 and set up house on a plantation near Ruleville, Mississippi. She was known by community members for her singing, work ethic, and knowledge of the Bible and the U.S. Constitution. After undergoing surgery to remove a small uterine tumor, she discovered that the doctor had performed an unauthorized hysterectomy. Later she learned that thousands of poor, rural black women were sterilized without consent at that time. By 1962, Hamer had experienced a lifetime of mistreatment born out of institutionalized racism. When the Student Nonviolent Coordinating Committee (SNCC) visited Ruleville that summer to encourage blacks to register to vote, Hamer was persuaded.

It did not take long for other civil rights champions to recognize that Hamer could be an instrumental participant in the movement. She was intelligent and persistent. She unified and inspired others with her singing. She embodied the movement leaders' claims that ordinary people can work for social change. She shared her stories with honesty and power. She explained her understanding of the intersections of race, economic power, and political efficacy. She did not hesitate to publicly denounce leaders, mimic public officials, or berate audience members who were not engaged in the movement. At the 1964 Democratic National Committee, she spoke as a representative of the Mississippi Freedom Democratic Party, exposing the brutality of life in Mississippi to a nation largely oblivious to the injustices in that state. She gained the attention of the nation.

Hamer's work was arduous. In 1963, she was jailed and beaten. She unsuccessfully ran for a seat in the U.S. House of Representatives in 1964 and Mississippi State Senate in 1971. Her work was all consuming: mentoring young people, traveling, and speaking with the purpose of gaining equal rights for black citizens. Visiting hostile communities made her work occasionally dangerous. She acknowledged the stress her work put on herself and her family but said, "Although we have suffered greatly, I feel that we have not suffered in vain. I am determined to become a first-class citizen" (Mills, 1996: 79).

In her later years, she went on speaking tours, focused on poverty as a social ill, and was embraced by second-wave feminists who turned to her for insight about how to resist sexism. She developed a strong relationship with citizens in Madison, Wisconsin, who supported her efforts to start a farm cooperative in Mississippi. Due to untreated cancer, hypertension, and diabetes, Hamer's health declined rapidly in her last year of life. Still, she traveled and spoke. She died at age 59, known then and now as a warrior for civil rights.

Lori Walters-Kramer

FURTHER READING

Brooks, Maegan Parker. 2014. *A Voice that Could Stir an Army: Fannie Lou Hamer and the Rhetoric of the Black Freedom Movement.* Jackson, MS: University Press of Mississippi.

Brooks, Maegan Parker, and Davis W. Houck, eds. 2011. *The Speeches of Fannie Lou Hamer: To Tell It Like It Is.* Normal, IL: Illinois State University.

Lee, Chana Kai. 1999. *For Freedom's Sake: The Life of Fannie Lou Hamer.* Urbana, IL: University of Illinois.

Mills, Kay. 1993. *This Little Light of Mine: The Life of Fannie Lou Hamer.* New York: Plume.

HELEN THOMAS (1920–2013)

Famous for asking blunt questions of famous men, Helen Thomas was one of the most well-known journalists in American history (1920–2013). As a White House correspondent, she reported the news about every president from John F. Kennedy to Barack Obama. During her career, Thomas overcame barriers of gender discrimination in the media industry and championed the watchdog role of the press in a democratic society. Thomas took pride in the American tradition of free speech that allows reporters to ask leaders difficult questions and hold them accountable to the people. Reporters are "guardians of the people's right to know," she wrote (2006, 201).

Thomas began her career as a reporter as men left to fight World War II, leaving behind jobs that had previously excluded women. She became a reporter in Washington, D.C., in 1958 and invented her high-profile position reporting on the president by simply showing up at the White House and refusing to leave.

Thomas became a reporter at a time when women were allowed to write lightweight stories for the "society pages," but not about topics like politics. The National Press Club, an elite club for reporters, where important people often gave speeches, was an exclusive men's club until 1971. Thomas became the first female president of the club in 1975. She was also the first woman recipient of the National Press Club's Fourth Estate Award, previously given to journalism superstars like Walter Cronkite.

Thomas lamented the rise of "news management" strategies that presidents use to control what the public knows about government policy. She felt strongly that reporters must remain skeptical of what presidents say, and have the courage to ask tough questions to get complete information for the public. Thomas argued that the news media have often failed to challenge falsehoods. The foremost example is the Iraq War. President George W. Bush claimed that Iraq supported the terrorist group Al Qaeda that attacked the United States in 2001. Bush also claimed Iraq threatened the United States with weapons of mass destruction. Although eventually proved false, these claims were effective in manipulating public opinion to support the American invasion of Iraq in 2003. The media generally failed to question the president's faulty reasoning and instead became what Thomas called "an echo chamber for White House pronouncements" (Thomas, 2006: 136).

Thomas's White House career ended abruptly in 2010 after she commented at a White House event that Israelis should stop occupying Palestinian land and go back to other countries in Europe and the United States. As a child of Lebanese parents, Thomas was well informed of Middle Eastern issues. She sympathized with the Palestinian experience in the conflict between Jewish Israel and Arab Palestine, in which Israel controls Palestinians in the West Bank with a military occupation. After her controversial remarks, she was accused of anti-Semitism. The backlash became so powerful that she was forced to resign her job as a columnist with Hearst Newspapers. For some scholars of news media, the political backlash Thomas received is evidence of the one-sidedness of the debate over Israel and Palestine in the United States. It was an ironic career ending for a woman who had devoted her life to free speech. Thomas died in 2013.

Dylan Bennett

FURTHER READING

Thomas, Helen. 1999. *Front Row at the White House: My Life and Times.* New York: Scribner.

Thomas, Helen. 2006. *Watchdogs of Democracy? The Waning Washington Press Corps and How It Has Failed the Public.* New York: Scribner.

BETTY FRIEDAN (1921–2006)

Betty Friedan's complex legacy for antisexist activists and students of feminist studies begins with her iconic work, *The Feminine Mystique*, published in 1963 to wide acclaim, popularity, and opposition. The book has often been credited with catalyzing the second-wave feminist movement, in which Friedan was a major figure and leader (she served as cofounder of the National Organization for Women [NOW], the National Women's Political Caucus, and the National Abortion and Reproductive Rights Action League [NARAL]). In *The Feminine Mystique*, she famously articulated "the problem that has no name," the condition of middle-class women in the United States at mid-century: this narrative revolves around the iconic figure of the (well-educated) housewife who, having sacrificed her potential career to support a husband and raise children, was left depressed and isolated, divorced in mid-life, and was struck with the impossibility of empowerment in the public sphere. Friedan's vision of liberation for the home-based reproductive laborer electrified many women who participated in feminist movements. But its exclusion of women whose lives and experiences of sexism did not fit this model has been the cause for further feminist theory and organizing. For instance, during the early formation of NOW, Friedan expressed horror at the presence and power of lesbians and lesbian politics in feminist networks, fearing that a movement focused on sex and sexual orientation would be the subject of ridicule. Her naming of lesbians as a "lavender menace" within feminism sparked outrage—and inspired a lesbian feminist organization, the Lavender Menace.

Friedan defined herself as an "equality" feminist for whom the passage of the ERA, equal pay legislation, and abortion access were the most natural and important movement goals. But her work was critiqued and opposed by those who understood their own identities (including intersectional notions of their identities as women) to be inextricable from structures of race, class, and nation—as well as gender/sex/sexuality. Friedan provided a foil for feminisms of color, working-class, socialist, anticolonial, and antiracist feminisms because she installed the white, well-educated, middle-class U.S. citizen woman as the privileged subject of feminism. Black feminist theorist bell hooks's 1984 *Feminist Theory: From Margin to Center* opens with a searing critique of Friedan's promotion of white, middle-class normativity as the basis of the feminist subject. For hooks, Friedan's importance to feminism dangerously marginalized working-class women who could never be "liberated" through exclusive focus on the realm of the private household, as it was not their (singular) site of oppression. As hooks argues, this model fails to account for working-class women who would be called on to perform the childcare and associated reproductive labor left behind by the liberated housewife who became a professional-class worker in a continually exploitative capitalist society.

Beginning in the 1970s, Friedan became an international activist focused on an "equal rights" agenda. As she and her fellow NOW members insisted, the problem of women's oppression was a part of, not an addendum to, other sociopolitical problems in need of radical reconfiguration. Paradoxically, in her work at the UN Conferences on Women, Friedan used this position to mobilize an essentialist notion of a "sisterhood" in which the realm of (public) "politics" would be sidelined in favor of a decontextualized focus on "women's issues." Friedan promoted policies that would influence the status of women across the globe; she also lauded U.S. feminism as an example for others, dismissing the contrary possibility that feminist movements in socialist or anticolonial formations might provide a model or partner for "first-world" feminists. Her legacy exemplifies both the power of an equal rights discourse and also white, liberal feminism's self-installation as the paradigmatic definition of feminism.

Brooke Lober

See also: Women's Liberation Movement.

FURTHER READING

Declaration of Mexico on the Equality of Women and Their Contribution to Development and Peace. 1975. Adopted at the World Conference of the International Women's Year, Mexico City, Mexico. June 19–July 2.
Friedan, Betty. 1963. *The Feminine Mystique*. New York: W.W. Norton.

Friedan, Betty. 1976. *It Changed My Life: Writing on the Women's Movement.* New York: Random House.

hooks, bell. 1984. *Feminist Theory: From Margin to Center.* Boston, MA: South End Press.

SHIRLEY CHISHOLM (1925–2005)

Shirley Chisholm challenged the status quo and advocated for the marginalized before, during, and after her political career. New York City residents elected her to the State Assembly in 1964. In 1968, she became the first black woman to be elected to the United States Congress. She ran for the presidency as a Democrat in 1972—the first woman to ever do so. The titles of her autobiographies, *Unbought and Unbossed* and *The Good Fight*, echo her tenacious approach to political office.

Chisholm's father encouraged her to see the beauty of her blackness; her mother instilled Christian values in her. As a child she was unafraid to speak her mind, and as an undergraduate she honed her speaking skills on the debate team at Brooklyn College. She was active in the National Association for the Advancement of Colored People (NAACP) and the League of Women Voters while attending Columbia University, where she earned a master's degree in elementary education.

Chisholm's political career spanned 18 years. Throughout, she concentrated on issues of concern in the black community and promoted programs to eradicate discrimination. At the 1972 Democratic National Convention, she declared her candidacy for president, knowing she had little chance to be chosen as the party's nominee. She later explained, "I ran because someone had to do it first," so that future women and non-whites would be regarded as serious candidates (Chisholm, 1973: 3). After the 1972 election she remained in Congress, serving seven terms for Brooklyn's 12th Congressional District, until 1982.

Chisholm was an impressive speaker. In the midst of the Vietnam War, she delivered her first speech as a member of Congress, where she proclaimed her decision to vote against any bill to fund the Department of Defense. Her speech attracted the attention of student groups, resulting in more than 100 visits to colleges where she was regularly encouraged to run for president. One of her better-known speeches was delivered to the House of Representatives. In it, she backed the Equal Rights Amendment and developed her thesis that "artificial distinctions between persons must be wiped out of the law" (Chisholm, 1970). Her campaign speeches often centered on economic justice for women and revealed her outrage at the discrepancy between men and women's salaries as well as the paucity of professional opportunities for women. She understood the intersectionality of race and sex. In one speech she asserted that "[t]he black woman lives in a society that discriminates against her on two counts. The black woman cannot be discussed in the same context as her Caucasian counterpart because of the twin jeopardy of race and sex which operates against her, and the psychological and political consequences which attend them" (Chisholm, 1974).

One of Chisholm's most controversial actions during her tenure in Congress was her visit to George Wallace, a political opponent and segregationist, in the hospital after an assassination attempt. She confided to him, "You and I don't agree, but you've been shot, and I might be shot, and we are both children of American democracy, so I wanted to come and see you" (Chisholm, 1973: 97). The controversy perplexed her and is one reason why, when she left office, she claimed she was often misunderstood.

Chisholm retired to Florida before her death in 2005. She continues to be known for her commitment to democratic ideals, social and economic justice, and living her life with integrity and courage.

Lori Walters-Kramer

FURTHER READING

Chisholm, Shirley. 1974. "The Black Woman in Contemporary America." America Radio Works. http://americanradioworks.publicradio.org/features/sayit-plain/schisholm.html.

Chisholm, Shirley. 1973. *The Good Fight*. New York: Harper & Row.

Chisholm, Shirley. 1970. "For the Equal Rights Amendment." American Rhetoric. http://www.americanrhetoric.com/speeches/shirleychisholmequalrights.htm.

Chisholm, Shirley. 1970. *Unbought and Unbossed*. New York: Avon.

DOLORES HUERTA (1930–)

Dolores Huerta is best known for her long career as a labor organizer and cofounder of the United Farm Workers union (UFW) alongside César Chávez (1927–1993). Though not as well known as many male leaders of the Civil Rights era, Huerta has been a powerful change agent for Mexican American men, women, and children laboring long hours in pesticide-rich fields and with little access to breaks, food, toilets, or shade.

Huerta was born in New Mexico to a father who worked as a coal miner, farm worker, and union activist before his election to the New Mexico state legislature. Although her father's activism influenced her, Huerta's parents divorced when she was young, and she was raised by her mother in Stockton, California. Huerta's mother was a cannery worker, waitress, and eventual owner of a restaurant and hotel; she modeled how a woman could make a public life for herself beyond the domestic space of the home and traditional motherhood. Huerta raised 11 children of her own, and her difficult experiences as both a mother and a woman in the fields provided insights into the gendered nature of farm worker's oppression. She raised awareness about sexual harassment, the impact of pesticides on women's bodies, and the need for women's leadership in unions and in government.

Huerta's influence in the UFW could be seen in the Delano grape pickers' strike (1965) and the coalitions she formed between strikers and consumers in the nationwide grape boycotts (1968–1969). In addition to organizing workers, Huerta sought political reform. She participated in voter registration campaigns and lobbied the federal and California state governments for the Aid to Dependent Children Bill (1963) and the Agricultural Labor Relations Act (1975); the latter act protected the collective bargaining rights of farm workers and established a board to review workers' grievances. She also advocated for stricter controls on pesticides known to be dangerous and sought improved public services, including health care access and bilingual driver's license exams.

After the success of the boycotts, Huerta became the first woman and Chicana/o to negotiate with the growers. As an outspoken Mexican American woman, she violated cultural expectations of submissiveness and domesticity, and as such she earned a number of nicknames, including *la pasionara* ("the passionate one"); *soldadera* (referencing women in the Mexican Revolution); and "dragon lady," given to her by opposing landowners. Huerta is unapologetic for her controversial negotiating style: "Why do we need to be polite to people who are making racist statements at the table, or making sexist comments?" (Chávez, 2005: 249).

In addition to her role in the UFW, Huerta cofounded the Coalition of Labor Union Women (1974), serves on the board of the Feminist Majority Foundation, campaigns on behalf of women seeking public office, and speaks on issues of social justice and public policy as the president of the Dolores Huerta Foundation. In recent years, she has been recognized for her diverse contributions for social, economic, and environment justice, and in 2011 she received the Presidential Medal of Freedom.

Christina Holmes

FURTHER READING

Chávez, Alicia. 2005. "Dolores Huerta and the United Farm Workers." In *Latina Legacies*, 240–54. Edited by Vicki Ruiz and Virginia Sanchez Korrol. New York: Oxford University Press.

Dolores Huerta Foundation. http://doloreshuerta.org/.

García, Mario T., ed. 2008. *A Dolores Huerta Reader.* Albuquerque: University of New Mexico Press.

Ruiz, Vicky. 1998. *From Out of the Shadows: Mexican Women in Twentieth-Century America.* New York: Oxford University Press.

RUTH BADER GINSBURG (1933–)

Supreme Court Justice Ruth Bader Ginsburg was the second woman ever to serve on the Supreme Court. Since graduating from law school in 1959, Ginsburg has fought for women's legal rights and equal protection under the law during her expansive career as a lawyer, a professor, and a judge.

Joan Ruth Bader was born on March 15, 1933, in Brooklyn, New York. Her mother, who died just before Ginsburg's high school graduation, taught her to value learning and encouraged her to invest in her education. She took her mother's encouragement to heart and studied government at Cornell University, graduating first among the women in her class. She married Martin Ginsburg right after graduation, and they both decided to pursue careers in law.

She enrolled in Harvard Law School with her husband, where she was one of nine women in a class of more than 500 students. She faced discrimination based on her gender while in law school—one Harvard dean asked her to justify taking the place where a man could be (Scanlon, 1999: 120). Despite such expressions of hostility and skepticism toward her, she was elected as the editor of the *Harvard Law Review*. After her husband graduated from Harvard and began work at a law firm in New York City, she transferred to Columbia Law School, where she tied for the top position in her graduating class.

Ginsburg struggled to find a job, despite her impressive performance in law school. She later said that "her status as 'a woman, a Jew, and a mother to boot' was 'a bit much' for prospective employers in those days" (Cushman, 2013: 487). She was eventually hired as a law clerk with a district court judge in New York, then went on to become the second woman to teach law at Rutgers University. Later, she became the first tenured woman law professor at the Columbia Law School.

Ginsburg did not become a lawyer intending to advance women's rights. However, after reading Simone de Beauvoir's *The Second Sex* in the early 1960s, she realized that much of the injustice she faced in her life was due to structural gender discrimination in American society, based on harmful gender stereotypes. She came to believe that the legal system should be a tool in fixing those inequalities.

In 1972, the American Civil Liberties Union (ACLU) established the Women's Rights Project and asked Ginsburg to lead its efforts. Over the next four years, she brought six gender discrimination cases to the Supreme Court and won five of them. Significantly, she fought for a heightened standard of review in gender discrimination cases, and finally won it in 1976, effectively establishing a legal framework for women's equality to men.

In 1980, President Jimmy Carter appointed her to the U.S. Court of Appeals for the District of Columbia Circuit. As a judge, she became known for her careful attention to detail and sensitivity to the fact that her decisions would affect real lives. She served on the U.S. Court of Appeals for 13 years and wrote more than 300 opinions that dealt with abortion rights, gay rights, and affirmative action. In 1993, President Bill Clinton nominated Ginsburg to serve on the Supreme Court. The Senate confirmed her with a 97–3 vote, and she was sworn in on August 10, 1993.

In 2014, she wrote the dissenting opinion in *Burwell v. Hobby Lobby Stores Inc.* The decision allowed closely held for-profit companies to refuse to include birth control in employees' health insurance plans. Instantly, Ginsburg's sharp dissent became an Internet sensation—especially after then-law student Shana Knizhnik started a Tumblr account called "Notorious R.B.G."—a reference to popular hip-hop artist Notorious B.I.G. The account became a "virtual shrine" to Ginsburg (Rand, 2015: 80) and turned her into a feminist icon.

Ginsburg's legal career has spanned more than 55 years. Over that time, she has helped create new legal precedent for equal protection for both men and women under the law and has become one of the most influential legal voices for women's rights.

Maggie Monson

FURTHER READING

Cushman, Clare, ed. 2013. *The Supreme Court Justices, Illustrated Biographies, 1789–2012*, 3rd ed. Los Angeles, CA: CQ Press.

Rand, Erin J. 2015. "Fear the Frill: Ruth Bader Ginsburg and the Uncertain Futurity of Feminist Judicial Dissent." *Quarterly Journal of Speech*, 101(1): 72–84.

Scanlon, Jennifer, ed. 1999. *Significant Contemporary American Feminists: A Biographical Sourcebook*. Westport, CT: Greenwood Press.

GLORIA STEINEM (1934–)

Gloria Steinem is an internationally acclaimed journalist and feminist. She studied government at Smith College and graduated Phi Beta Kappa. In the late 1950s and early 1960s, she served as director of the Independent Research Service, an organization funded in secret by the CIA (1976). In 1960, *Esquire* offered Steinem her first journalistic assignment, a story on the issue of contraception. Steinem's 1962 "Moral Disarmament" article, concerning the pressure women face to choose between marriage and a career, was published a year before Betty Friedan's *Feminine Mystique*. In 1963, Steinem worked undercover as a Playboy Bunny to expose the sexism employees faced at the New York Playboy Club. After the article "A Bunny's Tale" was published (accompanied by a photo of Steinem in costume), Steinem struggled to secure other assignments. Ironically, because she had appeared in print as a sex object, she was dismissed as too sexual to be taken seriously. Steinem persevered, however, and eventually secured journalistic success, cofounding the feminist magazine *Ms.* in 1972 (*Outrageous*, 1983: 74).

Today, Steinem is best recognized for her longstanding activism for women's rights, including abortion. In 1969, she covered an abortion speak-out for *New York Magazine* and felt what she called a "big click" (Pogrebin, 2011). Steinem had terminated a pregnancy at 22 and wished to help other American women secure safe and legal abortions without shame. Her fight for reproductive rights remains controversial today. When, for example, Steinem was interviewed by Land's End for their March 2016 feature, "Legends," anti-choice consumers expressed outrage. The clothing company promptly removed Steinem's interview from their website—a response that then angered pro-choice shoppers, who considered the decision an affront to women's rights. (Significantly, the interview did not address abortion. Steinem spoke instead for the need for an Equal Rights Amendment to secure gender equity) (Bukszpan, 2016).

Although abortion remains a central concern, Steinem has also campaigned for the Equal Rights Amendment, testifying before the 1970 Senate Judiciary in its favor. She also has raised awareness about the damage pornography poses to women and the endemic of female genital cutting, in such books as *Outrageous Acts and Everyday Rebellions* (1983), as well as in countless speeches, interviews, articles, and public appearances. Steinem advocated for same-sex marriage as early as 1970. Although she long rejected heterosexual marriage as oppressive to women, in 2000 she married David Bale at the home of Wilma Mankiller, the first woman principal chief of the Cherokee Nation. (Bale succumbed to cancer in 2003.)

Steinem has also forged lasting connections with other feminist leaders, notably Bella Abzug, an American lawyer who, alongside Steinem and Friedan, founded the National Women's Political Caucus. Today, Steinem continues to champion this collaborative spirit. When asked in a 2016 interview what advice she had for young feminists, Steinem emphasized: "Don't worry about what you *should* do; do whatever you can. And seek companions with shared values. If we're isolated, we come to feel powerless when we're not."

Some feminists critique Steinem for a white and cisgender focus, suggesting that she conflates "feminism" with the aims of white and straight women, excluding women of color and transwomen from her purview (Grey, 2016). In 2016, Steinem again stirred controversy when, in an interview with Bill Maher, she characterized young women who supported presidential candidate Bernie Sanders over Hillary Clinton as boy-crazy, remarking: "When you're young, you're thinking, 'Where are the boys? The boys are with Bernie.'" Later, Steinem claimed her words had been "misinterpreted."

In 1993, Steinem was inducted into the National Women's Hall of Fame in Seneca Falls, New York. Despite occasional mishaps and accusations of exclusionism, she remains at the forefront of the women's movement today.

Eden Elizabeth Wales Freedman

See also: *Ms.* Magazine; Women's Liberation Movement.

FURTHER READING

Bukszpan, Daniel. 2016. "How Land's End Suddenly Became an Abortion Battleground." *Fortune.* February 26.

Grey, Sarah. 2016. "An Open Letter to Gloria Steinem on Intersectional Feminism." *The Establishment*, February 8.

Harrington, Stephanie. 1976. "It Changed My Life." *The New York Times*, July 4.

Marcello, Patricia. 2004. *Gloria Steinem: A Biography.* Westport: Greenwood.

Pogrebin, Abigail. 2011. "How Do You Spell Ms." *New York*, October. http://nymag.com/news/features/ms-magazine-2011-11/.

Steinem, Gloria. 1983. *Outrageous Acts and Everyday Rebellions.* New York: Holt.

Steinem, Gloria. 2015. *My Life on the Road.* New York: Random House.

GERALDINE A. FERRARO (1935–2011)

Geraldine A. Ferraro was an esteemed trailblazer for women in American politics and held numerous political positions from the 1970s until her death in 2011. She was the first woman and first Italian American in American history to be nominated by a major political party (Democratic Party), as a candidate for national office. In the 1984 presidential election, Ferraro campaigned with Walter Mondale to be vice president and president, respectively. Many credit Ferraro's candidacy as shifting the political and social landscapes in America and permanently changing the gendered climate of American politics. Ferraro has been widely acknowledged as having paved the way for future generations of female politicians.

Originally from New York, Ferraro worked as a public school teacher before earning a law degree in 1960. Ferraro worked in real estate and did pro bono work for women, and eventually led the Special Victims Bureau of the Queens County District Attorney's Office, responsible for the prosecution of every case involving sex crimes, domestic violence, and/or child abuse. During the early years of Ferraro's legal career, Ferraro and her husband, John Zaccaro, had three children and worked to balance their personal and professional lives.

Ferarro was elected to the U.S. House of Representatives as a Democrat in 1978 and then reelected in 1980 and 1982. In the House, she worked in support of the Equal Rights Amendment and the Women's Economic Equity Act. As the child of an Italian immigrant, Ferraro's support of pro-choice policies caused major tensions within Italian Catholic communities. In the 1984 presidential election, Mondale and Ferraro lost to Ronald Reagan and George H. W. Bush. After the election, the House Ethics Committee announced that Ferraro and Zaccaro had misreported important financial information. Many supporters have claimed that the degree of scrutiny to which Ferraro was subjected was based largely on Ferraro's gender.

Ferraro campaigned unsuccessfully for a New York Senate seat in 1992 and again in 1998. Between these campaigns, President Bill Clinton appointed Ferraro as a United States Ambassador for the United Nations Commission on Human Rights, a position Ferraro occupied for four years. In 1994, Ferraro was elected into the National Women's Hall of Fame. Following a 1998 cancer diagnosis, Ferraro became an outspoken advocate on the disease. In 2008, Ferraro worked on Senator Hillary Clinton's 2008 presidential campaign against Senator Barack Obama, during which Ferraro took heat from supporters and opponents alike for making comments that some deemed to be racist. When Governor Sarah Palin received the Republican nomination for vice president in the 2008 election, Palin became the first woman since Ferraro to be nominated by a major political party for vice president.

Over the years, Ferraro published many articles and authored multiple popular books, including *My Story* in 1985 and *Changing History: Women, Power, and Politics* in 1993. In 2014, *Geraldine Ferraro: Paving the Way*, a feature documentary about Ferraro's life and career, premiered on Showtime in honor of Women's History Month.

Viki Peer

FURTHER READING

Ferraro, Geraldine. 1993. *Changing History: Women, Power, and Politics.* Wakefield, RI: Moyer Bell.

Geraldine Ferraro: Paving the Way. 2014. "Geraldine Ferraro: Paving the Way." http://www.ferraropavingtheway.com.

History, Art and Archives: United States House of Representatives. n.d. "Ferraro, Geraldine Anne." http://www.history.house.gov/People/Detail/13081.

Queens District Attorney's Office. 2014. "Special Victims Bureau." http://www.queensda.org/specialvictims.html.

ROSIE THE RIVETER

Rosie the Riveter lingers in the American imagination as a symbol of the fresh-faced bravery, patriotism, and selflessness of the American women who gamely stepped into manufacturing jobs vacated by new soldiers after the United States entered World War II. Beyond her context in WWII history, Rosie the Riveter has persisted as a feminist icon, a sign of women's workplace liberation, and a metaphor for American women's participation in the nation as citizens and workers.

The iconic "We Can Do It!" poster featuring the image of Rosie the Riveter sporting a red and white polka dot bandana and rolling up her blue uniform sleeve was created by J. Howard Miller for Westinghouse Electric and Manufacturing Company in late 1942. Norman Rockwell also created a Rosie the Riveter for the May 1943 cover of the *Saturday Evening Post.* Although "We Can Do It!" emerged as the most easily recognizable version of Rosie after the mid-1980s, during the war, Rockwell's Rosie vastly overshadowed Miller's. It is likely that the popular tune, "Rosie the Riveter," sung by Kay Kyser on radios across the nation in 1942, inspired both images. Though remarkably different in their composition, purpose, and style, audiences often conflate the two best-known Rosie the Riveter images. Both have contributed to the mythos of the young, white, female, American war worker.

Despite Rosie the Riveter's continued cultural position as a feminist icon, her liberation possibilities have been largely exaggerated in the American cultural imagination. Although the advertising and government propaganda campaigns (of which Rosie the Riveter was part) rapidly expanded the parameters of acceptable feminine behavior in response to the dramatically changing needs of the economy, the images of working women did not replace traditional expectations about the sexual division of labor or the limitations of proper femininity. Contrary to popular images, most women did not work as riveters; much higher percentages worked in "pink-collar" jobs as nurses, secretaries, and other female-designated positions. Even at the height of the war, only 37 percent of women worked (McEuen, 2011: 35). Furthermore, Rosie the Riveter imagery obscures the classed and racial reality of women workers. Contrary to popular images, the female workforce consisted largely of working-class wives, widows, divorcees, women of color, and students whose work arose from economic necessity more often than patriotic duty. Both

Miller's and Rockwell's Rosies are white women. Although women of color were much more likely than their white counterparts to work, they remain absent from mainstream wartime imagery.

This idealized image of the female wartime worker bolstered several facets of the American imagery surrounding the war, particularly in the decades since its conclusion. First, pretty, young, unmarried women war workers were meant to inspire courage among soldiers abroad and to imply that bravery on the battlefield guaranteed soldiers new sweethearts upon their safe return. Related to this message was the metaphor of the woman as the besieged nation. As such, she—and the nation—deserved all citizens' protection, dedication, and loyalty. Second, the war worker embodied the ideal spirit of the home front: hardworking, stoic, long suffering, and united for victory. Lastly, Rosie the Riveter reminded women that traditionally feminine qualities best equipped them to fulfill their civic and moral responsibilities as citizens. These messages became indelible components of the American ethos, and as such Rosie the Riveter endures as a symbol of American values, women's liberation, and the Greatest Generation.

Samantha L. Vandermeade

FURTHER READING

Gluck, Sherna Berger. 1987. *Rosie the Riveter Revisited: Women, The War, and Social Change.* Boston, MA: Twayne Publishers.

Honey, Maureen. 1984. *Creating Rosie the Riveter: Class, Gender, and Propaganda during World War II.* Amherst, MA: University of Massachusetts Press.

Kimble, James J. 2006. "Visual Rhetoric Representing Rosie the Riveter: Myth and Misconception in J. Howard Miller's "We Can Do It!" Poster." *Rhetoric & Public Affairs,* 9(4): 533–69.

Knaff, Donna B. 2012. *Beyond Rosie the Riveter: Women of World War II in American Popular Graphic Art.* Lawrence, KS: University of Kansas Press.

McEuen, Melissa A. 2011. *Making War, Making Women: Femininity and Duty on the American Home Front, 1941–1945.* Athens, GA: The University of Georgia Press.

BILLIE JEAN KING (1943–)

Billie Jean King's professional tennis career goes hand in hand with her fight for women's rights. In tennis and in all sports, King has actively worked to ensure women's rights and, later, LGBT rights. Arguably, her highest profile battle for equality was her 1973 tennis match against Bobby Riggs, dubbed the Battle of the Sexes, which aired on primetime television.

King's lengthy (1959–1990) tennis career was impressive, with 67 singles titles and 101 doubles titles (WTA, 2016). Her tennis prowess earned her the title of the *Sports Illustrated* Sportsman [sic] of the Year in 1972, becoming the first-ever female athlete to earn the honor. However, she became arguably even better known and respected for her tireless activism for women's rights, especially in the world of sports.

On September 20, 1973, King played an exhibition tennis match against Bobby Riggs, a retired top men's tennis player. King agreed to the match after Riggs's repeated public statements that women's tennis was inferior to men's and that he could beat any of the then-top players despite his age (at the time, Riggs was 53). The Battle of the Sexes match was televised live on ABC, with Howard Cosell calling the high-profile match. It attracted an estimated audience of over 50 million people (Tennis Channel, 2003). King beat Riggs in straight sets, 6–4, 6–3, 6–3. In interviews since the match, King has repeatedly acknowledged that for the advancement of women's rights, she had to win the match. " 'This was about history, getting us on to a more level playing field because of Title IX and the women's movement, all that was very close to my heart and very important to me,' " recalled King (Tennis Channel, 2003). King's victory, along with the passage of Title IX, are major landmarks in the public acceptance of women in sports.

In the early 1970s, King watched as tennis money increased for the networks and the male players while the female players' salaries languished. In 1973, just before Wimbledon, King, along with a few other female players, founded the Women's Tennis Association (WTA) in order create one tour for women's tennis and create a unified voice for more equitable pay. Today, the WTA is the governing body for women's tennis.

In 1974, King expanded her equal rights activism by founding the Women's Sports Foundation (WSF). Still active today, the WSF works to ensure women and girls access to sport. In 1981, King became the first professional athlete to publicly identify as a lesbian. She was outed as a result of a lawsuit. The revelation of King's sexual orientation cost her endorsements, money, and friendships. However, since that time, King has become a spokeswoman for LGBT rights, and in 2009 she earned the Presidential Medal of Freedom for "champion[ing] gender equality issues not only in sports, but in all areas of public life."

Still a well-respected activist, King has earned many honors, including being named one of the "100 Most Important Americans of the 20th Century" by *Life* Magazine (1990) and receiving the Arthur Ashe Courage Award (1999). King has been regularly cited as an idol and mentor to many high-profile tennis players, such as Chris Evert, Martina Navratilova, and Venus Williams.

Allison L. Harthcock

See also: Williams, Venus and Serena.

FURTHER READING

King, Billie Jean, and Christine Brennan. 2008. *Pressure Is a Privilege: Lessons I've Learned from Life and the Battle of the Sexes.* New York: LifeTime Media.

Naify, Marsha. 2013. "Billy Jean King." *Lesbian News*, 39(2).

"The Tennis Channel to Air Exclusive Event Marking 30th Anniversary of Historic Billie Jean King vs. Bobby Riggs 'Battle of the Sexes' Tennis Match." 2003. September 10. http://tennischannel.com/press_releases/the-tennis-channel-to-air-exclusive-event-marking-30th-anniversary-of-historic-billie-jean-king

-vs-bobby-riggs-battle-of-the-sexes-tennis-match-seotember-20-beginning-at-8-p-m-et-2/.

"'You've Got to Give People a Spectacle.'" 1998. *Business Week*, 3591: 66.

ANGELA DAVIS (1944–)

Angela Y. Davis, who was born in Birmingham, Alabama, is an American activist, writer, scholar, and public speaker. Initially deeply involved in activism regarding both civil rights and communism, Davis continues to dedicate herself to working for social and political rights, with a current focus on the prison system. As a radical black feminist activist who has at times championed black nationalism, Davis is a controversial figure for some, but her revolutionary contributions to feminist theory, prison abolition, and anti-imperialism movements are undeniable.

Davis completed her undergraduate degree in French at Brandeis University, studying under Herbert Marcuse (1898–1979). After studying at the Marxism-based Institute for Social Research in Frankfurt, Germany, with Theodor Adorno (1903–1969), a leading figure in theorizing cultural studies and cultural critique, Davis attended the University of Paris before returning to the United States. She resumed study with Marcuse at the University of California at San Diego, where she earned her master's degree. She then secured a PhD in philosophy from Humboldt University.

Davis began her academic career at the University of California, Los Angeles, and has also taught at San Francisco State University and the University of California Santa Cruz, where she currently holds the status of distinguished professor emerita in the history of consciousness and feminist studies departments.

In popular culture, Davis may be best known due to her 1970 arrest, subsequent time in prison, and eventual acquittal. During the August 1970 trial of the three men commonly known as the Soledad Brothers, weapons registered in Davis's name were used during a failed escape attempt. Davis was placed on the FBI's Most Wanted List and fled; she was eventually captured in New York City and imprisoned in California. A massive, multi-pronged movement for Davis's release began, raising awareness of her situation among the public, and after 16 months in prison, Davis was eventually released on bail and then acquitted of the charges.

In 1974, Davis published *Angela Davis: An Autobiography*, which detailed her incarceration and acquittal; *The New York Times* described it as "exemplary," and labeled it "an act of political communication" (Langer, 1974). While many of her books and essays draw on autobiographical material, Davis has no other fully autobiographical works; some biographies exist, but none appear to be sanctioned and acknowledged by Davis. The arrest and trial were also examined in a documentary coproduced by Jada Pinkett Smith, *Free Angela and All Political Prisoners* (2013), which featured interviews with Davis. The film won the NAACP Image Award for Outstanding Documentary. Other tributes and works about her include the Rolling Stones' song "Sweet Black Angel," which is dedicated to Davis, and John Lennon's song "Angela."

Davis has been a member of a number of organizations working toward social and political change over the years, including the Communist Party USA (primarily as part of the Che-Lumumba Club, an all-black part of the party), the Student Nonviolent Coordinating Committee (SNCC), and the Black Panthers. In 1980 and 1984, Davis ran for vice president of the United States on the Communist Party ticket. More recently, she helped found Critical Resistance, a group focused on prison abolition in the United States; she is also affiliated with an Australian organization that advocates for the rights of women in prison. In addition to her activist work, Davis has published significant scholarly work, including nine books as well as a number of essays and articles. Her work addresses gender, racial, LGBT, and economic inequality, focusing on the relationships between capitalism, imperialism, and inequality. As early as 1971, Davis identified the "judicial system and . . . the penal system" as "key weapons in the state's fight to preserve the existing conditions of class domination, therefore racism, poverty, and war" (Davis, 1998: 44). Today, this idea is more generally known as the prison-industrial complex to recognize that the penal system provides mutual profit for government and industry, and is also a means of enforcing racial and social control.

Jessica E. Birch

FURTHER READING

Davis, Angela Y. 1998. *The Angela Y. Davis Reader.* Edited by Joy James. Malden, MA: Blackwell Publishers.

Davis, Angela Y. 2013. *Angela Davis: An Autobiography.* New York: International Publishers.

Free Angela and All Political Prisoners. Film. Directed by Shola Lynch. Lionsgate, 2013.

Langer, Elinor. 1974. "Autobiography as an Act of Political Communication." *The New York Times.* https://www.nytimes.com/books/98/03/08/home/davis-auto-bio.html.

SALLY RIDE (1951–2012)

Sally Ride is most widely known as the first American woman astronaut to go into space. In addition to her success as an astronaut, Ride excelled as a tennis player, a scientist, a researcher, an educator, and an advocate for helping young women see their potential in the fields of science and technology.

From an early age, Ride excelled at athletic competition and briefly considered the possibility of becoming a professional tennis player. It was at Stanford University that she decided to refocus her efforts on astrophysics. During her doctoral studies, Ride and 8000 other individuals responded to NASA's job advertisement for mission specialists. For the first time, NASA explicitly encouraged both minority and female candidates to apply. After enduring grueling interviews and physical and psychological tests, Ride joined the 1978 class of astronauts.

During training, Ride learned to fly T-38 jets and spent hours in a simulator, learning to operate the space shuttle's robotic arm used for releasing and retrieving satellites. Her skills at manipulating the arm, along with her calm demeanor, earned her a spot on the STS-7 crew. The press was relentless. Reporters asked Ride questions ranging from "How does it feel to be a woman on an otherwise all-male crew?" to the more presumptuous, "Did you ever want to be a boy?" Ride and her crewmates tried to emphasize that gender made little difference in the shuttle and that Ride was chosen because of her qualifications. However, even NASA was uncertain how to accommodate a woman in space. At one point, for instance, NASA officials asked her if 100 tampons would suffice for her seven-day flight. "No. That would not be the right number," Ride said in response (Sherr, 2014: 145).

Ride proved that women could be successful in space, as she put her many hours of simulation practice to use releasing satellites into orbit. On June 24, 1983, she returned from her first space shuttle mission. However, her work for NASA was far from over. She served on a second shuttle crew in 1984 and played a critical role in the investigations following the deadly 1986 Challenger explosion and 2003 Columbia disaster.

After retiring from NASA in 1987, Ride became a professor at University of California San Diego. She also wrote children's books and founded Sally Ride Science, an organization intended to support student interest in science and technology. Ride understood that young girls and minorities often could not picture themselves as scientists. Through her books and lectures, Ride shared her experiences, hoping to demonstrate to students and educators that "scientists and engineers are diverse men and women with exciting careers" (Ride, 2009: 21).

Following Ride's death from pancreatic cancer in 2012, the public learned of her private, long-term relationship with Tam O'Shaughnessy, a woman whom Ride met playing tennis. Though some criticized Ride for not using her fame to further LGBTQ activism, others supported her choice to remain private because of her ties to NASA, a traditionalistic, conservative organization averse to public relations controversies.

Madelyn Tucker Pawlowski

FURTHER READING

Ride, Sally. 2009. "For the First Woman in Space, Science Is the First Frontier for Students' Dreams." *American School Board Journal*, 196: 21.
Sherr, Lynn. 2014. *Sally Ride: America's First Woman in Space.* New York: Simon & Schuster Paperbacks.

SONIA SOTOMAYOR (1954–)

Sonia Sotomayor was the first Latina and third woman to be appointed to the United States Supreme Court. As a self-described "Nuyorican" (UC Berkeley News, 2009), growing up in New York with the strong influence of her Puerto Rican–born parents and their cultural traditions, Sotomayor's identity and activist background came into play during her Supreme Court confirmation hearings. Since joining the Supreme Court in 2009, Sotomayor has often sided with the other justices who are considered liberal leaning in their interpretations of the law.

Sotomayor grew up in public housing in New York and attended Cardinal Spellman High School. She earned her undergraduate degree from Princeton University and her J.D. from Yale Law School. After serving in the District Attorney's office and in private practice, Sotomayor was nominated to the U.S. District Court by then-president George H. W. Bush. Here, she famously wrote the decision that ended the Major League Baseball strike, siding with the players. *The New York Times* noted that "she was widely

Justice Sonia Sotomayor is the first judge of Hispanic heritage to be appointed to the Supreme Court of the United States. She was nominated by the first African American president, Barack Obama. (Steve Petteway, Collection of the Supreme Court of the United States)

celebrated, at least in those cities with major-league teams, as the savior of baseball" (Stolberg, 2009). Sotomayor then went on to serve on the United States Court of Appeals from 1998 until her nomination to the Supreme Court in 2009.

Following her nomination to the Supreme Court by President Barack Obama, Sotomayor was critiqued by conservatives for a statement she made during a speech at the University of California Berkeley School of Law in 2001. Sotomayor, then serving as a federal appeals court judge, addressed gender and ethnicity in the judiciary. She said that "[w]hether born from experience or inherent physiological or cultural differences . . . our gender and national origins may and will make a difference in our judging." Conservatives asserted that Sotomayor's stance appeared to conflict with expectations that a judge should be impartial and objective. Noting that "there can never be a universal definition of wise," she added, "I would hope that a wise Latina woman with the richness of her experiences would more often than not reach a better conclusion than a white male who hasn't lived that life" (UC Berkeley News, 2009).

During her confirmation hearing, Sotomayor sought to clarify her comments. She told the Senate Judiciary Committee that her record demonstrated that life experience and personal views do not guide her judgments, adding that judges should "test themselves to identify when their emotions are driving a result, or their experiences are driving a result, and the law is not" (Goldstein, 2009). Her nomination to the Supreme Court was approved in the Senate by a 68–31 vote that broke down largely along party lines.

Supreme Court Justices seldom achieve celebrity status, but Sonia Sotomayor is an exception. Her memoir, *My Beloved World*, was published in 2013 and topped *The New York Times* bestseller list. At standing-room-only appearances on her book tour, Sotomayor spoke warmly and openly to audiences about her life and her career. Even the White House accommodated her busy public schedule: the swearing-in ceremony for Vice President Joe Biden's second term of office, with Justice Sotomayor presiding, was held in the morning instead of the afternoon because of a conflict with her scheduled reading at a Barnes & Noble in Manhattan. She has also appeared on *The Daily Show*, *The Colbert Report*, and *Sesame Street*, in an effort to make the Supreme Court more familiar and accessible.

Linda Levitt

FURTHER READING

Goldstein, Amy, Robert Barnes, and Paul Kane. 2009. "Sotomayor Emphasizes Objectivity, Explains 'Wise Latina' Remark." *Washington Post*, July 15. http://www.washingtonpost.com/wp-dyn/content/article/2009/07/14/AR2009071400992.html.

Sotomayor, Sonia. 2013. *My Beloved World*. New York: Knopf.

Stolberg, Sheryl Gay. 2009. "Sotomayor, a Trailblazer and a Dreamer." *The New York Times*, May 26. http://www.nytimes.com/2009/05/27/us/politics/27websotomayor.html?pagewanted=all&_r=0&module=ArrowsNav&contentCollection=Politics&action=keypress&region=FixedLeft&pgtype=article.

UC Berkeley News. "A Latina Judge's Voice: Judge Sonia Sotomayor's 2001 Address to the 'Raising the Bar' Symposium at the UC Berkeley School of Law." http://www.berkeley.edu/news/media/releases/2009/05/26_sotomayor.shtml.

WINONA LADUKE (1959–)

Two-time Green Party vice-presidential candidate Winona LaDuke is an internationally renowned scholar and activist best known for her work on Native American rights and environmental issues. LaDuke, an Anishinaabekwe (Ojibwe) enrolled member of the Mississippi Band Anishinaabeg, was born in Los Angeles, California, on August 18, 1959, and raised in Ashland, Oregon. In 1977, 18-year-old LaDuke spoke at the International Non-Governmental Organization Conference on Discrimination Against Indigenous Populations in the Americas, which marked a pivotal moment in the then burgeoning indigenous peoples' movement. For the first time in history, the United Nations (UN) opened its doors to indigenous delegates who called for a number of stipulations including, but not limited to, the establishment of a UN Working Group on Indigenous Populations. LaDuke's expert testimony on how the exploitation of natural resources impacts the indigenous peoples of North America set the stage for her continued activism at the intersection of Native American and environmental issues.

After graduating from Harvard University in 1982, she moved to the White Earth Reservation in Minnesota, where she later founded the White Earth Land Recovery Project (WELRP). Dedicated to recovering the original reservation territory—land that belongs to White Earth tribal members—WELRP directs a wide range of community-based programs focusing on cultural conservancy and, in particular, traditional agriculture (LaDuke, 1999: 115–39). LaDuke's work draws attention to the fact that for Anishinaabeg—indeed, for all indigenous peoples—land is inextricably linked to culture. By restoring local food systems as well as sacred foods (e.g., *manoomin*, or wild rice), the Anishinaabeg not only preserve and protect this link, they also fight against ecological destruction (LaDuke, 2005: 167–91).

Of particular importance to WELRP's mission is seed sovereignty, or the right of farmers to cultivate seeds versus the right of corporations to own them. LaDuke frequently speaks out about how native seeds, in addition to heritage crops, contain life as well as indigenous people's culture, history, and even ancestry. In 2013, she rode horseback along the Enbridge Corporation's proposed oil pipeline expansion, which would have cut through tribal treaty territory, including the White Earth reservation as well as two wild rice lakes. LaDuke remains at the forefront of this ongoing battle against Enbridge to protect indigenous people's land and the planet at large from further destruction caused by faulty pipes.

LaDuke likewise connects the violation of indigenous people's land to the violation of indigenous women's bodies, further contributing to the scope of environmental justice activism. In an effort to amplify and unite the voices of indigenous women on environmentalism, she established the Indigenous Women's Network alongside more than 200 indigenous women in 1985. In 1993, she cofounded Honor the Earth with The Indigo Girls (Amy Ray and Emily Saliers) to promote national awareness about Native environmental issues and fundraise for grassroots Native environmental groups. Among the organization's many groundbreaking initiatives is a campaign to end sexual violence against indigenous women in the Great Lakes region, where natural resource extraction is at an all-time high. For LaDuke, both resource extraction and the alarming rates of sexual violence in extraction zones evidence the enduring legacy of settler colonialism in North America.

LaDuke is a former board member of Greenpeace USA, an international environmental nonprofit organization. In 1994, *Time* Magazine named her one of America's 50 most promising leaders under 40 years of age, and in 1997 LaDuke was named *Ms.* Magazine Woman of the Year for her work with Honor the Earth. She has received many prestigious fellowships and awards, among them the Thomas Merton Award, the BIHA Community Service Award, the Ann Bancroft Award for

Women's Leadership Fellowship, the Reebok Human Rights Award, the Global Green Award, and the International Slow Food Award. In 2007, LaDuke was inducted into the National Women's Hall of Fame.

Tala Khanmalek

FURTHER READING

LaDuke, Winona. 1999. *All Our Relations: Native Struggles for Land and Life.* Cambridge, MA: South End Press.

LaDuke, Winona. 2005. *Recovering the Sacred: The Power of Naming and Claiming.* Cambridge, MA: South End Press.

Nelson, Melissa K., ed. 2008. *Original Instructions: Indigenous Teachings for a Sustainable Future.* Rochester, VT: Bear and Company.

Notes, Akwesasne, ed. 1978. *A Basic Call to Consciousness.* Summertown, TN: Native Voices.

Smith, Andrea. 2005. *Conquest: Sexual Violence and American Indian Genocide.* Cambridge, MA: South End Press.

WOMEN'S LIBERATION MOVEMENT

The women's liberation movement is a term often used to describe the quest undertaken by American women activists in the 1960s and 1970s to lift women up to a position of social, political, and legal equality with men. Among some feminist activists and historians, however, the term is sometimes used to reference the most radical and anti-patriarchal segments of that movement.

Prior to the 1960s, the opportunities for most American women to chart their own paths in life were circumscribed by cultural traditions and legal restrictions that were deeply entrenched in American society. This state of affairs was generally defended by its male architects, who benefited from their advantageous position in a host of ways. But in the late 1950s and early 1960s a confluence of events and trends laid the foundation for a political and cultural uprising against this male-dominated society. These factors included simmering resentments against a world in which women were expected to willingly accept subordinate roles in marriage and society and make due with employment in a handful of low-wage, traditionally "female" professions. During the economic boom of the 1950s and early 1960s, though, the sheer demand for workers became so great that women were increasingly able to break out of the "homemaker" straitjacket and find jobs outside the home. Women also drew inspiration—and experience in political organizing and activism—from the American Civil Rights Movement.

Even women who managed to gain a foothold in the world outside their homes, though, often found themselves at a disadvantage. Women in the workplace had no legal recourse when confronted with gender discrimination or sexual harassment, and they ran the risk of being fired if they became pregnant. Meanwhile, girls and women who chose to pursue non-traditional dreams still found themselves subjected to harassment, hostility, and ridicule. Women of color had it even worse, typically unable to land jobs beyond the service sector.

The women's liberation movement of the 1960s and 1970s—sometimes called the second wave of feminism (the first being the original suffragist movement)—emerged in response to this environment of continued inequality. Some of these early activists, such as Betty Friedan and the women who embraced the National Organization for Women (NOW) after its founding in 1966, were primarily interested in pursuing gender equality in American institutions and laws. As NOW itself stated, its goal was "to take action to bring women into full participation in the mainstream of American society, exercising all privileges and responsibilities thereof in true equal partnership with men." Others had an even more ambitious goal—to completely uproot the patriarchal foundations of American thought and thus "liberate" women to have complete agency over their own lives. These latter activists "popularized the idea that 'the personal is political'—that women's political inequality had equally important personal ramifications, encompassing their relationships, sexuality, birth control and abortion, clothing and body image, and roles in marriage, housework, and childcare" (Tavaana, n.d.).

Together, these linked but distinct campaigns had a transformative impact on American society, despite the fact that the relationship between the two wings was often strained. Utilizing everything from court challenges in order to end legally sanctioned gender discrimination in employment, education, high school and college sports, and financial lending to provocative demonstrations that took aim at beauty pageants and bridal fairs, activists registered a series of gains that helped break down many barriers confronting women in the United States. These victories were made possible in large measure because of their success in enlisting public support for their goals. But their quest to pass an Equal Rights Amendment (ERA) that would formally enshrine gender equality in the U.S. Constitution fell short—perhaps because the sense of urgency that drove support for the ERA in the first place diminished as women tallied victories in America's political, legal, and cultural arenas.

Ann M. Savage

See also: Betty Friedan; Gloria Steinem.

FURTHER READING

Collins, Gail. 2009. *When Everything Changed: The Amazing Journey of American Women from 1960 to the Present*. New York: Little, Brown.

Echols, Alice. 1989. *Daring to Be Bad: Radical Feminism in America, 1967–1975*. Minneapolis, MN: University of Minnesota Press.

Freeman, Jo. 1975. *The Politics of Women's Liberation: A Case Study of an Emerging Social Movement and Its Relation to the Policy Process*. New York: Longman.

Tavaana. n.d. "The 1960s–1970s American Feminist Movement: Breaking Down Barriers for Women." Accessed May 8, 2017. https://tavaana.org/en/content/1960s-70s-american-feminist-movement-breaking-down-barriers-women.

VENUS WILLIAMS (1980–) AND SERENA WILLIAMS (1981–)

Venus and Serena Williams have been trendsetters since they entered the professional tennis circuit in 1994 and 1995, respectively. Throughout their lengthy professional careers, they have fought for equal pay and stood up to racism in a largely white sport. In addition to their activism, they have also been innovators off the court. Both have engaged in entrepreneurial and philanthropic endeavors throughout their tennis careers.

Simply by virtue of their presence as African Americans in a largely white sport, the Williams sisters have changed the face of U.S. tennis. Coached by their father, Richard Williams, and playing on public courts in Compton, California, the Williams sisters took a nontraditional path to the professional tennis circuit. Early in their careers, their background was presented as a detriment or disadvantage to the sisters. However, the Williams sisters have dominated the Women's Tennis Association (WTA) for over two decades. Despite or perhaps, in part, because of their domination, the sisters have been subject to racist coverage, depictions, and statements throughout their careers.

Venus Williams has been ranked number one repeatedly, earned 49 singles titles, 22 doubles titles, four Olympic gold medals (one for singles and three for doubles) and has earned over $34 million in career prize money to date, making her the third highest earning woman tennis player (WTA, 2016).

In 2005, Venus Williams met with Wimbledon officials to demand equal pay for women, to no avail. In 2006, Venus published an essay in *The Times* (London), entitled "Wimbledon has sent me a message: I'm only a second-class champion," which sparked then–prime minister Tony Blair and several members of Parliament to publicly endorse her position. Later that year, Venus was asked to lead a joint WTA and UNESCO campaign for gender equality in sports. In 2007, Wimbledon gave into public pressure to award equal pay to women. Shortly thereafter, the French Open followed suit. Many people argue that it was Venus's public pressure during a time of her professional dominance that resulted in this significant shift toward equal rights for women in tennis.

Beyond her on-court accomplishments, Venus is an entrepreneur, starting her own fashion line, Ele11en, and interior design company, V*Starr.

Serena Williams's professional accomplishments are unparalleled: she has been ranked number one repeatedly, earned 71 singles titles, 23 doubles titles, four Olympic gold medals (one for singles and three for doubles), and has earned over $80 million in career prize money to date, making her the highest earning woman in tennis by over $50 million (WTA, 2016).

Serena's entrepreneurial endeavors include creating an athletic fashion line designed for Nike; a clothing line for HSN; and, most recently, launching her own clothing line, Aneres. Serena's philanthropic endeavors include being named a UNICEF Goodwill Ambassador in 2011, opening two secondary schools in Kenya, and backing the Equal Justice Initiative, which works to end mass incarceration and challenge racial and economic injustice in the United States.

As competitors, the sisters have faced controversy compounded by racism. At the 2001 Indian Wells Masters tournament in California, Venus withdrew from her semifinal match against her sister. Rumors swirled that their father, Richard, was arranging which sister should win the tournament. After the withdrawal, Serena played Kim Clijsters in the finals the next day. During that match, Serena was booed by the crowd throughout the match and her championship presentation. Venus and her father were booed as they entered the stands to watch Serena's match. Citing the racist vitriol they faced from the crowd, neither Williams sister played the tournament again until 2015, when Serena returned to Indian Wells. In an essay she wrote for *Time* Magazine, Serena shared her terrifying experience at the 2001 Indian Wells tournament. Citing the changes in tennis, such as the WTA's and U.S. Tennis Association's (USTA) swift and public condemnation of racist and sexist comments from a Russian tennis official, along with her own professional growth and accomplishments, Serena decided it was time to return to Indian Wells. To make her return even more powerful, Serena raffled off the opportunity to stand with her at Indian Wells. All proceeds went to the Equal Justice Initiative.

Allison L. Harthcock

See also: Billy Jean King.

FURTHER READING

Djata, Sundiata A. 2008. *Blacks at the Net: Black Achievement in the History of Tennis, Volume 2: Sports and Entertainment.* Syracuse, NY: Syracuse University Press.

Williams, Serena. 2015. "I'm Going Back to Indian Wells," *Time* Magazine, February 4. http://time.com/3694659/serena-williams-indian-wells/.

Williams, Serena, and Daniel Paisner. 2010. *My Life: Queen of the Court.* London: Pocket.

Williams, Venus. "Wimbledon Has Sent Me a Message: I'm Only a Second-Class Champion," *The Times* (London), June 26, 2006. http://www.thetimes.co.uk/tto/sport/tennis/article2369985.ece.

ALISON BECHDEL (1960–)

Alison Bechdel is a critically acclaimed writer and cartoonist. Her first successful publication, considered a cult classic, was the long-running, witty, and controversial comic strip on lesbian culture called *Dykes to Watch Out For (DTWOF)*. The comic strip, which ran from 1983–2008, appeared in several gay and lesbian newspapers, such as the *Chicago Tribune*'s WomanNews and Between the Lines, and was later published on the Web.

Considered to be one of the first North American pop culture representations on lesbians, *DTWOF* offered a comical, yet critical, commentary on topical political issues. Characters discussed contemporary events, including gay pride parades, popular protests, and women's marches as well as their experiences of love, intimacy, trauma, sexism, and homophobia. Importantly, these topics were regularly debated among a diverse group of characters who came from different racial groups and class backgrounds. Based on their different social locations, each character offered a unique perspective on various political issues. The representation of different identities and intersectional politics (the interconnections of oppression, such as sexism and racism) in *DTWOF* challenged the stereotypical overgeneralization that categorized lesbian feminists as a monolithic group of white middle-class women. Other works by Bechdel include *The New York Times* best-selling graphic memoir *Fun Home* (2006), which chronicles her childhood relationship with her gay father, who committed suicide, and her award-winning companion novel *Are You My Mother?*, which was published in 2012.

Bechdel is also well known for her development of the so-called Bechdel Test to assess the active presence of women in a work of fiction. Although mainly applied to movies, the test—which was first introduced in Bechdel's 1985 comic strip entitled "The Rule" from *DTWOF*—has also been used to assess the representation of women in video games and novels. In order to pass the Bechdel Test three criteria must be satisfied: (1) there must be at least two women; (2) the women must talk to each other; and (3) they must talk about something other than a man. Some variations of the test require that the two women have names and that they talk to each other for at least 60 seconds.

Bechdel credits the idea for the test to her friend Liz Wallace, and therefore the test is also sometimes referred to as the Bechdel-Wallace Test. Other names include the Bechdel Rule and the Mo Movie Measure (the latter is named after the main character in *DTWOF*). The test gained mainstream popularity in 2009, when feminist cultural critic Anita Sarkeesian referenced "The Rule" in a video on her YouTube channel *Feminist Frequency*. Although the test is a quick and easy way to gauge the presence of women in fictional works and, as such, has become a standard feminist tool to analyze media, the test does not indicate whether a work has sexist content or not. It is also possible that a fictional work about women or with predominantly female characters can also fail the test. However, the Bechdel Test is useful because it helps point out that the lack of relevant and meaningful roles of women in mainstream media is a systemic issue and reoccurring pattern. Several studies have applied the Bechdel Test to box office movies and found that approximately half of the films fail the test (see Hunt, Ramon, and Proce, 2014; Smith et al., 2014). The Bechdel Test has inspired several other tests, including the Russo Test, which analyzes the representation of LGBTQ characters in fictional work, and the POC (people of color) Test, which examines the development and presence of characters of color in television and movies.

Andie Shabbar

FURTHER READING

Bechdel, Alison. 2001. "Dykes to Watch Out For." *Dykestowatchoutfor.com*. http://dykestowatchoutfor.com.

Bechdeltest.com. 2014. "Bechdel Test Movie List". http://bechdeltest.com.

Hunt, Darnell, Ana-Christina Ramon, and Zachary Proce. 2014. *2014 Hollywood Diversity Report: Making Sense of the Disconnect.* California: Ralph J. Bunche Center for African America Studies at UCLA. http://www.bunchecenter.ucla.edu/wp-content/uploads/2014/02/2014-Hollywood-Diversity-Report-2-12-14.pdf.

Sarkeesian, Anita. 2009. *The Bechdel Test for Women in Movies.* Video. https://www.youtube.com/watch?v=bLF6sAAMb4s.

Smith, Stacy, Marc Choueiti, Katherine Pieper, Traci Gillig, Carmen Lee, and Dylan DeLuca. 2016. *Inequality in 700 Popular Films: Examining Portrayals of Character Gender, Race, & LGBT Status from 2007 to 2014.* Media, Diversity, & Social Change Initiative. California: USC Annenberg School for Communication and Journalism. http://annenberg.usc.edu/pages/~/media/MDSCI/Inequality%20in%20700%20Popular%20Films%208215%20Final%20for%20Posting.ashx.

UNITED STATES V. WINDSOR (2013)

United States v. Windsor is a 2013 decision of the United States Supreme Court that paved the way for the legalization of same-sex marriage two years later in *Obergefell v. Hodges* (2015). In *Windsor*, the Supreme Court declared unconstitutional Section 3 of the 1996 Defense of Marriage Act (DOMA), which defined marriage for federal purposes as the legal union between one man and one woman. Because of DOMA, same-sex couples that were treated as married under the law of the state where they lived were not treated as married for federal purposes.

This became a problem for Edith Windsor, the surviving member of a married same-sex couple who lived in New York. Windsor's spouse, Thea Spyer, died and left her entire estate to Windsor. Ordinarily, spouses are allowed to leave each other money tax-free upon death, but the Internal Revenue Service denied Windsor's claim, saying that the couple had not been married for federal purposes. Windsor successfully sued for a tax refund in the United States District Court for the Southern District of New York, on the grounds that DOMA was unconstitutional. The Court of Appeals for the Second Circuit affirmed the District Court's judgment. The case was appealed to the United States Supreme Court by a Bipartisan Legal Advisory Group (BLAG) of the House of Representatives.

The involvement of the BLAG was precipitated by the refusal of the attorney general of the United States to defend the constitutionality of DOMA (although the Attorney General said that the government would continue to uphold the law). The BLAG decided to intervene in the case to defend DOMA, so the first issue before the Supreme Court was whether the Court had jurisdiction to hear an appeal, given the Department of Justice's decision not to defend the law. The second issue was whether the BLAG had the authority to intervene in the case. The third, and perhaps more controversial, issue was whether Section 3 of DOMA violated the

Fifth Amendment's guarantee of equal protection in treating only married opposite-sex couples as spouses for federal tax (and other) purposes.

In a 5–4 decision, the Supreme Court ruled that it had proper jurisdiction, that BLAG was a proper party to the case, and that DOMA was unconstitutional. Writing for the majority, Justice Anthony Kennedy emphasized the "equal dignity of same-sex marriages, a dignity conferred by the States in the exercise of their sovereign power" (*Windsor*, 2013: 133). In liberal and progressive circles, the immediate reaction to the *Windsor* decision on June 26, 2013, was one of outright jubilation, as this represented a tremendous stride forward for LGBT rights in general and for same-sex marriage in particular. Windsor and her attorney, Roberta Kaplan of Paul, Weiss Rifkin, Wharton & Garrison LLP, immediately went on a "triumphal lap" around Manhattan, during which people swarmed their car and chanted Windsor's name in triumph (Levy, 2013).

For many people, the *Windsor* decision represented the culmination of a multi-decades quest for marriage equality. Others, such as conservatives, were dismayed at the federal recognition of same-sex marriage. Both before and after the *Windsor* decision, even some supporters of lesbian and gay civil rights were critical of the investment of institutional and political resources in securing a right for same-sex couples to marry. In 1989, attorney Paula Ettelbrick famously asked, "Since when is marriage a path to liberation?" drawing attention to the patriarchal and historically oppressive aspects of the institution of marriage (1989). Edith Windsor also fit many socially acceptable and preferred norms. She is white, attractive, wealthy, well educated and was in a long-term, monogamous relationship. Substantively speaking, her case involved the estate tax, which applies only to the wealthiest Americans. The case nevertheless has historic importance. It represented formal Supreme Court recognition of same-sex couples and laid the groundwork for same-sex marriage.

Aurora Grutman

FURTHER READING

Ettelbrick, Paula. 1989. "Since When Is Marriage a Path to Liberation?" *Out/Look*, 9: 14–16.

Levy, Ariel. 2013. "The Perfect Wife." *The New Yorker*, September 30. http://www.newyorker.com/magazine/2013/09/30/the-perfect-wife.

Obergefell v. Hodges, 135 S. Ct. 2584 (2015).

United States v. Windsor, 133 S. Ct. 2675 (2013).

SIX

On the Web

The introduction of the World Wide Web transformed the flow of information and how human beings communicate with each other and to the world. Long-established organizations working on behalf of women's rights could now develop a Web presence and reach out to the public like never before. Reproductive rights organizations, such as Planned Parenthood and NARAL Pro-Choice America, developed and maintain websites as a way to promote their cause. Print publications moved to the Web too. *Our Bodies, Ourselves* was the go-to resource for women seeking more information about women's health since the 1970s. The website now allows for greater accessibility to an even wider audience. Established feminist print magazines *Ms.* as well as *Bitch Media* (formerly *Bitch Magazine*) developed an online presence and made online journalism an important part of their profile. General feminist women's advocacy organizations such as the Feminist Majority Foundation also moved online. Finally, the advent of the Internet age also spurred the creation of new women's advocacy organizations like Feminist.com, Feministing.com, Jezebel.com, and Feministfrequency.com.

PLANNED PARENTHOOD (PLANNEDPARENTHOOD.ORG) (1916–)

Planned Parenthood Federation of America (PPFA) is rooted in the feminist reproductive politics, movements, and history of the United States. PPFA is a national and international nonprofit organization. It offers reproductive health care, social services, educational resources, research, and policy advocacy for reproductive health, justice, and rights for women, men, and adolescents. It was founded by Margaret Sanger (1879–1966), a nurse from a working-class background, who first used the term "birth control." In 1916, when contraception was still illegal, Sanger opened the first U.S. birth control clinic in Brooklyn, New York, to distribute information on contraception.

Since 2015, the *I Stand With Planned Parenthood* slogan has become a widespread cultural-political symbol of the pro-choice public's support for Planned Parenthood against disparaging action by *anti-choice* activists and conservative government leaders. Through material production and social media such as hashtags, Twitter, and Facebook, the slogan promoted the pro-choice public's desires for reproductive freedom. Sanger once said, "The problem of birth control has arisen directly from the effort of the feminine spirit to free itself from bondage"(Sanger, 1931). Sanger understood "bondage" through witnessing, as a nurse, extreme health conditions from immigrant families in New York City's Lower East Side as a result of unwanted pregnancy and illegal abortions. Sanger opened her birth control clinic because of society's unwillingness to attend to these deplorable health and social conditions for many families. Today, *I Stand With Planned Parenthood* and its supporters resists such historical bondage and addresses similar contemporary social concerns.

Furthermore, *I Stand With Planned Parenthood* silently reconciles Planned Parenthood's controversial adverse history. Margaret Sanger's beliefs and intentions to reduce unwanted pregnancies were not just among married middle- and working-class white women but also among poor women of color. In the 1920s, Sanger believed that poor women exposed to too many pregnancies were a health and social problem. This contributed to the rise of eugenic beliefs in breeding superior, "wanted" children and elimination of the "unfit" as a solution to social problems (Freedman, 2002). Although Sanger briefly allied herself with leaders of the eugenics movement, popular in the United States and Europe at that time, Planned Parenthood has long committed to combat such oppressive racial theories.

I Stand With Planned Parenthood is recognition of social and medical progress. For example, during the Great Depression of the 1930s, women relied on the diaphragm, either fitted in doctors' offices or in the expanding number of birth control clinics sponsored by Planned Parenthood. In the 1960s, as more women entered the workforce, feminists challenged society's rigid sexual mores toward women's right to choose voluntary motherhood. By 1965, when the U.S. Supreme Court decision *Griswold v. Connecticut* guaranteed the right of married couples nationwide to use contraception, many women were already controlling their fertility with the new oral contraceptive pill, which had been approved in 1960. Planned Parenthood fought heavily to legalize abortions in the 1970s. After the *Roe v. Wade* Supreme Court decision in 1973, Planned Parenthood leaders pushed to protect the abortion rights of vulnerable women by supporting legislation to keep such procedures private and affordable.

Supporters of Planned Parenthood characterize *I Stand With Planned Parenthood* as a cultural and political recognition of a rich history of advocacy and resistance against governmental control of reproductive rights during the presidential years of Richard Nixon, Ronald Reagan, George H. W. Bush, and George W. Bush. *I Stand With Planned Parenthood* is both a cultural production and a movement because of its wide reach. In 2013, Planned Parenthood served 2.7 million women, men, and young people in the United States, Latin America, and the Caribbean. Only 3 percent of the services provided by the organization are for abortions.

Nessette Falu

See also: Margaret Sanger; Feminist Majority Foundation; Women's Liberation Movement.

FURTHER READING

Freedman, Estelle B. 2002. *No Turning Back: The History of Feminism and the Future of Women.* New York: Ballantine Books.

Planned Parenthood Federation of America. 2016. "History & Successes." https://www.plannedparenthood.org/about-us/who-we-are/history-successes.

Roberts, Dorothy E. 1997. *Killing the Black Body: Race, Reproduction, and the Meaning of Liberty.* New York: Vintage Books.

Sanger, Margaret. 1920/1991. "Birth Control: A Parent's Problem or Woman's?" In *The Gender Reader*, edited by E. Ashton-Jones and Gary A. Olson. Boston: Allyn and Bacon.

Sanger, Margaret. 1931. "Awakening and Revolt." In *The Gender Reader*, edited by E. Ashton-Jones and Gary A. Olson. Boston: Allyn and Bacon.

NARAL PRO-CHOICE AMERICA (NARAL.ORG) (1969–)

From its inception in 1969, NARAL, a pro-choice advocacy group, has publicly pledged its mission of protecting and preserving reproductive freedom for women, specifically the right to a safe, legal abortion. Although the acronym behind NARAL has changed many times to reflect the status of abortion laws, it has remained the leading abortion rights organization in America. NARAL is the principal source of choice-related information at the state level, with 22 state chapters and affiliates, and works to secure reproductive rights for future generations in the face of anti-choice legislation (NARAL, 2016). This organization recognizes that reproductive rights are at the heart of gender inequality, arguing that women cannot be fully equal without control over their own reproduction. Therefore, it promotes abortion as a fundamental right that must be secured through education, training, organization, legal action, and public policy.

NARAL was founded by American doctor Bernard Nathanson (1926–2011) and feminist scholar Betty Friedan (1921–2006) as the National Association for the Repeal of Abortion Laws. After the U.S. Supreme Court ruled in the monumental abortion case *Roe v. Wade* (1973) that women should be able to personally decide whether to have an abortion based on their constitutional right to privacy, the organization shifted its focus. It moved from an emphasis on making abortion legal to protecting the right against legislative efforts to weaken it, such as the Hyde Amendment (1976), which banned the use of federal funds for abortion except in the cases of incest, rape, or to save the life of the mother. Although the organization continues to concentrate on legal disputes, it changed its name to NARAL Pro-Choice America in 2003 to highlight how America is a pro-choice nation. Because over half of Americans support legal access to abortion, the organization rebranded itself to reflect popular opinion while opposing abortion stigma and antichoice cultures (NARAL, 2016).

Although NARAL has always been dedicated to abortion rights, it has expanded its focus to include birth control, sexual education, and healthy pregnancies, including preventing unintended pregnancies and bearing healthy children. These four areas are interconnected, as they impact access to reproductive health care, gender inequality, and women's ideological positioning in society. Additionally, this organization works to shatter the stigma and silence around abortion through education, especially for younger generations, and legal action. Its fight for equal and safe access to abortion has intensified with the implementation of what many refer to as Targeted Regulation of Abortion Provider (TRAP) laws. NARAL's controversies typically manifest politically, through efforts to shape policy; and socially, through stigma, denouncement, and violence from groups whose opposition to abortion or access to birth control is undertaken in the name of a 'pro-life' philosophy. In the face of opposition, this organization exposes pro-life anti-choice legislation and access barriers to reproductive health services while working to develop and sustain a political constituency dedicated to guaranteeing autonomy in sexual health.

Supporters of NARAL Pro-Choice America describe it as an important historical, social, and political organization working to support and protect a woman's freedom to make personal decisions regarding reproductive choices. Moreover, defenders say that the organization is an important voice for equality and fundamental human rights for all people.

Skye de Saint Felix

See also: Margaret Sanger; Women's Liberation Movement.

FURTHER READING

Condit, Celeste. 1990. *Decoding Abortion Rhetoric: Communicating Social Change.* Urbana, IL: University of Illinois Press.

Marty, Robin, and Jessica Mason Pieklo. 2013. *Crow after Roe: How "Separate but Equal" Has Become the New Standard in Women's Health and How We Can Change That.* Brooklyn: Ig Publishing.

"NARAL Pro-Choice America." n.d. http://www.prochoiceamerica.org.

Page, Cristina. 2006. *How the Pro-Choice Movement Saved America: Freedom, Politics, and the War on Sex.* Cambridge, MA: Basic Books.

OUR BODIES OURSELVES (OURBODIESOURSELVES.ORG) (1969–)

The Internet and the Web have played critical roles in disseminating women's health information globally. There is an abundance of online publications, specifically about women's sexual and reproductive health. However, online information is sometimes inaccurate, unclear, untrustworthy, biased, and out of date because it is continually changing. Yet access to it can have a profound impact on a woman's quality of life and serve as an impetus for cultural, political, and social change.

Among the myriad women's health resources online, many experts consider Our Bodies Ourselves to be the indispensable companion to the book with the same name. In 1998, the Boston Women's Health Book Collective officially launched the website, which serves as a portal of health information, including up-to-the-minute news on abortion, birth control, childbirth, domestic violence, gender identity, menopause, relation-

Nancy Miriam Hawley, founder of the Boston Women's Health Book Collective, Inc., pictured with copies of *Our Bodies, Ourselves*, the first book of its kind by women and about women's health. (AP Photo/Bizuayehu Tesfaye)

ships, and other issues related to human rights and social justice.

Our Bodies Ourselves' origins date back to the late 1960s, when a group of 12 women gathered in May 1969 during a women's rights conference in Boston. After sharing like-minded concerns and frustrations about their experiences with physicians, they formed the Doctor's Group, later known as the Boston Women's Health Book Collective.

Determined to make a difference, they printed a 193-page booklet titled "Women and Their Bodies: A Course" in 1970. It was radical and controversial for the era because it openly discussed taboo topics like homosexuality, masturbation, miscarriage, and abortion, which was still illegal throughout most of the United States. The authors also encouraged women to "take a mirror and examine yourself. Touch yourself, smell yourself, even taste your own secretions. After all, you are your body and you are not obscene" (Boston Women's Health Collective, 1970: 14).

Just one year later, in 1971, the booklet was republished as *Our Bodies, Ourselves*, selling more than 250,000 copies. It was reissued in 1973, and since that time it has been translated into 30 languages, sold more than 4 million copies, and received numerous accolades, including recognition from *Time* Magazine as one of the best 100 nonfiction books since 1923. Although the book *Our Bodies, Ourselves* is frequently described as the women's health bible, the companion website serves as a platform for advocacy, global outreach, and women's rights as human rights; the site facilitates access to 10–15 percent of the book's content for free. This online tool embodies the idea that information is power, and sharing it can transform lives.

Heidi Abbey Moyer

See also: *The Handmaid's Tale* by Margaret Atwood; TheFeministWire.com; Women's Liberation Movement.

FURTHER READING

Angier, Natalie. 1999/2014. *Woman: An Intimate Geography*. New York: Mariner Books.

Boston Women's Health Collective. 1970. "Women and Their Bodies: A Course." Boston: Author. http://www.ourbodiesourselves.org/cms/assets/uploads/2014/04/Women-and-Their-Bodies-1970.pdf.

Boston Women's Health Book Collective. 1973/2011. *Our Bodies, Ourselves*. New York: Simon & Schuster.

MS. MAGAZINE (MSMAGAZINE.COM) (1971–)

Ms. is an internationally circulating print and online magazine for feminists. The publication covers women's rights; legal, economic, and cultural status; and viewpoints across the world. *Ms.* is one of the longest-running magazines with an openly feminist perspective. The slogan of *Ms.* is "More than a Magazine—A Movement!"

The first issue of *Ms.* was a supplement in *New York Magazine* in December 1971, with a print run of 300,000 copies. There was a tremendous response to the first issue; the magazine received 20,000 letters to the editor, and 26,000 people purchased subscriptions. The first stand-alone issue was published in 1972 and featured an image of Wonder Woman on the cover. The cofounding editors of the magazine were Patricia Carbine (1931–), Joanne Edgar (1943–), Nina Finkelstein (1927–2013), Mary Peacock (1942–), Letty Cottin Pogrebin (1939–), and Gloria Steinem (1934–). Unlike most feminist magazines of the 1960s and 1970s, *Ms.* entered the marketplace with the goal of competing directly against other commercial women's magazines. By September 1973, *Ms.* had a subscription base of 350,000 and an estimated 1.4 million readers. By 1975, the publication had grown to 400,000 subscribers.

Ms. became a not-for-profit publication in 1978 and was published by the Ms. Foundation for Education and Communication. In 1987, the magazine was sold to the Australian company Fairfax, and Anne Summers (1945–) took the reins as editor. After the sale, *Ms.* was widely perceived as having lost its critical feminist voice. During this time, the magazine also attracted criticism due to its heavy reliance on tobacco and alcohol advertising. The magazine was put on temporary hiatus in 1989 because of increasing losses in revenue. The magazine relaunched in 1990 as an ad-free publication under the editorial leadership of Robin Morgan (1941–).

In the 1990s, *Ms.* recommitted to representing greater diversity among women and established a Board of International Advisors. Marcia Ann Gillespie (1944–)

became the first African American to serve as editor of *Ms.* in 1993. Since 2001, Liberty Media for Women has published *Ms.* Liberty Media is owned by the Feminist Majority Foundation, a United States-based nonprofit organization.

Ms. has an online presence through msmagazine.com. The website includes access to selected articles also appearing in the print magazine, a store, a blog, and links to other feminist news stories and resources. *Ms.* also has a program called "*Ms.* in the Classroom," which promotes the magazine as a teaching tool for educators in women's studies, sociology, and media and communication studies. A Committee of Scholars and an Advisory Board also help steer the magazine.

Elizabeth Groeneveld

See also: Feminist Majority Foundation; Gloria Steinem.

FURTHER READING

Farrell, Amy Erdman. 1998. *Yours in Sisterhood:* Ms. *Magazine and the Promise of Popular Feminism.* Chapel Hill, NC: University of North Carolina Press.

Ferree, Myra, and Patricia Yancey. 1995. "Like a Tarantula on a Banana Boat: Ms. Magazine, 1972–1989." In *Feminist Organizations: Harvest of the New Women's Movement.* Philadelphia: Temple University Press.

Thom, Mary. 1997. *Inside* Ms.: *25 Years of the Magazine and the Women's Movement.* New York: Henry Holt and Company.

FEMINIST MAJORITY FOUNDATION (FEMINIST.ORG)
(1987–PRESENT)

Founded in 1987, the Feminist Majority Foundation (FMF) is a nonprofit organization committed to advancing women's empowerment economically, socially, and politically through research, education, and political action. Primary focal areas for the organization include reproductive health, nonviolence, and women's equality. A 1986 Newsweek/Gallup opinion poll showing that 56 percent of women in the United States self-identifying as feminists inspired the organization's name, and current polls suggest that this majority continues today (Feminist Majority Foundation, 2014). Eleanor Smeal (1939–), cofounder of the organization and past president of the National Organization for Women, currently serves as president of FMF, leading its research and activism efforts.

Since the mid-1990s, Internet use has expanded rapidly across the globe, becoming a valuable platform for advancing knowledge, engagement, and activism around social issues related to women's rights. Through its site Feminist.org, FMF has been able to promote initiatives with which it is involved: encouraging women to enter law enforcement through the National Center for Women and Policing; advocating for eliminating violence toward women in the United States and globally; organizing to protect the Domestic Violence Offender Gun Ban; and developing the National Clinic Access project to train thousands of defense volunteers at women's health clinics where physicians perform abortions. FMF has collaborated with other antiviolence entities, lawmakers, marketing experts, and celebrities in these efforts and media campaigns. Further, in 2001, FMF purchased Liberty Media for Women, which publishes *Ms.* Magazine. This publication, launched in the 1970s, is committed to critical feminist journalism and serves as a platform for the liberal feminist movement. FMF has also engaged young feminists on college campuses through the Choices Campus Leadership Program and Feminist Majority Leadership Alliances. It has promoted leadership development through its National Young Feminists Leadership Conference and Girls Learn International, which also addresses issues of access to education nationally and globally.

Along with the praise FMF has received for advancing important causes, its initiatives and approaches have also been criticized. For example, FMF's global initiatives for the empowerment of women and girls have been criticized for employing a definition of gender equality informed by a Western imperialist and ethnocentric lens. In the early 2000s, FMF supported the U.S.-NATO war on Afghanistan on the premise of "saving" Afghani women. The FMF also supported President Barack Obama's (1961–) decision to delay the drawdown of U.S. troops in Afghanistan. As late as 2009, the FMF stood firm in its stance and did not support antiwar advocates' push for the military to leave Afghanistan. The FMF argued that the United States needed to stay in Afghanistan so as not to desert Afghani women and girls. In 2015, FMF was part of a group filing a Title IX complaint against a university for failing to protect students from threats of violence and sex-based cyberassaults after they spoke out condemning sexual assault. This was met with some media criticism suggesting that the organization was trying to suppress speech contrary to its views by condemning remarks allegedly protected by free speech. Despite this backlash, the organization continues leveraging the power of the Web to achieve gains toward gender equality.

Krista L. Prince

FURTHER READING

Adams, J. 2011. "Feminist Majority Foundation." *The Multimedia Encyclopedia of Women in Today's World.* Edited by Mary Zeiss Stange, Carol K. Oyster, and Jane E. Sloan. Thousand Oaks, CA: SAGE Publications.

Feminist Majority Foundation. 2014. http://feminist.org/default.asp.

Russo, Ann. 2006. "The Feminist Majority Foundation's Campaign to Stop Gender Apartheid." *International Feminist Journal of Politics*, 8(4): 557–80.

FEMINIST.COM (1995–)

Founded in 1995, the website Feminist.com was one of the first online resources for feminist issues. Under the leadership of founder and executive director Marianne Schnall (1967–), Feminist.com developed into a not-for-profit organization that is home to a host of resources for individuals interested in learning more about feminism, receiving updates on current events, and becoming involved in activism. The newsfeed on Feminist.com is supplied in cooperation with the Women's Media Center, another website that is invested in giving women a voice and changing stigmas surrounding women. Among the website's resources is also an independent section titled "Marketplace," where employment-seeking women can access a directory of women-owned businesses and job postings.

Feminist.com was launched at a crucial time when women's and diversity issues received growing coverage in news media. With its rather informal beginnings as a conversation in Schnall's kitchen, Feminist.com has become a growing destination for individuals who care about women's issues and wish to stay informed on upcoming events. Gloria Steinem (1934–), longtime feminist activist and media icon, once thanked the website for "putting the .com in feminism." Feminist.com was able to position itself as a premier resource for anyone interested in the feminist cause.

Since its inception in 1995, Feminist.com has adapted to its audience's needs. According to Amy Richards (1970–) and Marianne Schnall, the website "learns from visitors what issues feminism should highlight" (Richards and Schnall, 2003: 519). The news media began covering Feminist.com several years after its launch. This delay is partially to be attributed to the novelty of online resources and a lack of understanding of the importance of online activism. Feminist.com reported in 2015 that the website receives more than a million clicks per year. Hence, the website furnishes information for students, educators, activists, and the public at large. Feminist.com is not to be confused with Feminist.org, which is the official website of the Feminist Majority Foundation, an advocacy organization that was launched eight years prior. Feminist.com developed and flourished entirely online and, as such, differs from other organizations that were born out of activist groups or forged in physical spaces.

Although Feminst.com does not engage in formal media monitoring on coverage of women, the website and its team have always been invested in consciousness-raising on feminist issues, including women's portrayal in the media. Through its exclusive online existence, Feminist.com can be placed in the category of feminist cyberactivism or cyberfeminism, which allows users to access useful information and also leads them from the virtual space into the streets (see also Everett, 2004; Richards and Schnall, 2003). As such, Feminist.com exists to raise awareness on contemporary issues, promote women's inclusion in all aspects of life, and offer valuable resources. Feminist.com is frequently featured on other feminist blogs and websites as a multifaceted resource for women and men alike.

Giuliana Sorce

FURTHER READING

Everett, Anna. 2004. "On Cyberfeminism and Cyberwomanism: High-Tech Mediations of Feminism's Discontents." *Signs*, 30(1): 1278–86.

Hess, Amanda. 2009. "Don't Know If You Were Raped? Ask Your Rapist." *Washington City Paper*, November 30.

McCaughey, Martha, and Michael D. Ayers, eds. 2013. *Cyberactivism: Online Activism in Theory and Practice.* London: Routledge.

Richards, Amy, and Marianne Schnall. 2003. "Cyberfeminism: Networking the Net." In *Sisterhood Is Forever: The Women's Anthology for a New Millennium*, 517–25. Edited by Robin Morgan. New York: Washington Square Press.

BITCH MEDIA (BITCHMEDIA.ORG) (1996–)

Bitch Media is a nonprofit, independent, feminist media organization headquartered in Portland, Oregon. The now multimedia organization started in 1996 as a zine (a self-published magazine with a small circulation) founded by Lisa Jervis (1972–), Benjamin Shaykin (birth date unknown), and Andi Zeisler (1972–). Provocatively titled *Bitch: Feminist Response to Pop Culture,* the zine set out to challenge the sexist representations of women in mainstream media. Jervis and Zeisler were recent college graduates and budding feminists who were fed up with the problematic representation of women and the feminine in movies, television, and advertising, and pined for fun and clever publications that opposed and criticized the avalanche of such lackluster and dated images. Finding nothing, they partnered with graphic designer Shaykin and launched a rudimentary formatted *Bitch*, which they initially distributed out of a station wagon. Their efforts received a big boost when nationally known newspapers and magazines like the *Chicago Tribune, The Nation,* and *Spin* published favorable reviews of the upstart publication.

With the invention of new technologies, the enterprise morphed into a multiplatform outlet, adopting the name Bitch Media in 2009 and developing an online presence with daily online articles and weekly podcasts in addition to its quarterly magazine. Bitch Media also hosts a community lending library and a Bitch on Campus program.

Despite the potential for criticism, Bitch creators deliberately adopted the controversial term "bitch" as the title of the magazine and organization in an effort to take away the word's power as a slur against women who voice opinions, challenge norms, and advocate for women's rights. Bitch is not only a strong feminist voice in the world of pop culture, but the organization also insists on making feminism fun with witty writing, pun-infused headlines, and provocative imaging. The magazine and website cover stories on activism, art, culture, music, politics, and film. Bitch also hosts an online shop where supporters can buy feminist-inspired mugs, books, and greeting cards. The organization also recognizes the complexities and diversity of contemporary feminism, welcoming debate and disagreement even as it encourages activism and social change. More than a magazine or organization with an online presence, Bitch also seeks to engage, educate, challenge, and encourage its readers to step out of their comfort zones and contest a world that consistently tells girls and women they are inadequate failures in an unattainable pursuit of a mythical idealized womanhood.

Ann M. Savage

FURTHER READING

Jervis, Lisa, and Andi Zeisler. 2006. *Bitchfest: Ten Years of Cultural Criticism from the Pages of Bitch Magazine*, 1st ed. New York: Farrar, Straus and Giroux.

Worland, Gayle. 2008. "Bitch Magazine Publisher Wants to Talk to You about Feminism." *McClatchy-Tribune Business News.*

Zeisler, Andi. 2008. *Feminism and Pop Culture*. Berkeley, CA: Seal Press.

FEMINISTING.COM (2004–)

A popular American Internet blog, Feministing.com is intended as "a place for younger feminists to build their careers and platforms" (Feministing, 2011). Since its inception in 2004, the blog's columnists and community writers have discussed a variety of barriers to women's equality. Feministing critiques multiple types of discrimination, noting how sexism intersects with racism, classism, ableism, transphobia, and homophobia. The blog has garnered both praise and criticism for its wide-ranging content on women's sexual empowerment, issues in reproductive rights, transgender rights, celebrity feminism, media representation, politics, and sexual violence, among many other topics. In 2011, the blog garnered upward of 20,000 visitors a day, and that same year was awarded the Sidney Hillman Prize for social and economic justice in blog journalism. Since then, the site has continued to attract hundreds of thousands of unique visitors per month, who have read, commented on, and contributed articles. The Community portal allows "anyone—from teens to national non-profits—[to] make their voices heard" (Feministing, 2016), fulfilling the blog's mandate to increase diversity within the feminist movement. As Feministing founder Jessica Valenti (1978–) describes, she intended the blog to allow once "misrepresented or ignored" young women a public podium previously reserved for "an elite few in the feminist movement" (Feministing, 2011).

Feministing's content has at times sparked heated debate about whether particular sexual representations and practices are empowering or oppressive to women (a long-standing, divisive issue within feminist circles). For instance, a controversy dubbed "boobgate" emerged after a political blogger, Ann Althouse (1951–), criticized Jessica Valenti's appearance at a luncheon with then-president Bill Clinton, stating: "She wears a tight knit top that draws attention to her breasts and stands right in front of him and positions herself to make her breasts as obvious as possible?" Many commenters disagreed with this focus and judgment of a young woman's outward appearance. In this widely debated and shared post, Althouse also described Feministing as a sexually graphic "breastblog," noting, "The banner displays silhouettes of women with big breasts" (Althouse, 2006). These comments expressed a concern some feminists have voiced concerning the website's reproduction of sexist symbols, namely, that it is depicting women as sexual objects. However, according to Feministing, the logo is intended to be an ironic and revised portrayal of the sexualized "mud flap girl," a curvaceous silhouetted woman who figuratively raises her middle finger at the patriarchy (Feministing, 2016).

Other recent feminist protests featured on Feministing critique pop cultural symbols in a similar tongue-and-cheek manner. Sexually charged images and words are given new meaning within the international SlutWalk movement, for instance, which critiques rape culture by using "slut" ironically. Feminists on- and offline are not sure if traditionally misogynist and sexual language can be successfully reclaimed to promote equality for all along gender, racial, sexual, and class lines. Controversies about Feministing's sexual image and content reflect contrary views about sexuality (as empowering and/or harmful) circulating in the contemporary feminist movement.

Emily L. Hiltz

FURTHER READING

Althouse, Ann. 2006. "Let's Take a Closer Look at Those Breasts," September 15. http://althouse.blogspot.ca/2006/09/lets-take-closer-look-at-those-breasts .html.

Feministing. 2016. "About Feministing." http://feministing.com/about.

Feministing. 2011. "Farewell, Feministing," February 2. http://feministing.com/ 2011/02/02/farewell-feministing.

Feministing. 2006. "The 'Dirty Pillow' Line of Attack," September 16. http://feministing.com/2006/09/16/the_dirty_pillow_line_of_attac.

Valenti, Jessica. 2011. "SlutWalks and the Future of Feminism," *The Washington Post*, June 3. https://www.washingtonpost.com/opinions/slutwalks-and-the-future-of-feminism/2011/06/01/AGjB9LIH_story.html.

JEZEBEL.COM (2007–)

Jezebel.com was launched on May 21, 2007, as a magazine blog with a feminist slant on women's popular culture and initially featured the tagline "Celebrity, Sex, Fashion for Women. Without Airbrushing." One of several online publications by Manhattan blog company Gawker Media, the site aims to provide women with a source of news, gossip, and celebrity content that takes "all the essentially meaningless but sweet stuff directed our way" by mainstream women's magazines "while taking more of the serious stuff and making it more fun, or more personal" (Jezebel, 2007). By December 2007, Jezebel.com was receiving 10 million monthly views and today receives more than 30 million hits per month in addition to maintaining a strong social media presence across Facebook, Reddit, Instagram, and Twitter.

Jezebel.com was created by former *InStyle* journalist Anna Holmes in response to Gawker Media's request for a woman-centered blog as part of its emerging blog network. Jezebel.com provides a blend of journalistic material, viewer-submitted articles, and shared content, often with a humorous or irreverent angle. Jezebel.com is known for a number of regular blog topics, including a biweekly advice column called "Pot Psychology," which offers herbal solutions to contemporary problems; "Crap Email from a Dude," in which viewers offer examples of their worst experiences of social media communication while dating; and "Photoshop of Horrors," where badly edited images of celebrities are compiled in a regular gallery and "Hall of Shame."

Jezebel.com has been the target of a range of media criticisms and continues to use controversy to bring issues of feminism, sexuality, and race to public attention. In 2007, the blog was criticized for offering $10,000 for an original celebrity photo to contrast with retouched photos that appear in celebrity magazines. In 2012, the blog caused a media backlash for publishing the names of a group of American high school students who had posted racist tweets when President Barack Obama was elected and, in the same year, for posting YouTube footage and still shots of a sexual assault of a foreign female journalist in Libya. On January 16, 2015, Jezebel .com generated attention for another offer of $10,000 for "pre-photoshopped" images from the glamorous photoshoot of actress Lena Dunham for *Vogue* magazine. Arguing that Dunham is known in popular culture for promoting body positivity and speaking out against unattainable beauty standards, Jezebel.com used the *Vogue* photographs as a platform for its overall critique of female body idealizations in mass media.

Rebecca Bishop

FURTHER READING

Hill, Kashmir. 2012. "This Week in Horrible Journalism: Jezebel's Rape Photos." Forbes, February 10. http://www.forbes.com/sites/kashmirhill/2012/02/10/this-week-in-horrible-journalism-jezebels-rape-photos/#1ab6365370b0.

Hill, Kashmir. 2012. "Should Teenagers Have Racist Election Tweets in Their Google Results for Life? Jezebel Votes Yes." Forbes, November 9. http://www.forbes.com/sites/kashmirhill/2012/11/09/should-teenagers-have-racist-election-tweets-in-their-google-results-for-life-jezebel-votes-yes/#4f89068435eb.

Holmes, Anna. 2013. *The Book of Jezebel: An Illustrated Encyclopedia of Lady Things.* New York: Grand Central Publishing.

Jezebel.com. 2007. "The Five Great Lies of Women's Magazines." November 1. http://jezebel.com/262130/the-five-great-lies-of-womens-magazines.

Jezebel.com. 2015. "We're Offering $10,000 for Unretouched Images of Lena Dunham in Vogue." January 16. http://jezebel.com/were-offering-10-000-for-unretouched-images-of-lena-d-1502000514.

FEMINISTFREQUENCY.COM (2009–)

In 2012, the Internet erupted with two separate but similarly themed events that exposed many underlying misogynistic attitudes in gaming culture: *Beat Up Anita Sarkeesian* and #1reasonwhy. The *Beat Up Anita Sarkeesian* game was a response to a Kickstarter campaign to fund a series of videos for Sarkeesian's (1983–) Feminist Frequency series titled "Tropes versus Women in Video Games." The series would build on the success of Sarkeesian's existing Tropes Versus Women series, which analyzed representations of women in pop culture and was first launched in 2011 for *Bitch Magazine*; the initial video series was an extension of the feminist criticism Sarkeesian had started when she first launched her website, Feminist Frequency, in 2009. According to Sarkeesian, the videos would explore feminist critiques of depictions of women in video games—particularly tropes like rescuing princesses, hypersexualized female characters, and the lack of character gender diversity. However, some gamers—a group often defined as heteronormative young males, even though women comprise approximately 50 percent of the gaming market—responded with vitriol. Not only did Sarkeesian receive threats of rape, violence, and death, but she became the literal punching bag in gamer Bendilin Spurr's video game *Beat Up Anita Sarkeesian*. In this game, Sarkeesian's face fills the screen, and the player "punches" her, disfiguring the face with bruises and lacerations.

Although this game brought Sarkeesian's plight to mainstream media, the controversy may have died down quietly had #1reasonwhy not followed on its heels. The #1reasonwhy hashtag appeared in response to Kickstarter Head of Games Luke Crane's (1985–) seemingly innocuous tweet "Why are there so few lady game creators?" What emerged was a flood of tweets that chronicled rampant sexism in the gaming industry. The hashtag campaign demonstrated that the industry as a whole, including game developers, marketers, and players, were complicit in marginalizing women at best and threatening to rape and kill them at worst. Even as the industry decried these problems, industry decision-makers continued to objectify women, leading to the very public resignation of two prominent International Game Developers Association (IGDA) members—Brenda Romero (1966–) and Darius Kazemi (1984–)—in 2013. Then-president Brenda Romero had just presented on the panel #1ReasonToBe at the Game Developers Conference, in which she and other developers discussed the many reasons for women to join the game workforce. But later that evening, an industry party cosponsored by IGDA and YetiZen featured scantily clad young female dancers (or models or paid gamers; reports vary) to entertain the audience.

Harassment in gaming continued to make headlines in 2014 after the hashtag #gamergate arose in response to an attack blog directed at Zoe Quinn (designer of *Depression Quest*) by her ex-boyfriend. The blog claimed that Quinn's success was due to her sleeping with game critics, even though none of the men Quinn was allegedly involved with had reviewed the game. Regardless, #gamergate supporters mobilized around ethics in games journalism, while dismissing any accusation of sexism. At the same time, however, several women, among them Quinn, Sarkeesian, and game developer Brianna Wu, endured sustained harassment from self-identified #gamergate supporters. Wu's personal address was posted online with invitations to rape and murder her, and Sarkeesian cancelled some public appearances due to threats, including a talk at Utah State University. Other women in and around the game industry were also harassed via social media, some with distressing photos of men standing outside their offices with knives or of their own images covered in semen tweeted under the guise of "games journalism."

Jennifer deWinter and Carly Kocurek

FURTHER READING

Chess, Shira, and Adrienne Shaw. 2015. "A Conspiracy of Fishes, or, How We Learned to Stop Worrying about #GamerGate and Embrace Hegemonic Masculinity." *Journal of Broadcasting and Electronic Media*, 59(1): 208–20.

Cross, Katherine Angel. 2014. "Ethics for Cyborgs: On Real Harassment in an 'Unreal' Place." *Loading... The Journal of the Canadian Game Studies Association*, 8(13): 4–21.

deWinter, Jennifer, and Carly Kocurek. 2012. "Rescuing Anita: Games, Gamers, and the Battle of the Sexes." *Flow Journal*, 17.03, December. http://www.flow-journal.org/2012/12/rescuing-anita.

Massanari, Adrienne. 2015. "#Gamergate and The Fappening: How Reddit's Algorithm, Governance, and Culture Support Toxic Technocultures." *New Media & Society*, October 9: 1–18.

THE SHRIVER REPORT (SHRIVERREPORT.ORG) (2009–)

The Shriver Report is an advocacy initiative founded by journalist and former California First Lady Maria Shriver (1955–) to raise awareness of the key social, economic, and political issues facing contemporary women and their families. Created in 2009 as a branch of the nonprofit organization A Woman's Nation, the Shriver Report aims to report on key events that impact women's lives, generate critical dialogue on women's issues, and serve as an advocate for women in areas of policy and political practice.

A key feature of the Shriver Report has been the publication of a series of book-length special editions in both online and print format, written and produced in partnership with academic, grassroots, and corporate organizations. The first of these, "The Shriver Report: A Woman's Nation Changes Everything" (Boushey and O'Leary, 2009), was published in partnership with the United States policy research and advocacy organization The Center for American Progress. This edited collection of 34 essays and chapters addressed the changing roles of women in the workplace and argued that both government policies and workplace practices were failing to address the fact that mothers were now the primary breadwinners for two-thirds of American families. The impact of this report was significant, with American broadcast company NBC Universal joining the project as a corporate sponsor and inviting Shriver to guest-edit a weeklong series about the study under the title "A Woman's Nation."

In 2010, the Shriver Report released the special edition "A Women's Nation Takes on Alzheimer's" (Geiger et al., 2010), which suggested that women constituted approximately two-thirds of Alzheimer's patients and two-thirds of Alzheimer's caregivers. Maintaining that the significant emotional and physical toll of the disease is compounded by financial burden, the report advocated both increased government funding into Alzheimer's research and a need to provide economic support to families impacted by the disease. Building on the findings of these earlier reports, "The Shriver Report: A Woman's Nation Pushes Back from the Brink" (Morgan and Skelton, 2014) broadly addressed the issue of social

Maria Shriver—journalist, activist, former First Lady of California, and member of the Kennedy family. Shriver launched The Shriver Report: A Woman's Nation Changes Everything, a continuing initiative to improve many facets of women's lives. (Sbukley/Dreamstime.com)

immobility and economic insecurity for American families and maintained that, although critical to the American workforce, a third of women in the United States lived in a state of poverty. The report offered a set of public policies that would boost women's economic potential, including a higher minimum wage, improved access to work and income supports, and better opportunities to access medium and high-paying jobs.

In addition to the release of special editions, the Shriver Report, alongside A Woman's Nation, has produced a series of special initiatives to enhance the well-being of American women. These have included initiatives like The Shriver Corps, an antipoverty national service program for women and their families, and Fund a 21st Century Boss, a micro-lending initiative formed with crowdfunding platform Kiva to provide start-up funds for women entrepreneurs.

Rebecca Bishop

FURTHER READING

Boushey, Heather, and Ann O'Leary, eds. 2009. *The Shriver Report: A Woman's Nation Changes Everything.* New York: Free Press.

Geiger, Angela Timashenka, Oliva Morgan, Kate Meyer, and Karen Skelton, eds. 2010. *The Shriver Report: A Women's Nation Takes on Alzheimer's.* New York: Simon and Schuster.

Morgan, Olivia, and Karen Skelton. 2014. *The Shriver Report: A Woman's Nation Pushes Back from the Brink.* New York: St Martin's Press.

THE FEMINIST WIRE (THEFEMINISTWIRE.COM) (2010–)

Promoting the feminist movement and its goals of equality, inclusion, solidarity, and social change, TheFeministWire.com (TFW) is an online feminist news site with corresponding social media presences that publishes and promotes writing by feminists of diverse backgrounds, ages, races, genders, and sexualities. Although most of the content on TFW is nonfiction and covers a range of topics—including politics, popular culture, law, religion, health and wellness, sexuality, body studies, activism, education, sports, fashion, and global issues—short fiction and poetry works are also published. TFW was cofounded by Hortense Spillers, PhD (1942–) and Tamura A. Lomax, PhD (1973–) in 2010. The site debuted on January 1, 2011.

TFW was created by Spillers and Lomax because of two key experiences: a lack of publication venues for scholar-activists and a general dissatisfaction with the ways conflicts of racial disparity were portrayed by the U.S. media in 2010. Spillers and Lomax claim they couldn't find a venue that would publish their "black feminist response" to the 2010 controversy and media coverage of Shirley Sherrod, an African American woman and former Georgia State Director of Rural Development for the U.S. Department of Agriculture (Lomax). Sherrod was forced to resign from the USDA after Conservative blogger Andrew Breitbart shared a heavily edited video of Sherrod speaking to the National Association of the Advancement of Colored People (NAACP) on his blog. The video depicted her as making racist comments and compelled the NAACP to demand her resignation. It was only after Sherrod's resignation that an unedited version of her speech was found. Viewed in this wider context, it became clear that Sherrod's remarks were focused on the importance of overcoming ingrained prejudices. The NAACP and White House subsequently apologized for their hasty reactions based on an "out-of-context" clip. Meanwhile, due to the immediacy and ease of online publishing, Spillers and Lomax were able to use TWF.com as a vehicle for commenting on these developments alongside unfolding U.S. media coverage.

Since the beginning of the 21st century, feminist scholars have commented on the lack of a "public feminist movement in the U.S." (Fernandez and Wilding, 2002: 17; Gajjala and Oh, 2012: 1). Unlike earlier feminist movements (or waves) occurring in the United States during the 19th and 20th centuries, 21st-century feminists are more divided by geography, material access, and cultural gaps. The affordances of the Web have been critical for the establishment and growth of TFW and for the feminist movement in the 21st century. Online websites and communities like TFW bridge material, spatial, and sociocultural (e.g., race, ethnicity, gender) divides between feminists while promoting solidarity over a given cause. Indeed, the Web provides 21st-century feminist scholar-activists a means of coalition and community building through social and digital media technologies. As of August 2015, TFW had more than 65,000 likes on Facebook and a claimed readership of more than 1 million readers a year (Advertise, 2015).

Mariana Grohowski

See also: Women's Liberation Movement.

FURTHER READING

Advertise with Us. n.d. TheFeministWire.com. http://www.thefeministwire.com/
advertise-with-us.

Fernandez, Maria, and Faith Wilding. 2002. "Situating Cyberfeminisms." In
Domain Errors! Cyberfeminist Practices, 17–28. Edited by Maria Fernandez,
Faith Wilding, and Michelle M. Wright. Brooklyn, NY: Autonomedia &
SubRosa.

Gajjala, Radhika, and Yeon Ju Oh. 2012. "Introduction: Cyberfeminism 2.0:
Where Have All the Cyberfeminists Gone?" In *Cyberfeminism 2.0*, 1–9. Edited
by Radhika Gajjala and Yeon Ju Oh. New York: Peter Lang.

Lomax, Tamura. 2015. Personal email requesting info on TFW for anthology.

She's Beautiful When She's Angry. DVD. 2015. Directed by Mary Dore. 2014. New
York: Cinema Guild.

THE MIS-ADVENTURES OF AWKWARD BLACK GIRL (AWKWARDBLACKGIRL.COM) (2011–2013)

A highly successful and innovative comedic Web series, *The Misadventures of Awkward Black Girl* (*ABG*) premiered on February 3, 2011, on the video hosting site YouTube. Jo-Issa Rae Diop, commonly known as Issa Rae (1985–), created and starred in the two-season, 24-episode series as the character "J." "J" is a heterosexual black woman in her mid-20s who works in an office environment, dates, and finds herself in a range of socially awkward situations—from situations specific to women of color, to the universally relatable. Though the series had a short run, it won the 2012 Shorty Award for Best Web Show, and after airing its sixth episode, it raised more than $40,000 in donations from fans via a Kickstarter campaign to help ensure the show's continuation. New episodes of the show, which contained explicit language and sexual content, premiered monthly and had an average run time of 15 minutes.

ABG's impact was substantial because Rae capitalized on the affordances of the Web in general, and YouTube in particular, to create and share the web series. As a social/digital media platform, YouTube has granted millions of users across the globe the opportunity to create, upload, and store video content that is then accessible to a global audience. YouTube offers a fast track for creating a series that otherwise entails standard television production processes (pitching an idea, making a pilot, getting funding, etc.).

Prior to the launch of *ABG* in 2011, Rae was no stranger to YouTube or film production. As a college student at Stanford University, Rae created and uploaded videos to YouTube that chronicled and parodied awkward moments of college life (Hua, 2012; Rae, 2015). Inspiration for *ABG* came to Rae as a way for her to find "confirmation that [she] wasn't alone" (Rae, 2015: 47), that is, that she was not the only young, black woman in the United States who felt excluded by cultural stereotypes and the lack of relatable television characters of color on network television.

According to Rae, *ABG* was created at a time in which network television did not star a diverse range of characters. YouTube allowed Rae to fill the void left by television while maintaining creative control over the content and enabling instant, global access on a tight financial budget. Though the web series ceased production with the February 28, 2013, series finale, Rae's memoir, which bears the name of the web series, has become a national bestseller. Through Issa Rae Productions and Color Creative, Rae is dedicated to increasing the voices of women and people of color in media entertainment content.

Mariana Grohowski

FURTHER READING

Hua, Vanessa. 2012. "Now Playing: Awkward Stage." *Stanford Alumni*, May/June. https://alumni.stanford.edu/get/page/magazine/article/?article_id=53330.

Kickstarter. 2011. "The Misadventures of Awkward Black Girl." https://www.kickstarter.com/projects/1996857943/the-misadventures-of-awkward-black-girl/posts/106068?ref=email&show_token=30c3f7fc3079b13c.

Rae, Issa. 2015. *The Misadventures of Awkward Black Girl.* New York: Atria Books.

About the Editor and Contributors

EDITOR

Ann M. Savage, PhD, is Professor of Critical Communication and Media Studies and an affiliate faculty member of Gender, Women & Sexuality Studies at Butler University, Indianapolis, Indiana. She earned her PhD from Bowling Green State University in Ohio. Dr. Savage teaches courses on queer film, women and rock, documentary film, and media literacy. Her research focuses on feminist and queer media studies. Her work has appeared in the *Journal for Excellence in Teaching*, *Journal of Popular Film and Television*, and *Atlantis: A Women's Studies Journal*. She is the author of *They're Playing Our Songs: Women Talk about Feminist Rock Music* (2003, Praeger).

CONTRIBUTORS

Dorian Adams is an independent researcher in Philadelphia. Their recent work includes designing professional development curricula about transgender issues at Drexel University, as well as speaking presentations on the history and current issues facing transgender students in higher education.

Jamie Anderson is a journalist and musician and writes about music when she isn't doing her own. Her work has appeared in *Acoustic Guitar, Curve*, and *Sing Out!* She is the author of a memoir, *Drive All Night*, and is currently working on her second book, about women's music of the 1970s and 1980s.

Dr. Gabrie'l J. Atchison holds a doctorate in women's studies from Clark University and has been teaching as an adjunct professor in sociology, Africana studies, communications and gender/women's studies at various colleges and universities in New York, Connecticut, and New Jersey.

Katie Sullivan Barak is an independent scholar in Denver, Colorado. She has a PhD in American culture studies and a master's in popular culture from Bowling Green State University. By day she works in higher ed administration; by night she researches media representations of gender and class.

Dylan Bennett is an associate professor of political science at University of Wisconsin–Waukesha. A former newspaper writer, he teaches a variety of courses in world politics.

Jessica E. Birch is a lecturer in Case Western Reserve University's English Department/SAGES, and she has a PhD in American studies from Purdue University. Her teaching and research focus on how cultural narratives justify and perpetuate social inequality.

Rebecca Bishop is an independent scholar and educator based in Sydney, Australia. She holds a PhD in interdisciplinary cross-cultural research and has expertise in the cultural politics of embodiment, digital cultures, and sexuality.

Ebru Cayir is a physician from Turkey who is currently a PhD candidate in the Department of Health Promotion, Education and Behavior of Arnold School of Public Health in the University of South Carolina. She is also a certificate student at the Women's and Gender Studies Program.

Casely E. Coan is a doctoral student in the Rhetoric, Composition and Teaching of English Program at the University of Arizona. She holds a master's degree in women's and gender studies from Rutgers University. Her work resides at the intersection of transgender studies, queer theory, and the rhetorics of performance.

Sarah E. Colonna is the associate faculty chair for Grogan College at the University of North Carolina at Greensboro. With a background in health care, women's and gender studies, and educational leadership, her research interests include feminist thought and pedagogy, leadership, and young adult literature.

Jayda Coons is a PhD candidate in English literature at the University of Arizona in Tucson, Arizona. Her research and teaching interests include 19th-century British literature, feminist theory, the novel, and psychoanalysis.

Angeline Davis has an MAT in English from Coastal Carolina University and is currently earning an MA in English from Morehead State. She is a domestic violence survivor and a member of the National Council of Teachers of English (NCTE) and the Conference on College Composition and Communication (CCCC), and has been a full-time English instructor at Brown Mackie College–Louisville since 2010.

Christine DeCleene is currently a graduate student in the field of history at the University of Nebraska at Kearney. She received her M.A. in sociology from Sam Houston University. Her research interests are in the area of African American studies.

Jennifer deWinter is an associate professor of rhetoric and the Director of Interactive Media and Game Development at Worcester Polytechnic Institute, and an associate in research at Harvard's Reischauer Institute of Japanese Studies. She researches game development, game distribution, and Japanese popular culture in global markets.

Nessette Falu is a postdoctoral fellow at the Institute for Research on the African Diaspora in the Americas and the Caribbean at CUNY Graduate Center.

Skye de Saint Felix is a master's candidate in the Department of Communication at the University of Arkansas–Fayetteville. Her primary academic interests are rhetoric and gender theory, specifically the social and political consequences of public discourse on abortion and reproductive health.

Kate L. Flach is a PhD candidate in the Department of History at The University of California, San Diego. Her dissertation, "Channeling Dissent: Prime-Time Television and Social Change in Post-War America," examines the politics of television from the 1950s–1970s as a medium that reflected and mediated social change.

Dr. Eden Elizabeth Wales Freedman is an assistant professor of multicultural American literature and diversity studies at Mount Mercy University (Cedar Rapids, Indiana) and an affiliate assistant professor of women's studies at the University of New Hampshire. She has published articles on the novels of William Faulkner, Zora Neale Hurston, and Toni Morrison.

Sarah E. Fryett, PhD, is a professor in the Department of English at the University of Tampa. Her recent work includes an analysis of female comedians ("Laudable Laughter" in *Introduction to Women's Studies Reader*) and a forthcoming essay on the representation of lesbian identity in the Netflix drama *Orange Is the New Black*.

Dr. Sanjukta Ghosh is professor of communication at Castleton University in Vermont. Her research and teaching is focused on race, gender, and sexuality. A founding member of the university's women's and gender studies program, she also served as its coordinator for eight years.

Eduardo Gregori (PhD in Spanish, Penn State, 2009) is Associate Professor of Spanish and of gender, sexuality, and women's studies at the University of Wisconsin–Marathon County. He has published on modernist and avant-garde

Spanish culture. His current research interests deal with the imbrication of masculinity and the avant-garde in Spain.

Elizabeth Groeneveld is an assistant professor in the Department of Women's Studies at Old Dominion University. Her book, *Making Feminist Media: Third-Wave Magazines on the Cusp of the Digital Age* (2016), examines the relationship between social movements and independent publishing in the 1990s.

Mariana Grohowski is an assistant professor of English at Indiana University Southeast. She received her PhD in rhetoric and writing from Bowling Green State University (Ohio). Her research explores the rhetorical practices of under- and misrepresented populations, including women veterans. She is founder and chief editor of the *Journal of Veterans Studies*.

Aurora Grutman is an independent writer who lives in New York City.

Allison L. Harthcock, PhD (University of Missouri–Columbia), is an associate professor at Butler University in Indiana. Her teaching and research focuses on the relationship between sports media and identity.

Emily L. Hiltz is a PhD candidate and Instructor of Communication within the School of Journalism and Communication at Carleton University, in Ottawa, Canada.

Christina Holmes, PhD, is an assistant professor of women's, gender, and sexuality studies at DePauw University. Her book *Ecological Borderlands* (University of Illinois Press, 2016) addresses Mexican American women's environmental activism.

Erica Horhn is a doctoral student in the Educational Leadership and Cultural Foundations Department at the University of North Carolina at Greensboro. Her research interests include African American womanhood and humor. She earned an MA in English and African American literature from North Carolina A&T State University (2009).

Daniela Hrzán is in the Department of English and American Studies at Humboldt-Universitaet zu Berlin and the Office of Women's Affairs and Equal Opportunities, University of Kassel, Germany.

Stephanie Leo Hudson is affiliated with the Cultural Foundations and Women's and Gender Studies Programs at the University of North Carolina at Greensboro.

Eleanor M. Huntington graduated with her Master's in Cinema and Media Studies from the University of Southern California. She currently works in cause marketing in Los Angeles.

Dr. Terri Jett has a BA in Ethnic Studies and a Master's in Public Administration from California State University, Hayward, and a PhD in Public Policy and Public Administration from Auburn University. Currently she is an associate professor of political science and affiliate faculty member of the Gender, Women & Sexuality Studies.

Priya Jha is Associate Professor of English at the University of Redlands. Her work focuses on postcolonialism and transculturalism in South Asian, Caribbean, and African literatures and cultures. A book chapter, entitled, "Mother, Insider: Katherine Mayo and the Problem of Transnational Feminism" is forthcoming in a collected volume, *What Is Feminism?* (Bloomsbury Press).

Dr. Tonia Kazakopoulou is an associate lecturer in film and television at the University of Reading, UK. She is the coeditor of *Contemporary Greek Film Cultures from 1990 to the Present* (Peter Lang, 2016) and the author of 'Women Screenwriters: Greece' in *Women Screenwriters: an international guide* (Palgrave Macmillan, 2015).

Holly M. Kent is an assistant professor of history at the University of Illinois–Springfield, where she teaches courses in U.S. women's history, nineteenth-century U.S. history, and slavery and abolition. Her monograph, *Her Voice Will Be on the Side of Right: Gender and Power in Women's Antebellum Antislavery Literature*, is forthcoming from Kent State University Press.

Tala Khanmalek received her PhD in Ethnic Studies at the University of California, Berkeley with a Designated Emphasis in Women, Gender, and Sexuality Studies.

Carly Kocurek is Assistant Professor of Digital Humanities and Media Studies and Director of Digital Humanities at the Illinois Institute of Technology. She is the author of *Coin-Operated Americans: Rebooting Boyhood at the Video Game Arcade* (University of Minnesota Press, 2015). Her research considers the intersections of games, gender, and culture.

Evan L. Kropp, PhD, is an assistant professor of communication and media studies at Reinhardt University.

Jennifer Hall Lee is a filmmaker, writer, and speaker. Her award-winning documentary film "Feminist: Stories from Women's Liberation" is distributed by Women Make Movies. She has been published in anthologies, including "Love Her, Love Her Not: The Hillary Paradox."

Linda Levitt is an associate professor of communication at Stephen F. Austin State University. Her research interests focus on the intersection of cultural memory and media. She has published essays about the depiction of women scientists in 1950s movies, mothers of evil children in Hollywood thrillers, and growing up as a reluctant feminist.

Melinda Lewis earned her PhD in American culture studies from Bowling Green State University in 2014. Her dissertation, "That's What She Said: Politics, Transgression, and Women's Humor in Contemporary American Television," discussed the ways in which women writers have helped form and transform the American sitcom. She is currently a visiting fellow at Drexel University.

Grace Lidinsky-Smith is an undergraduate at Indiana University. She is studying environmental feminist geography. She has presented at the 2015 Seneca Falls convention and the 2014 Indiana University Gender Studies Conference. She has also been published in Kinsey Confidential.

Brooke Lober is Visiting Assistant Professor in Women's and Gender Studies at Sonoma State University. Her research addresses relations between late 20th-century U.S.-based feminist, anticolonial, and anti-imperialist activist formations. In partnership with the Freedom Archives in San Francisco, Lober currently directs the Women Against Imperialism Oral History Project.

Rachel R. Martin is Assistant Professor of English and Women's and Gender Studies at Northern Virginia Community College in Alexandria, Virginia. She has published in *Feminism in the Worlds of Neil Gaiman: Essays on Comics, Poetry and Prose* (McFarland & Co, 2012). Currently, she is working on the manuscript entitled *Alison Bechdel: Conversations*, due out in early 2017 (University Press of Mississippi).

Angel Daniel Matos is a Consortium for Faculty Diversity Postdoctoral Fellow in English at Bowdoin College, interested in young adult literature, affect, narrative, and LGBTQ fiction and media. He obtained his PhD in English with a graduate minor in gender studies from the University of Notre Dame.

Andrea McClanahan, PhD, is a professor of communication and the coordinator of Women & Gender Studies at East Stroudsburg University of Pennsylvania. She teaches courses in communication, media, and feminist theory. Her research focuses on critical analysis of media representations.

Maggie Monson earned her BA in Critical Communications and Media Studies at Butler University. She currently works in Global Employee Communications at Eli Lilly and Company in Indianapolis, Indiana.

Heidi Abbey Moyer is the Archivist and Humanities Reference Librarian and Coordinator of Archives and Special Collections at the Penn State Harrisburg

Library in Middletown, Pennsylvania, and a tenured faculty librarian with the Penn State University Libraries. She is the author of *Penn State Harrisburg* (Arcadia Publishing, 2016).

Monica Murtaugh has a master's degree in women's studies from San Diego State University.

Madelyn Tucker Pawlowski is an English PhD student at the University of Arizona, where she also teaches composition. In 2010, she completed an internship at the National Air and Space Museum in Washington, D.C.

Viki Peer is currently pursuing an MA in Women's and Gender Studies at the University of South Florida and is interested in feminism and disability, LGBTQ issues, race and racism in America, motherhood, and prison abolition.

Krista L. Prince works professionally in student affairs while concurrently pursuing doctoral work in educational studies and women's and gender studies. She is a past directorate member of the Coalition for Women's Identities with American College Personnel Association-College Student Educators International.

Michele Ren is an associate professor of English and the associate director of Women's and Gender Studies at Radford University in Radford, Virginia.

Erica Robak is a graduate student of the English Literature Department at Morehead State University.

Jeanette Sewell is a cataloging and metadata librarian at a public library in Houston, Texas. She is published in *More Library Mashups: Exploring New Ways to Deliver Library Data* (2015, Information Today Inc.) and gives presentations on a variety of topics related to libraries and digital projects.

Andie Shabbar is a PhD candidate and lecturer at Western University, Canada. Her research focuses on queer-feminist public artwork and its capacity to mobilize political action through affect, autonomous networks, and antiauthoritarian politics. She teaches courses on digital media, gender, virtual worlds, and new media art.

Leah Shafer is an assistant professor of Media and Society at Hobart and William Smith Colleges, where she teaches courses on television and new media. Her work has appeared in: *Cinema Journal Teaching Dossier, The Journal of Interactive Technology & Pedagogy, Flow: A Critical Forum on Television and Media Culture*, and *Teaching Media Quarterly*.

Suzan Neda Soltani is a professional in the field of social work and public health. Her work includes counseling at-risk children and victims of domestic violence.

She has collaborated with the Women's Well-Being Initiative of the University of South Carolina to divert female adolescents from entering the juvenile justice system.

Giuliana Sorce is a PhD candidate in the College of Communications and Department of Women's, Gender, and Sexuality Studies at The Pennsylvania State University. Her research centers feminist media studies and international communication. Sorce's work has appeared in the *Global Media Journal, Women's Studies in Communication*, and *Feminist Media Studies*.

Kristin A. Swenson (PhD, University of Minnesota) is an associate professor in critical communication and media studies, and an affiliated faculty member in the Gender, Women, and Sexuality Studies Department at Butler University. She is the author of *Lifestyle Drugs and the Neoliberal Family* (Peter Lang, 2013).

Mary Thompson is Associate Professor of English and the coordinator of the Women's and Gender Studies program at James Madison University, where she teaches courses in women's literature and feminist theory. Her research examines popular and literary representations of reproductive justice issues.

Samantha L. Vandermeade is a PhD student in Gender Studies at Arizona State University. She earned a Master of Arts in history at North Carolina State University. Her research focuses on the intersections of gender, belonging, nationalism, and religion in American history and politics.

Lori Walters-Kramer is an assistant professor of communication studies at Monmouth College in Monmouth, Illinois. She earned her PhD from Bowling Green State University, where her focus on feminist rhetoric and women's studies culminated in the dissertation "Performing Emancipatory Rhetorics: The Possibilities of Michelle Shocked's Musics, Discourses and Movements."

Sarah Wyman is an associate professor of English and creative writing at the State University of New York at New Paltz. As a faculty affiliate in women, gender, and sexuality studies, she teaches courses on contemporary poetry and women's writing.

Index